OUTDOOR LEARNING ENVIRONMENTS

'Little, Elliot and Wyver's *Outdoor Learning Environments* is a much needed and comprehensive resource for pre-service teachers and educators of young children that encompasses philosophies, theories, pedagogy and practice for purposeful engagement of children in all kinds of outdoor spaces in Australia. From the beach to the bush, from early childhood outdoor spaces to On Country Learning, this book is culturally sensitive and inclusive, and clearly reflects children's voices, ensuring it will become the go-to resource for educators, early childhood service providers and policy makers. The authors are leaders in the field and this is evident in the inclusion of the most current research and the distinctive, rich narrative of each and every chapter.'
—**Dr Kumara Ward, Director of Academic Program: Early Childhood Education, School of Education, Western Sydney University.**

'At a time when outdoor play is still seen as an option rather than an imperative, in some contexts, this book brings provocation, planning, pedagogy and practice together to burst open the doors and get outdoors. The voice of the child is loud and clear.'
—**Leanne Grogan, Lecturer: Early Childhood Education, School of Education, La Trobe University.**

OUTDOOR LEARNING ENVIRONMENTS

Spaces for exploration, discovery and risk-taking in the early years

Edited by
Helen Little, Sue Elliott and Shirley Wyver

ALLEN&UNWIN
SYDNEY·MELBOURNE·AUCKLAND·LONDON

First published in 2017

Copyright © Helen Little, Sue Elliott and Shirley Wyver 2017

Allen & Unwin
83 Alexander Street
Crows Nest NSW 2065
Australia
Phone: (61 2) 8425 0100
Email: info@allenandunwin.com
Web: www.allenandunwin.com

Cataloguing-in-Publication details are available
from the National Library of Australia
www.trove.nla.gov.au

ISBN 978 1 76029 685 8

Internal design by Post Pre-press Group, Australia
Index by Puddingburn Publishing Services Pty Ltd
Set in 11.5/15 pt Minion Pro by Post Pre-press Group, Australia
Printed and bound in Australia by SOS Print + Media Group

10 9 8 7 6 5 4 3 2 1

Contents

List of tables and figures

Tables

Figures

Contributors

Anne Bell is the Director of Conservation and Education at Ontario Nature, a charitable conservation organisation based in Toronto, Canada. She holds a PhD in environmental studies, where her research focused on naturalising school grounds. She has worked for over twenty years as an environmental educator, researcher and advocate.

Anita Bundy has a joint appointment as Professor and Department Head in the Department of Occupational Therapy at Colorado State University, United States, and Professor of Occupational Therapy in the Faculty of Health Sciences at the University of Sydney, Australia. As an occupational therapist, Anita has a particular interest in children's everyday activity, and especially in play. For more than a decade, Anita has been involved with research examining the effectiveness of interventions to promote physical activity, social skills, play, resilience and coping in young typically developing children and children with disabilities.

Victoria Carr is Professor of Early Childhood Education and Human Development and Executive Director of the Arlitt Center for Education, Research and Sustainability at the University of Cincinnati, United States. She teaches education courses and provides leadership for the laboratory preschool and sustainability initiatives at the Arlitt Center. Victoria serves as Co-Editor for *Children, Youth & Environments* and studies the design of and children's experiences in outdoor play and learning environments, specifically playscapes, with a focus on research to practice.

Meredith Chan completed an undergraduate degree in early childhood education and a postgraduate degree in children's literature at Macquarie University, Sydney. She is currently the lead teacher in the birth to 2-year-olds room at Mia Mia Child and Family Study Centre, Department of Educational Studies, Macquarie University, Sydney, Australia.

Barbara Chancellor is an independent researcher who has conducted and participated in an extensive body of scholarly research in the fields of children's play, children's geographies and histories, outdoor playspace design and management in school playgrounds, early childhood settings and public open spaces. Barbara has several ongoing research collaborations with scholars in Australia and many other parts of the world, and publishes in peer-reviewed academic journals and books, regularly presenting her research at international forums. She is the Director of Outdoor Playspace Consultancy. With more than 35 years' teaching experience in the early childhood, primary and higher education sectors, she draws on her academic research and industry links to provide practical support to those responsible for the provision of outdoor playspaces for children.

Julie Davis is an Adjunct Professor in the School of Early Childhood, Queensland University of Technology, Brisbane, Australia. Her academic interests are early childhood education for sustainability (ECEfS) and embedding sustainability into teacher education. She is particularly interested in forms of education for sustainability that promote decision-making and action-taking by young learners. In 1996, Julie co-founded the Queensland Early Childhood Environmental Education Network, a state-based network for those with an interest in education for sustainability in the early years. Julie is keenly interested in promoting research in ECEfS. She led the Transnational Dialogues in Research in Early Childhood Education for Sustainability in 2010, 2011 and 2015. New interests in ECEfS revolve around advocating for, and engaging in, interdisciplinary and transdisciplinary research and teaching.

Janet Dyment is a Senior Lecturer and Deputy Head of School in the Faculty of Education, University of Tasmania, Hobart, Australia. In her teaching, she adopts an interdisciplinary approach in various curriculum contexts, and she seeks to make her teaching thematic, integrated and situated in real-life contexts. She is recognised for her high-quality scholarship in educational research and her strong publication record in the areas of teacher education, education for sustainability, interdisciplinary teaching and learning, and reflective practice.

Leyla Eide is a PhD candidate in the Department of Educational Studies, Macquarie University. Before undertaking her doctoral study, she was an early childhood teacher for six years, working with children aged from birth to 2 years and 3–5 years in long day care settings. Her current research interests focus on the association between preschool-aged children's self-efficacy beliefs and engagement in physical risk-taking in the context of outdoor play. Her current research is being conducted with child and adult participants from Sydney (Australia) and Bergen (Norway).

Sue Elliott is a Senior Lecturer and Course Coordinator in Early Childhood Education at the University of New England, Armidale, Australia. She is a long-term advocate of education for sustainability and, in particular, natural outdoor playspaces. Sue is an acknowledged author and researcher in the early childhood education field, with interests in outdoor playspaces, Bush Kinder, sustainability and action research approaches. In 2016, Sue was awarded life membership of Play Australia for her contributions to outdoor play.

Lina Engelen is a Research Fellow in the Faculty of Health Sciences, University of Sydney. She manages the Sydney Playground Project, a research project aimed at increasing physical activity and social skills in primary school children by means of a school playground intervention. Lina's research interests span children's health, physical activity, oral physiology, interaction with and perceptions of food, and nutrition. She is the author of journal articles and book chapters and her research has been presented at international conferences.

Karen Fong completed an undergraduate degree in early childhood education and is currently a teacher in the birth to 2-year-olds room at

Mia Mia Child and Family Study Centre, Department of Educational Studies, Macquarie University.

Monica Green is a Senior Lecturer in the School of Education, Federation University Australia, Gippsland, Australia. Her teaching and research focuses on community- and place-based sustainability pedagogies in primary schools, and university–school partnerships as pedagogical frameworks. She has conducted extensive research in Victorian schools, investigating sustainability curriculum and practice, focusing specifically on the impact of teaching and learning in diverse environments, such as school grounds, food gardens and local settings. Her latest book, *Children, Place and Sustainability*, gives close and careful attention to the nature of children's sustainability learning in the context of their local places.

Elizabeth Jackson-Barrett is a Whadjuck Wudjari woman who is a Lecturer in the School of Education, Murdoch University, Perth, Australia. Libby's research passion is to have schools in Australia commit to Aboriginal education through an On Country Learning (OCL) approach. Libby is currently teaching in the initial education program at Murdoch University, as well as working alongside a remote community school in the upper Gascoyne to assist them to develop their own unique OCL approach.

Sharon Jameson is currently Director of Ocean View College Children's Centre for Early Childhood Development and Parenting, South Australia. Prior to 2017, Sharon was Manager of Assessment, Rating and Compliance for the Education Standards Board. The Board is responsible for the regulation of education and care services, including the National Quality Standards (NQS) in South Australia. Sharon has worked as both an adviser and in various leadership positions in preschools, long day care and family day care. Sharon has a special interest in outdoor learning environments and has been involved in a number of initiatives to support the sector, including developing a vision and values statement for early childhood education and is a member of the Department for Education and Child Development (DECD) Preschool Outdoor Learning Project Taskforce.

Mary Jeavons is the Director of Jeavons Landscape Architects, specialising in the design of children's outdoor environments (in early childhood centres, school grounds, parks/playspaces, hospitals and so on) and broader landscape projects, especially with recreational and sustainable objectives. Mary represents Play Australia on the Standards Australia Committee for Playgrounds and Play Equipment, and contributed to the review of Australian Play Equipment Standards AS4685 (2014).

Jennifer Kent is a Postdoctoral Research Fellow in the Urban and Regional Planning program at the University of Sydney. Previously, she was a lecturer at Macquarie University and a Research Associate in the Healthy Built Environments Program at the University of New South Wales, Sydney. She has also worked as a town planner in New South Wales, both in local government and as a consultant. Her research interests lie primarily in the intersections between planning and health, including planning for active transport and attachments to the private car as a form of mobility.

Libby Lee-Hammond is Associate Professor of Early Childhood Education at Murdoch University. Libby's work in the early years field spans twenty years. Her primary research area is Aboriginal education and care in the early years. Libby's interest in outdoor play and learning began during a visit to Norway, when a clear connection to her work with Aboriginal families was made. This work is now recognised internationally and is currently funded by the Froebel Trust and includes an investigation into how Froebel's gifts may be used in a remote community context.

Helen Little is a Senior Lecturer and Early Childhood Program Director in the Department of Educational Studies, Macquarie University, where she teaches in child development and outdoor learning environments. Prior to this, she was an early childhood teacher with experience teaching in preschools and primary schools in Sydney. Her main research interest focuses on the individual, social and environmental factors influencing children's engagement in risk-taking in outdoor play. Her current focus is on how the physical features of the outdoor environment and pedagogical practices in early childhood settings impact on children's experiences of risk-taking in play. Helen is also currently the Early Childhood Australia representative on the Standards Australia Committee for Playgrounds and Play Equipment.

Glynne Mackey is a Senior Lecturer in Early Childhood Education at the University of Canterbury, New Zealand, teaching and researching in sustainability, social justice and early childhood education. Her research explores ways in which young children participate in action within their communities and how teachers can support them to be agents of change.

Elisapesi Manson is Dean of School of Education at Pacific Adventist University, Papua New Guinea. An experienced academic and administrator, Elisapesi is currently involved in several research studies investigating teaching and student learning, and enhancing agricultural knowledge and practices in primary schools. Elisapesi has also coordinated major curriculum reviews including facilitating national senior capacity trainings in conjunction with the European Union and the Government of Papua New Guinea.

Deborah Moore recently completed her PhD at the Australian Catholic University in Melbourne, with a scholarship in the Early Childhood Futures Research team, and is currently working as a Lecturer in Early Childhood/ Primary Education at Deakin University. With a background of over 25 years as a preschool teacher and preschool field officer, Deborah was also the inaugural Early Years Sustainability Officer for a Victorian local government body working on the creation of a sustainability program to be implemented in early childhood settings with children, their families and educators. In conjunction with this role, Deborah has worked for many years as an early childhood consultant, presenting on the importance of children's natural play places in early childhood environments. Deborah's research interests include education for sustainability with young children; children's outdoor play places; and children's imaginative play places and practices, particularly children's private and secret play places.

Geraldine Naughton is a Professor in Paediatric Exercise Science in the School of Exercise Science, at the Melbourne campus of the Australian Catholic University. Her research focuses on improving health-related outcomes through physical activity in young people. She has researched with a range of young populations from overweight and obese children to intensively training adolescents. Geraldine has been part of several multi-disciplinary school-based interventions to reduce sedentary behaviour and improve the physical and social health of children and adolescents.

Janet Robertson is currently the outdoor teacher at Mia Mia Child and Family Study Centre, Department of Educational Studies, Macquarie University, where she has taught for 21 years. Her interests range from the educational experience of the schools of Reggio Emilia, the Scandinavian Forest school movement and social justice. With colleagues Alma Fleet and Catherine Patterson, she has co-edited three books on pedagogical documentation.

Lalen Simeon is Director of the Postgraduate and Research Office, Pacific Adventist University, Papua New Guinea. Lalen is an experienced researcher, has over 15 years experience as an ethnographer and academic and is involved in several research studies including an Australian Centre for International Agricultural Research (ACIAR) project with researchers from the University of Canberra.

Kym Simoncini is an Assistant Professor of Early Childhood and Primary Education at the University of Canberra, Australia. Prior to her academic career, Kym was a primary school teacher. She taught in both government and Catholic schools in North Queensland and England. Kym's current research focuses on children's and family learning and play. Much of her research is located in Papua New Guinea investigating family learning, playgrounds, playgroups and school readiness. Her research in Australia examines early childhood science, technology, engineering and mathematics (STEM) learning and she is part of the Early Learning STEM Australia project.

Kam Tara is an economist, a transportation specialist and an urbanist with over twenty years' experience in project management and facilitation. He has been responsible for the preparation of guidelines, strategies and policy analysis in regional urban planning, transport planning and urban design. He has developed special competence in the optimisation of multi-modal transportation facility operations and in the development of major business case studies for urban infrastructure management. Kam has worked on and coordinated major projects in Australia and internationally, including in China, Indonesia and the United States.

Paul Tranter is Associate Professor in Geography at the Australian Defence Force Academy, University of New South Wales, where his research and teaching interests are in social and transport geography, and global change. His research has made a pioneering contribution to the literature in areas of child-friendly environments, active transport, and healthy and sustainable cities.

Shirley Wyver is a Senior Lecturer in child development in the Department of Educational Studies, Macquarie University. Her research interests are in early play and cognitive/social development. She also conducts research in the area of blindness/low vision and development. She is a lead investigator in a large multidisciplinary outdoor play project known as the Sydney Playground Project.

Chapter 1

Why do outdoor play and learning matter?

Helen Little, Sue Elliott and Shirley Wyver

This chapter presents an overview of outdoor environments as spaces for promoting children's learning, development and wellbeing. It examines the historical and contemporary outdoor play literature and looks at the status of outdoor play in the early years across early childhood education centres and schools, particularly in relation to how outdoor play is viewed within the Early Years Learning Framework (EYLF) (DEEWR, 2009), the National Quality Standard (NQS) (ACECQA, 2016a) and the Australian Curriculum (ACARA, 2015). The chapter also provides an overview of contemporary issues impacting on children's outdoor play and the chapter perspectives presented in this book.

Provocation

When examining the history of early years education, it is apparent that the seminal thinkers understood the unique and important contribution of the outdoors in early learning and development. While the most documented early education philosophies are mainly European, it is recognised that most, if not all, cultural groups traditionally have supported children's learning by establishing connections with nature. Rapid urbanisation and opportunities for relocation/migration have brought about many changes, but at the same time have made it more difficult for children to have high-quality outdoor experiences. Connections with nature and local communities are being lost through shifts from rural to urban contexts and immigration. For example, people from culturally and linguistically diverse (CALD) backgrounds are considered to be at high risk of drowning in Australia. This is partly because most other countries lack the surf lifesaving resources available in Australia and therefore these are not accessed; it is also due to a lack of understanding of Australian aquatic conditions (Australian Water Safety Council, 2012). When the transmission of knowledge from one generation to the next is lost, or is not as useful due to change in context, it becomes easy to see the 'new nature' and 'new social communities' as dangerous. These types of fears, along with changed traffic conditions and similar disruptions within communities, have led to reduced opportunities for children to engage in outdoor play (Carver, Timperio, & Crawford 2008; Wyver et al., 2010).

Early years education in settings such as long day care, preschools and schools has two important and sometimes conflicting responsibilities:

1. Early education settings provide holistic programs offering experiences that may stimulate all areas of children's learning and development. Settings—particularly those prior to school—focus on key skills, such as social interaction, conflict-resolution, creativity and the development of autonomy. Outdoor environments are dynamic and offer spontaneous learning opportunities, such as finding a dead baby bird that has fallen from a nest high in a tree. Such experiences frequently elicit extended questions and discussions that are unlikely to be captured in more formal contexts, and may include questions about the perspectives of other species and the moralities of life and death in nature.

2. Early education settings may also be viewed as compensatory for deficits in other areas of children's lives. In particular, education settings can be seen as contexts in which healthy behaviours are established (Adelman & Taylor, 2006; Keshavarz et al., 2010). A focus on sound nutrition, physical activity and other behaviours that promote lifelong health and sustainable

living is therefore seen as important, and many argue that outdoor play offers the best way to achieve these outcomes (Bundy et al., 2011; Davis, 2015; Ginsburg, 2007).

Historical influences on contemporary approaches to outdoor learning

Outdoor play has been a feature of early years education for centuries. The educational philosophies and pedagogical approaches of Rousseau (1712–78) and Froebel (1782–1852) have been influential in emphasising the unique contribution of the natural environment as an important resource and context, within which children learn through their sensory interactions with the physical world. Underlying these approaches was the belief that, through their engagement and observations within the environment, children actively solved problems through play and constructed knowledge through experimentation and exploration (Änggard, 2010; Lascarides & Hinitz, 2000). In particular, through these experiences children learned to love nature early, coming to understand natural objects by using their senses, rather than through the explanations and words of their teachers (Änggard, 2010; Herrington, 2001).

Froebel's philosophy was particularly influential in the establishment of early childhood education in Australia. Largely in response to concerns for the welfare and education of young children living in poverty, early educational pioneers, including Maybanke Anderson, Lillian de Lissa and Frances Newton, established kindergartens in New South Wales, South Australia, Western Australia and Queensland, while in Victoria the first free kindergartens were established mainly by church-based organisations. In keeping with Froebelian philosophy, the outdoors was prominent in these kindergartens (Press & Wong, 2013).

Access to outdoor play was also on the agenda in the wider community context. For example, in the United Kingdom, Lady Marjorie Allen of Hurtwood (1897–1976) was principally responsible for introducing the concept of adventure playgrounds after visiting this type of playground in Copenhagen, Denmark. These community playgrounds were recognised as spaces where children could enjoy being able to move things around, utilising loose parts such as sticks, stones, boxes, ropes and other open-ended play materials, and testing themselves in response to new challenges (Allen, 1968). Adventure playgrounds still thrive as community hubs for children and families in some Australian inner-city areas today. Further, as an architect, Lady Allen of Hurtwood was concerned about trends occurring in the 1960s, such as increasing housing density and the lack of open spaces, which were impinging on children's play (Allen, 1968). One can only imagine what she might have said today.

Each of these pioneers challenged the ideas and practices of their time. They are a reminder that while traditional practices have their place, we also need to question current practices and be prepared to consider, and even argue for, alternative ways. Pedagogical and curriculum approaches in the early years are diverse and dynamic, constantly evolving in response to current contexts and issues. The chapters in this book present a range of provocations and ideas drawing on contemporary theories, research and practice to challenge the reader to adopt a critically reflective examination of outdoor learning and pedagogy.

Outdoor play in children's lives today

A number of social and environmental factors are impacting on children's lives today, ranging from mobility to urban planning and design, and increasingly indoor-focused attractions. A range of studies have uncovered an astonishing reduction in children's independent mobility. For example, in England in 1971, 55 per cent of children aged under 10 years were allowed to travel alone to destinations other than school that were within walking distance, whereas almost no children were allowed to travel alone by 2010 (Shaw et al., 2015). In order to map changes over time, Schoeppe and colleagues (2016) examined five separate Australian cross-sectional studies conducted in 1991, 1993, 2010, 2011 and 2012. The studies were comparable in terms of collecting data from children and parents, and having a focus on primary school children (aged 8–13 years). The percentage of children travelling to school independently dropped from 61 per cent in 1991 to 32 per cent in 2012, and significantly fewer girls than boys travelled independently. Detailed studies with small numbers of participants have also revealed significant changes. A study of three generations from two families in Sheffield in the United Kingdom, in which a grandparent, parent and child (aged 6 and 10 years) from each family were interviewed, revealed that grandparents and parents had options of places to go 'without permission', a freedom no longer available to the children in this study. The number of places to which children could go independently with permission was reduced compared with parents and grandparents (Woolley & Griffin, 2015). While parents remember their positive experiences of playing outdoors and recognise the benefits, their desire to protect their children means that parents increasingly are restricting children's unsupervised play and playspaces (Little, 2015). The mothers in Little's (2015) study recalled their childhood play environments were many and varied, both in terms of locations and the activities in which they engaged. Exploration of their neighbourhood and the natural environment, and activities such as bike riding, bushwalking and climbing trees, were common in their descriptions of childhood play experiences. In comparison, their own children experience fairly restricted environments. Despite acknowledging that the neighbourhood in which they live was reasonably safe, many of the parents indicated that they would not allow their child to experience the same freedom they enjoyed. These studies have identified recurrent themes in the sources of parental fears, with 'stranger danger' figuring very strongly in their concerns, followed by hazards related to increased traffic and exposure to bullying and other anti-social behaviour from older children.

A number of other social and environmental factors have been identified to explain these changes in children's outdoor play. Poor urban planning when neighbourhoods have been redeveloped has led to children not only having fewer outdoor places to play, but also having difficulty accessing those that are available without assistance (see Chapter 14). Housing blocks are becoming smaller and high-density housing with limited outdoor space is becoming more prevalent. In 2004, the Australian Bureau of Statistics' analysis of building approvals demonstrated a steady decrease in the size of building blocks—in the period from 1994 to 2004, the average site area for new homes decreased by almost 70 square metres from 802 to 735 square metres. At the same time, the floor area of new houses increased by 39 square metres. In other words, we are building bigger houses on increasingly smaller blocks, and Australia currently is the world leader in house sizes. As a result, the space traditionally available for children to play in their own backyards has decreased—not to mention the negative ecological, health and wellbeing impacts of reduced backyards (Hall, 2010). When considered alongside the trend for these outdoor spaces to be entertainment areas (Wyver et al., 2010), with adults in mind, the appeal as a playspace for a child is somewhat questionable.

There are also many more indoor-focused attractions for children, whether these be organised extra-curricular classes or screen-based technologies, drawing children away from outdoor pursuits. This is an increasingly researched field and indicates some causative factors of childhood obesity along with nutrition concerns (Vandewater et al., 2007; Rutherford, Biron & Skouteris, 2011). Magarey, Daniels and Boulton (2001) found that 25 per cent of children in Australia were overweight or obese, and this level has been sustained according to more recent reports, with childhood obesity still considered an issue (Commonwealth DHA, 2014). The Commonwealth government has published *Healthy Eating and Physical Activity Guidelines for Early Childhood Settings* (Commonwealth DHA, 2009), among a range of resources to support educators working with families, to address this significant public health concern.

Evidence is accruing that inexpensive improvements in outdoor play can lead to increases in children's physical activity (Engelen et al., 2013; Hyndman et al., 2014). Recently, a systematic review of eighteen separate studies of risky outdoor play—that is, outdoor play that is thrilling, exciting and has the possibility of physical injury (see Chapter 2)—found this type of play to be associated with positive effects on a range of health indicators, including social health and behaviours, injuries and lower aggression (Brussoni, Brunelle et al., 2015; Brussoni, Gibbons et al., 2015). Findings from the systematic review have led to an important position statement:

> Access to active play in nature and outdoors—with its risks— is essential for healthy child development. We recommend increasing children's opportunities for self-directed play outdoors in all settings—at home, at school, in child care, the community and in nature (Tremblay et al., 2015, p. 6476).

Outdoor learning environments in the early years

Early years settings represent a significant context for outdoor play opportunities in children's lives. The historical traditions of valuing outdoor learning environments is reflected in the early years curriculum documents of many countries (e.g. Australia, New Zealand, Norway and Scotland); however, with the emphasis on academic outcomes-based approaches, the potential of the outdoor learning environment is often under-recognised. The Australian Early Years Learning Framework (EYLF) (DEEWR, 2009), the NQS (ACECQA, 2016a) and National Regulations (ACECQA, 2016b) all recognise the importance of outdoor play environments as an integral part of the early childhood curriculum, with attention given to promoting access to, flexible use of and interaction between indoor and outdoor environments, as well as ensuring that outdoor spaces allow children to explore and experience the natural environment. Similarly, the Australian Curriculum (ACARA, 2015) recognises the unique learning opportunities provided by the outdoors. Teachers are encouraged to utilise natural outdoor learning environments to integrate learning across the curriculum. In particular, the Australian Curriculum (F–10) (ACARA, 2015) for Health and Physical Education; Humanities and Social Sciences; Geography; Science; general capabilities (ACARA, n.d.) and cross-curriculum priorities can be organised and delivered through learning in the outdoors.

The significance of the outdoors as a context for learning is also evident in the curriculum documents of other countries. The prominence of outdoor play within Scandinavian early childhood education curricula reflects the importance of outdoor life as a core value underpinning Scandinavian early childhood education provision (Sandseter, 2014). However, a 2012 survey of over 2000 early childhood education settings in Norway found that a growing focus on child safety and injury prevention within Norwegian society was beginning to have a detrimental impact on the experiences of children in early childhood settings, with activities that previously had been allowed becoming increasingly restricted (Sandseter & Sando, 2016). In New Zealand, the outdoors has traditionally had an integral role in the learning environment, but here too Stephenson (2014) notes a shifting focus with changes to licensing criteria having a detrimental impact on children's free-flow access to the outdoors as well as space allocation for outdoor play provision. In the

United Kingdom, Scotland's strong commitment to the provision of outdoor experiences is evidenced by the publication of a school curriculum for learning outdoors. The Welsh government has a similar commitment to the provision of outdoor experiences for children in the early years, but this is countered to some extent by the content-based outcomes for children aged 3 to 7 years associated with the Foundation Phase curriculum (Waters & Maynard, 2014). Waters and Maynard also note the even more limited prominence given to outdoor learning in the Northern Ireland Foundation Stage curriculum and the Early Years Foundation Stage curriculum in England. The importance of outdoor play appears to be less visible in other curriculum and accreditation documents. For example, the National Association for the Education of Young Children (NAEYC) Early Childhood Program Standards and Accreditation criteria in the United States requires early childhood services to have a curriculum or curriculum framework that includes the provision of both indoor and outdoor experiences on a daily basis, 'when weather, air quality, and environmental safety conditions do not pose a health risk' in environments that include natural elements (NAEYC, 2016, p. 50).

The NQS (ACECQA, 2016a), which applies to all early childhood services, comprises seven Quality Areas, two of which relate to outdoor spaces: Quality Area 2: Children's health and safety; and Quality Area 3: Physical Environment. Since the introduction of the NQS in 2012 (ACECQA, 2016a), quarterly snapshot reports have offered an indication of how services are progressing in meeting the various standards and elements within each quality area. Overall, 83 per cent of services have met or exceeded Quality Area 2 and 82 per cent have met or exceeded Quality Area 3, leaving the remainder of services working towards these quality areas (ACECQA, 2016c, p. 14), which appears somewhat positive. More specifically within Quality Area 3, though, just under 30 per cent of services are not yet meeting the requirements of Element 3.2.1: Outdoor and indoor spaces are designed and organised to engage every child in quality experiences in both built and natural environments (ACECQA, 2016c, p. 15). Another area where services are likely to receive a rating of 'working towards' is Standard 3.3: The service takes an active role in caring for its environment and contributes to a sustainable future. Both Elements 3.3.1 and 3.3.2, relating to sustainable service operation and children becoming environmentally responsible and respectful, are elements where just under half of services nationally are not meeting the requirements (ACECQA, 2016c, p. 15). There is a need for improvement in these Quality Area 3 elements and both ACECQA and other professional early childhood environmental organisations are working to address this.

Despite the recognition of the importance of outdoor learning environments within the EYLF (DEEWR, 2009) and NQS (ACECQA, 2016a), growing populations are impacting on early childhood centres as well. Urban density and shifting populations from the suburbs to inner-city/city locations, and the resultant growing demand for childcare, have seen an increase in centres located in commercial buildings with limited (if any) access to outdoor environments—often the outdoors is just another room set up with 'outdoor activities'. These spaces are often devoid of natural elements or access to natural lighting. Such pretend outdoor spaces have been facilitated by a state government regulatory waiver (Victorian State Government Education and Training, 2016), but have also provoked social media action from concerned educators (Outside Play Everyday Facebook page).

Even when efforts are made to overcome this, there are still significant issues to consider in relation to children's health and wellbeing. For example, several research studies investigating the rise in myopia (short-sightedness) have identified a lack of time spent outdoors as a contributory factor. The issue relates to both exposure to natural sunlight as well as opportunities for viewing objects over greater distances (Sherwin et al., 2012). Another area of concern for children's health and wellbeing is levels of vitamin D, with daily exposure to sunlight being important to promote vitamin D production. The Cancer Council of Australia notes that many individual, geographical and behavioural factors can impact vitamin D levels, and a balanced approach is essential given the risks of skin cancer (Cancer Council of Australia, 2016).

Another aspect is children's physical and motor fitness, and the contribution of the environment and task demands to the development of body system structures and processes (e.g. musculo-skeletal components, sensory systems, central sensori-motor integrative mechanisms) that promote motor development. Access to natural environments with diverse vegetation and topographies (slope and roughness) is positively associated with increases in children's motor fitness, especially balance and coordination abilities

(Fjørtoft, 2004). Physical movement in diverse sensory environments, such as walking on uneven surfaces or climbing trees, is advocated, when much of children's play lives are restricted to flat, even, non-trippable surfaces and ergonomically designed manufactured climbing structures. There is also well-documented evidence of the health and wellbeing impacts of green spaces for children and adults alike (Chawla, 2015; Kellert, 2012; Townsend & Weerasuriya, 2010), and this is now being realised in an international nature play movement spawning naturalised outdoor playspaces, forest preschools and schools, and nature playgroups (Knight, 2013). There are many reasons why early years educators must be advocates for outdoor play, particularly in authentically natural environments (Nelson; 2012; Rivkin & Schein, 2014). This publication offers a basis for building strong arguments with colleagues, management and the wider community about children's outdoor play needs.

OVERVIEW

In developing this publication, as editors we have identified key areas about outdoor play and playspaces to be addressed, and invited experienced authors, researchers and practitioners to contribute. Beyond this introductory first chapter, the following thirteen chapters are collated into five parts: Part 1: Outdoor environments as pedagogical spaces; Part 2: Designing and planning for outdoor learning; Part 3: Children's voices; Part 4: Cultural perspectives; and Part 5: The outdoors and beyond. We believe this comprehensively addresses outdoor play and playspaces across the early years for early childhood centres and school-based settings, and both pre-service and in-service educators/teachers.

Part 1 focuses on how educators pedagogically engage with children in outdoor spaces. We leave behind misconceptions that outdoors is a time for management-style supervision of children's safety only. Chapter 2, by Helen Little, makes a strong case for positive approaches to risk-taking, aligned with current international trends promoting the benefits of risk. Chapter 3, by Janet Dyment, Anne Bell and Monica Green, brings to the fore the health and wellbeing aspects of outdoor play—an increasingly important issue given children's sedentary indoor lifestyles. In Chapter 4, Julie Davis raises education for sustainability as critical in working collaboratively towards sustainable futures with children. Lastly, in this part, Janet Robertson, Meredith Chan and Karen Fong illustrate the potential of outdoors for children from birth to two years through engaging narratives in Chapter 5.

Part 2 presents Chapters 6 and 7 led by Mary Jeavons, a landscape architect with significant expertise in designing playspaces and an ongoing role with Standards Australia. These chapters create a framework for thinking about designing and planning a physical space that is 'fit for purpose for all users'. They also address the issue of ensuring that outdoor spaces and equipment align with relevant regulations and safety requirements, while at the same time inviting challenges and recognising children's innate appetite for risk (Stephenson, 1998) and the key professional decision-making roles of educators and teachers.

Stemming from the earlier work of Hart (1997) and the United Nations Convention on the Rights of the Child (UNCRC) (OHCHR, 1989) Part 3 is integral to discussing outdoor play and playspaces. In particular, Glynne Mackey identifies the role of children in public outdoor playspaces in Chapter 8, and Deborah Moore offers children's descriptions of secluded or private spaces outdoors—places where imagination abounds—in Chapter 9. In Chapter 10, Sue Elliott and colleagues describe how young children's voices informed the design and development of their school playspace in Papua New Guinea.

A further misconception is that outdoor playspaces are physical spaces only. By including Part 4, we recognise the cultural embeddedness of outdoor play and playspaces. Chapter 11 by Libby Lee-Hammond and Elizabeth Jackson-Barrett, and Chapter 12 by Leyla Eide offer cultural insights for consideration across Australia and Norway.

Finally, Part 5 comprises two chapters by Sue Elliott and Barbara Chancellor (Chapter 13) and Shirley Wyver and colleagues (Chapter 14) alerting readers to the potential of outdoor spaces beyond the fence of typical educational settings. Underlying these chapters is consideration not only of children's activity levels, and their health and wellbeing within broader community concerns, but children being visibly active participants in their local communities.

There is much to celebrate in the expertise about outdoor play and playspaces shared in these chapters. We invite you to build and extend on this expertise and be vital advocates for children and outdoor play, whatever your particular setting or role. We believe outdoor learning environments are unique spaces for exploration, discovery and risk-taking in childhood.

REFERENCES

Adelman, H.S. & Taylor, L. (2006). Mental health in schools and public health. *Public Health Reports, 121*(3), 294–8. Retrieved 12 January 2017 from <www.pubmedcentral.nih.gov/articlerender.fcgi?artid=1525289&tool=pmcentrez&rendertype=abstract>.

Allen, Lady of Hurtwood (1968). *Planning for play.* London: Thames and Hudson.

Änggard, E. (2010). Making use of 'nature' in an outdoor preschool: Classroom, home and fairyland. *Children, Youth and Environments, 20*(1), 4–25.

Australian Bureau of Statistics (2004). *Building approvals, Australia, July 2004,* cat. no. 8731.0. Retrieved 4 January 2017 from <www.abs.gov.au/ausstats/abs@.nsf/0/15cdfb6cdb264658ca256f02007967be?OpenDocument>.

Australian Children's Education & Care Quality Authority (ACECQA). (2016a). *Guide to the National Quality Standard.* Retrieved 20 December 2016 from <files.acecqa.gov.au/files/National-Quality-Framework-Resources-Kit/NQF-Resource-03-Guide-to-NQS.pdf>.

——(2016b). *Guide to the Education and Care Services National Law and the Education and Care Services National Regulations 2011.* Retrieved 20 December 2016 from <files.acecqa.gov.au/files/National-Quality-Framework-Resources-Kit/NQF-Resource-02-Guide-to-ECS-Law-Regs.pdf>.

——(2016c). *NQF snapshot Q3 2016.* Retrieved 12 January 2017 from <files.acecqa.gov.au/files/Reports/2016/NQF_Snapshot_Q3_2016.PDF>.

Australian Curriculum Assessment and Reporting Authority (ACARA). (2015). *Health and physical education: Sequence of content F–10.* Retrieved 31 October 2016 from <www.acara.edu.au/_resources/Health_and_Physical_Education_-_Sequence_of_content.pdf>.

——(n.d.). *Personal and social capability learning continuum.* Retrieved 31 October 2016 from <www.acara.edu.au/_resources/General_capabilities_-PSC_-_learning_continuum.pdf>.

Australian Water Safety Council (2012). *Australian water safety strategy 2012–2015.* Sydney: Australian Water Safety Council.

Brussoni, M., Brunelle, S., Pike, I., Sandseter, E.B.H., Herrington, S., Turner, H., . . . Ball, D.J. (2015). Can child injury prevention include healthy risk promotion? *Injury Prevention: Journal of the International Society for Child and Adolescent Injury Prevention, 21*(5), 344–7.

Brussoni, M., Gibbons, R., Gray, C., Ishikawa, T., Sandseter, E.B.H., Bienenstock, A., ... Tremblay, M.S. (2015). What is the relationship between risky outdoor play and health in children? A systematic review. *International Journal of Environmental Research and Public Health, 12*(6), 6423–54.

Bundy, A.C., Naughton, G., Tranter, P., Wyver, S., Baur, L., Schiller, W., ... Charmaz, K. (2011). The Sydney Playground Project: Popping the bubblewrap—unleashing the power of play: A cluster randomized controlled trial of a primary school playground-based intervention aiming to increase children's physical activity and social skills. *BMC Public Health, 11*(1), 680.

Cancer Council of Australia (2016). *Position statement: Sun exposure and Vitamin D.* Retrieved 20 March 2017 from <wiki.cancer.org.au/policy/Position_statement_-Risks_and_benefits_of_sun_exposure#Key_messages_and_recommendations>.

Carver, A., Timperio, A. & Crawford, D. (2008). Playing it safe: The influence of neighbourhood safety on children's physical activity—a review. *Health & Place, 14*(2), 217–27.

Chawla, L. (2015). Benefits of nature contact for children. *Journal of Planning Literature, 30*(4), 433–52.

Commonwealth DHA (2009). *Get up & grow: Healthy eating and physical activity for early childhood.* Canberra: Commonwealth Government. Retrieved 28 March 2016 from <www.health.gov.au/internet/main/publishing.nsf/content/phd-early-childhood-nutrition-resources>.

—— (2014). *Obesity: Prevalence trends in Australia.* Retrieved 20 March 2017 from <sydney.edu.au/medicine/research/units/boden/ANPHA%20Obesity%20 Prevalence%20Trends.pdf>.

Davis, J. (ed.) (2015). *Young children and the environment: Early education for sustainability* (2nd edn). Melbourne: Cambridge University Press.

Department of Education Employment and Workplace Relations (DEEWR). (2009). *Belonging, being and becoming: The Early Years Learning Framework for Australia.* Canberra: Commonwealth Government.

Engelen, L., Bundy, A.C., Naughton, G., Simpson, J.M., Bauman, A., Ragen, J., ... van der Ploeg, H.P. (2013). Increasing physical activity in young primary school children—it's child's play: A cluster randomised controlled trial. *Preventive Medicine, 56*(5), 319–25.

Fjørtoft, I. (2004). Landscape as playscape: The effects of natural environments on children's play and motor development. *Children, Youth and Environments, 14*(2), 21–44.

Ginsburg, K.R. (2007). The importance of play in promoting healthy child development and maintaining strong parent–child bonds. *Pediatrics, 119*(1): 182–91.

Hall, T. (2010). *The life and death of the Australian backyard.* Melbourne: CSIRO Publishing.

Hart, R.A. (1997). *Children's participation: The theory and practice of involving young citizens in community development and environmental care.* London: Earthscan & UNICEF.

Herrington, S. (2001). Kindergarten: Garden pedagogy from romanticism to reform. *Landscape Journal, 20*(1), 30–47.

Hyndman, B.P., Benson, A.C., Ullah, S., Telford, A., Butcher, K., Sallis, J., . . . Stratton, G. (2014). Evaluating the effects of the Lunchtime Enjoyment Activity and Play (LEAP) school playground intervention on children's quality of life, enjoyment and participation in physical activity. *BMC Public Health, 14*(1), 164.

Kellert, S.R. (2012). *Birthright: People and nature in the modern world.* New Haven, CT: Yale University Press.

Keshavarz, N., Nutbeam, D., Rowling, L. & Khavarpour, F. (2010). Schools as social complex adaptive systems: A new way to understand the challenges of introducing the Health Promoting Schools concept. *Social Science and Medicine, 70*(10), 1467–74.

Knight, S. (ed.) (2013). *International perspectives on forest school: Natural spaces to play and learn.* London: Sage.

Lascarides, V.C. & Hinitz, F. (2000). *History of early childhood education.* New York: Falmer Press.

Little, H. (2015). Mothers' beliefs about risk and risk-taking in children's outdoor play. *Journal of Adventure Education & Outdoor Learning, 15*(1), 24–39.

Magarey, A. Daniels, L.A. & Boulton, J.C. (2001). Prevalence of overweight and obesity in Australian children and adolescents: Assessment of 1985 and 1995 data against new standard international definitions. *Medical Journal of Australia, 174*, 561–4.

National Association for the Education of Young Children (NAEYC). (2016). *NAEYC Early Childhood Program Standards and Accreditation Criteria & Guidance for Assessment.* Retrieved 30 March 2016 from <www.naeyc.org/academy/content/access-naeyc-accreditation-standards-and-criteria>.

Nelson, E. (2012). *Cultivating outdoor classrooms.* St Paul, MN: Redleaf Press.

Office of the United Nations High Commissioner for Human Rights (1989). *Convention on the Rights of the Child.* Retrieved 21 May 2016 from <www.ohchr.org/EN/ProfessionalInterest/Pages/CRC.aspx>.

Press, F. & Wong, S. (2013). *A voice for young children: 75 years of Early Childhood Australia*. Canberra: Early Childhood Australia.

Rivkin, M. & Schein, D. (2014) *The great outdoors: Advocating for natural spaces for young children*. Washington, DC: NAEYC.

Rutherford, L., Biron, D. & Skouteris, H. (2011). Children's content regulation and the 'obesity epidemic'. *Media International Australia, 140*, 47–60.

Sandseter, E.B.H. (2014). Early years outdoor play in Scandinavia. In T. Maynard & J. Waters (eds), *Outdoor Play in the Early Years* (pp. 114–26). Maidenhead: Open University Press.

Sandseter, E.B.H. & Sando, O.J. (2016). 'We don't allow children to climb trees'. How a focus on safety affects Norwegian children's play in early childhood education and care settings. *American Journal of Play, 8*(2), 178–200.

Schoeppe, S., Tranter, P., Duncan, M.J., Curtis, C., Carver, A. & Malone, K. (2016). Australian children's independent mobility levels: Secondary analyses of cross-sectional data between 1991 and 2012. *Children's Geographies, 14*(4), 408–21.

Shaw, B., Bicket, M., Elliott, B., Fagan-Watson, B., Mocca, E. & Hillman, M. (2015). *Children's independent mobility: An international comparison and recommendations for action*. Retrieved 13 March 2017 from <http://westminsterresearch.wmin.ac.uk/15650>.

Sherwin, J., Reacher, M., Keogh, R., Khawaja, A., Mackey, D. & Foster, P. (2012). The association between time spent outdoors and myopia in children and adolescents: A systematic review and meta-analysis. *Ophthalmology, 119*(10), 2141–51.

Stephenson, A. (1998). *Opening up the outdoors: A reappraisal of young children's outdoor experiences*. Unpublished Master of Education thesis, Victoria University of Wellington.

—— (2014). Outdoor play in New Zealand centres: Protecting, defending, extending. In T. Maynard & J. Waters (eds), *Exploring outdoor play in the early years*. (pp. 127–40). Maidenhead: Open University Press.

Townsend, M. & Weerasuriya, R. (2010). *Beyond blue to green: The benefits of contact with nature for mental health and well-being*. Melbourne: Beyond Blue.

Tremblay, M.S., Gray, C., Babcock, S., Barnes, J., Bradstreet, C.C., Carr, D., . . . Brussoni, M. (2015). Position Statement on Active Outdoor Play. *International Journal of Environmental Research and Public Health, 12*(6), 6475–505.

Vandewater, E.A., Rideout, V.J., Wartella, E.A., Huand, X., Lee, J.H. & Shim, M. (2007). Digital childhood: Electronic media and technology use among infants, toddlers and preschoolers. *American Academy of Pediatrics Journal, 119*(5), 1006–15.

Victorian State Government Education and Training (2016). *Waivers of outdoor space requirements for centre-based services located in the Melbourne Central Business District (CBD).* Retrieved 29 March 2017 from <www.education.vic.gov.au/Documents/childhood/providers/regulation/waiversoutdoorspaceJan16.docx>.

Waters, J. & Maynard, T. (2014). Introduction: Outdoor play in early years settings. In T. Maynard & J. Waters (eds), *Exploring outdoor play in the early years.* (pp. 1–13). Maidenhead: Open University Press.

Woolley, H.E., & Griffin, E. (2015). Decreasing experiences of home range, outdoor spaces, activities and companions: Changes across three generations in Sheffield in north England. *Children's Geographies, 13*(6), 677–91.

Wyver, S., Tranter, P., Naughton, G., Little, H., Sandseter, E.B.H. & Bundy, A. (2010). Ten ways to restrict children's freedom to play: The problem of surplus safety. *Contemporary Issues in Early Childhood, 11*(3), 263–77.

Part 1

Outdoor environments as pedagogical spaces

Chapter 2

Risk-taking in outdoor play
Challenges and possibilities

Helen Little

Play is an integral part of children's lives, through which they learn and develop. Many children are drawn to risky play wherein they can challenge themselves and engage in experiences that take them out of their 'comfort zone' (Stephenson, 1998). This chapter examines current research into the significant benefits of engaging in risky play and the environments that support this type of play. The chapter concludes by examining how educators can provide challenging physical outdoor play for children by taking a risk–benefit approach to managing risk in play.

Provocation

A great deal of research has focused on the association between children's risk-taking and unintentional injury on the assumption that this behaviour results in consequences that are detrimental to children's health (Morrongiello, Corbett & Brison, 2009). On the other hand, risk avoidance and protection are equated with safeguarding children's health to ensure that they grow up to become healthy adults (Christensen & Mikkelsen, 2008). This focus on safety highlights the contradictory discourses in contemporary constructions of childhood. On the one hand, children are deemed to have greater autonomy, are viewed as capable and are seen as having the right to be involved in decisions that affect them and to make a difference in their own lives. On the other hand, their autonomy is constrained as the emphasis on safety positions children as vulnerable and in need of protection (Madge & Barker, 2007; Waller, 2007). Parental and societal concerns for children's safety has seen a reduction in children's engagement in outdoor play, the demise of many childhood activities that previous generations took for granted and the emergence of an experience of childhood where children's lives are increasingly regulated, supervised and controlled (Brussoni et al., 2012; Gill, 2007). Further, Kelley, Hood and Mayall (1998, p. 20) believe that 'adult control might be viewed as "protective" when necessary to prevent the child's exposure to dangers/hazards within the environment, but as "constraining" and a "source of risk" to the child's autonomy when unnecessary.'

The impact of this safety focus on children's play has been challenged, with researchers highlighting the positive outcomes of risk-taking for children's learning and development. Smith (1998) initially questioned the way in which adults view risk in relation to children's playground activities, challenging adults to redefine their notions of risk and to recognise the role of risk in fostering children's growth towards maturity. More recently, Niehues and colleagues (2013) have argued that adults need to reframe their notions of risk to recognise the benefits of healthy risk-taking and to value the learning associated with the decision-making and actions in situations where the outcome is uncertain. The challenge, then, is for educators to find the balance between risk, challenge and safety in their early childhood and school settings.

Risk: A situation or event where something of value is at stake and where the outcome is uncertain.

Understanding risk and risk-taking

Part of the issue surrounding the competing discourses of promoting children's autonomy on the one hand and the need for protection on the other is the way in which risk is commonly viewed. The term 'risk' is often associated with some probability of loss or negative outcomes (Aven & Renn, 2009). From this perspective, risk-taking involves engagement in behaviours that are potentially dangerous and result in adverse outcomes; however, engaging in risk-taking behaviours can result in outcomes that are either positive or negative (Boyer, 2006). In other words, the outcomes of the risky behaviour are uncertain. So perhaps risk and risk-taking are more accurately defined as events, behaviours and consequences that are associated with some degree of uncertainty about the outcomes (Aven & Renn, 2009). All aspects of our daily lives involve an element of risk, and every day we make decisions with uncertain outcomes. In these situations, we base our decisions on our assessment of the potential benefits against any potential undesirable outcomes along with a judgement of our likelihood of success. Without a willingness to engage with this uncertainty, we would never have learned to walk, climb stairs, ride a bicycle, swim, drive a car or many other far 'riskier' activities (Little & Eager, 2010). What sets these activities apart from what we might commonly see as risk is that they are viewed in a much more positive light as being part of the inevitable challenges we face throughout our lives to learn, develop and improve ourselves.

In the context of children's play, the focus on the potential adverse outcomes associated with injury risk has had a detrimental impact on the provision and quality of outdoor play linked to the regulation of playspaces. The safety legislation for children's playground equipment in the form of standards (e.g. EN 1176:2008; AS 4685:2014) has focused on physical features, such as maximum fall height, impact-absorbing surfaces, fall zones, sharp edges, and tripping, crushing and entrapment hazards (Ball, 2002). While the elimination of hazards is important, early childhood educators consider that the problem in the past was that play value was compromised in complying with these standards (Little, Wyver & Gibson, 2011). The revised Australian Standards, (AS 4685:2014, see Chapter 7) include a recognition of the importance of risk-taking in children's play with regard to children's development and children learning to make risk judgments for themselves (Standards Australia, 2014).

Despite these changes, the legacy of this regulation of playspaces has had an unfavourable impact on play in many ways. First, play provision has been impacted through the removal of playground equipment and natural elements from playspaces. In prior-to-school settings, early childhood educators report equipment such as swings and taller climbing equipment being removed, trees being cut down and natural elements such as rocks being removed or banned, as well as limits being placed on climbing heights (Little, 2017). In primary schools, playgrounds have similarly been lacking in opportunities for play in natural environments and play has been restricted by rules that prevent children climbing trees, exploring bushy areas or playing with loose materials, such as sand, dirt, stones and sticks (Chancellor, 2013). The problem with this approach to removing 'risks' from the environment is that it assumes children will be safer as a consequence, but the opposite is more often the result. The implementation of safety regulations has been associated with risk-compensation behaviour. Children and the adults supervising them change their perceptions of the risks involved in activities when safety gear is worn (Morrongiello, Walpole & Lasenby, 2007). For example, children's behaviour on an obstacle course while wearing safety gear (helmets, wrist guards) showed increased risk-taking (greater speeds and recklessness, such as tripping, bumping into things and falling) compared with when they were not wearing safety gear (Morrongiello, Walpole & Lasenby, 2007).

The outdoor play environment as a context for risk and risk-taking

The outdoor environment is inherently a dynamic, constantly changing space in response to the weather, the seasons, the time of day and the interaction of humans and the environment. As a consequence, it is unpredictable and typically involves some element of risk. The risks and challenges of being outdoors provide rich opportunities for learning and problem-solving. In this context, children continually test the limits of their physical, intellectual and emotional development (Little & Wyver, 2008).

Belonging, Being and Becoming: The Early Years Learning Framework for Australia (EYLF) (DEEWR, 2009) for prior-to-school settings describes outdoor learning environments as spaces that invite risk-taking. It acknowledges that taking calculated risks and dealing with uncertainty is one way by which children become confident, resilient and involved learners. This type of play contributes to their emerging autonomy, interdependence, sense of agency and social and emotional wellbeing, as they deal with change and cope with failure and the unexpected (DEEWR, 2009). Educators support children in becoming confident and involved learners by providing 'learning environments with appropriate levels of challenge where children are encouraged to explore, experiment and take appropriate risks in their learning' (DEEWR, 2009, p. 35). Although there is no explicit mention of outdoor environments and risk-taking, the Australian Curriculum (ACARA, 2015) general capabilities identify becoming confident, resilient and adaptable as one of the sub-elements of the personal and social capability continuum. For children in the early years of school (Foundation to Year 2), this means being able to identify situations that feel safe or unsafe, having the confidence to approach new situations, and undertaking and persisting with tasks within the limits of their personal safety—experiences provided by risk-taking in the context of outdoor play (ACARA, n.d.). This view is not unique to the Australian context—for example, in the United Kingdom, the Early Years Foundation Stage curriculum similarly promotes children taking risks and learning by trial and error in enabling environments supported by educators who encourage children to try new activities and to judge risks for themselves (Early Education, 2012).

What is risky play and why is it important for children's learning and development?

Risky play can be described as a form of play that involves physically challenging activities where there is potential for injury. These activities also provide a sense of fun, enjoyment and exhilaration. In her observational study of outdoor play in New Zealand preschools, Stephenson (1998, p. 127) described aspects of play reflecting children's noticeable desire to physically challenge themselves and extend their skills by 'riding bikes very fast, climbing around the outside of the fort structure of the fixed play equipment, running across the obstacle course, swinging very high, dangling off the edge of the fixed slide and dropping to the ground'. In these situations, the children appeared to be very aware of their own skill level and competence. At times, they were intently focused on the task at hand with the aim of testing their own limits. At other times, they wanted to display their mastery of skills, calling for others—particularly the adults—to look at them (Stephenson, 1998).

> **Risky play:** A form of play that involves physically challenging activities where there is a potential for injury.

So, in general terms, we can think of risky play as situations where children have an obvious desire to challenge themselves, and extend their skills by moving out of their comfort zone. A key element of this type of risky play involves attempting something never done before; feeling on the borderline of being out of control (perhaps due to height or speed); and consequently overcoming fear (Stephenson, 2003).

The types of behaviours and play environments that distinguish risky play are described further by Sandseter (2007) in her observational study of Norwegian children's outdoor play. As with Stephenson's observations of children's play, Sandseter (2009b) highlights the sensation of being on the borderline of being out of control and the dual emotions of exhilaration and fear that accompany such experiences. Sandseter (2007) identified six categories of risky play, involving, (1) play with heights (where there is a risk of falling); (2) play with high-speed (situations involving uncontrolled speed and pace, potentially leading to collision with people or objects); (3) play with dangerous tools (where there is a risk of injury); (4) play near dangerous elements (involving the possibility of falling into or from something); (5) rough-and-tumble play (where children can harm each other); and (6) play where children can 'disappear' or be out of the sight of adults.

Benefits of risk-taking in play

Through these types of risky play, children experience a range of learning and development benefits. The physicality of many of the play experiences described by Sandseter (2007) potentially provides opportunities for children to acquire and ultimately master a wide range of fundamental movement skills, as well as developing muscle and skeletal strength, motor fitness and endurance. The experience of negotiating their way around their environment at speed and climbing high presents a new perspective on the world that contributes to the development of perceptual abilities, including depth, shape, size, movement perception and general spatial-orientation abilities (Fjortoft & Sageie, 2000). The decisions that children make, and learning to take responsibility for their actions during risky play, support children in developing 'their emerging autonomy, interdependence, resilience and sense of agency' (DEEWR, 2009, p. 22). As described by Sandseter (2007), during risky play children experience simultaneous emotions of exhilaration and fear. Learning to deal with these emotions as well as coping with frustrations, change and unexpected outcomes in the context of risky play support children to become 'strong in their social and emotional wellbeing' (DEEWR, 2009, p. 31).

Finally, risky play provides a context in which children are presented with real, but managed, risks that support the emergence of risk-appraisal skills necessary for handling risks and dangers in other contexts. As Sandseter (2009c, p. 8) highlights, risky play is a 'serious risk-management exercise'. The skills children gain through risk-taking in play don't just support their learning and development in childhood; this type of play also provides a supportive context in which they acquire problem-solving skills, coping strategies and resilience to face the challenges and uncertainties that they will encounter throughout life.

The importance of risk-taking in play as a context for learning about safety and risk assessment is acknowledged within early childhood education documents. For example, the United Kingdom Early Years Foundation Stage Framework (Early Education, 2012) describes the child at 3–5 years as one who shows understanding of the need for safety when tackling new challenges, considers and manages some risks, and practises some appropriate safety measures without direct supervision (Early Education, 2012). Similarly, the Australian National Quality Standard (NQS) outlines the significant role of educators in encouraging children 'to develop the skills to assess and minimise risks to their own safety' (ACECQA, 2016a, p. 68). In the Australian Curriculum, the Health and Physical Education learning area's sub-strand on making healthy and safe choices focuses on children from Foundation to Year 2 identifying knowledge, skills and understandings, and describing actions that can help them to stay safe and healthy in a range of environments, including how to be safe during play while outdoors in natural environments (ACARA, 2015).

Environments that support risky play

The EYLF describes outdoor play environments as spaces that 'invite open-ended interactions, spontaneity, risk-taking, exploration, discovery and connection with nature' (DEEWR, 2009, pp. 15–16). This theory of the environment *inviting* certain behaviours can be explored through Gibson's (1979) notion of affordances (see also Chapter 12). Affordances relate to the functional properties of the physical environment that invite us to do something or to undertake a particular action. Affordances within the environment are dynamic and unique to the individual, varying in response to the individual's changing body size, strength, capabilities and motivation (Kytta, 2004). Consequently, different individuals will perceive different affordances, and therefore use the same elements within the environment in different ways. For example, in relation to environments that support risky play, a tree with a solid trunk and appropriate branches at a height that can be accessed from the ground affords climbing possibilities. The same feature might have multiple affordances—for example, the same tree branches may afford swinging opportunities because it is at an appropriate height with branches of a diameter that a child can readily fit their hand around (Heft, 1988).

Affordances: Functional properties of the environment that invite particular actions.

Environments that promote risky play include a diverse range of both natural and manufactured affordances, such as:

- fixed or moveable manufactured playground equipment or natural elements in the environment that afford a variety of climbing opportunities—for example, the problem-solving challenge involved in climbing up trees, ladders and ropes or scrambling over mounds and rocks, as opposed to the predictability of a fixed or moveable climbing apparatus
- platforms, logs, trees, rocks, mounds, fixed or moveable equipment for jumping down from heights
- manufactured balance beams, logs, repurposed loose parts, such as pipes or timber off-cuts, that afford balancing
- traditional manufactured swings or improvised tyre or rope swings attached to branches or trees with branches at a height, and with a diameter, that children can grasp to afford swinging
- slides at different gradients, to provide variations in the sensation of speed
- slopes to afford sliding, running, cycling and the sensation of speed
- uneven ground; rocks for clambering; grassy slopes for rolling; tunnels for crawling; and stepping stones for leaping
- elements that give the sensation of instability—features such as swaying rope bridges and ladders to offer unpredictability
- tools, such as real carpentry tools (hammers, saws and hand drills)
- secluded spaces where children have a sense of being away from the watchful eyes of adults, where they can create their own worlds (see Chapter 9 for further discussion on children's secret spaces) (Heft, 1988; Sandseter, 2009a).

Balancing risk, challenge and safety

As the excerpts from the EYLF presented earlier in this chapter illustrate, contemporary approaches to early childhood education view children as capable and resourceful, and their autonomy is encouraged (DEEWR, 2009). Young children can identify hazards and appraise risky behaviours (Little & Wyver, 2010). Although younger children may be slower to make these judgements, and may not be able to suggest preventative measures or fully understand the severity of potential injury outcomes, they can nevertheless identify and understand varying degrees of risk associated with different behaviours; consequently, play environments provide an important context for developing risk-appraisal skills and safety awareness. Indeed, both the Australian Curriculum general capabilities and the NQS recognise children's capacity to develop risk-assessment skills and the importance of learning to take responsibility for their own safety (ACARA, n.d.; ACECQA, 2016a). It is important to note, however, that risks need to be visible/obvious for children to enable them to make appropriate decisions. For example, the inclusion of rocks in a natural playspace presents a visible risk that children learn to negotiate, whereas surfacing such as artificial grass may present a risk that is not obvious, depending on whether or not it has impact-attenuating properties.

Despite this, recent research (Little, 2017) suggests that few early childhood education settings in Australia have outdoor environments that promote the types of risky play described earlier in this chapter to facilitate risk-assessment skills. For example, while the early childhood centres in Little's (2017) study provided some natural elements, playspaces or resources that afforded risk-taking, very few provided a diverse range of these elements in their outdoor environments (e.g. trees, rocks, contrasting ground surfaces, uneven ground and slopes, flat areas, digging patches, sand play, water play, large open spaces, areas for gross motor equipment, secluded spaces, balancing and climbing, trampolines, swings, slides and bikes). Furthermore—particularly in relation to play with heights—almost half the centres did not permit tree climbing and restricted climbing heights (on equipment and trees) to less than 1 metre (despite allowable height under the Play Equipment Standards being 1.5 metre for moveable and 1.8 metre for fixed equipment—see Chapter 7).

A number of factors have been identified in the literature that potentially lead to risk minimisation in children's outdoor play environments, including high child-to-staff ratios; external regulations restricting activities; poorly designed outdoor environments; inadequate understanding by educators of the benefits of risk-taking; and fear of litigation (Little & Wyver, 2008). Australian early childhood educators have identified factors associated with the quality of the outdoor environment, regulatory requirements and a litigious environment as constraints on their pedagogical practice. Educators often raise issues related to safety concerns associated with risky play and the inclusion of natural elements within the environment, resulting in reduced opportunities for physical activity. Also, they believe their supervision duties often prevent them from actively engaging children in physical activity or setting up additional physical play opportunities for the children (Coleman & Dyment, 2013; Dyment & Coleman, 2012; Little, 2010). Their focus is more often about compliance with regulations than the provision of challenging play environments for children, due to the risks that might be associated with this type of play (Fenech, Sumsion & Goodfellow, 2006; Little, 2010). The impact of external regulations and fear of litigation, restricting activities and children's opportunities for risky play, is evident in other countries as well. Waters and Begley (2007) found that the Welsh preschool teachers focused on the negative aspects of risk-taking and felt the need to exert a high level of control to ensure the children's safety and meet curriculum goals. Tovey (2007) found variations in the impact of external regulations and fears of litigation on pedagogical practice. While some English early childhood educators expressed anxiety about the risk-taking behaviour of the children, others openly encouraged risky play.

The challenge for educators is to overcome these barriers to provide the best possible play opportunities, and to create playspaces that will attract children, capture their imagination and give them scope to play in new, more exciting and more creative ways while considering children's safety.

Implications for practice: Managing risk in play

Conventional approaches to risk-assessment are focused on injury prevention; consequently, their purpose is to determine whether the level of risk is acceptable or tolerable by considering: (1) the likelihood of a person coming to harm; and, (2) the potential severity of the harm (Ball, Gill & Spiegel, 2008). This approach focuses on the adverse outcomes without any consideration of the benefits of the activity. One potential consequence of such an approach is that it results in 'surplus safety', whereby excessive safety measures are put in place to counter injuries (no matter how minor) and regardless of the cost (Wyver et al., 2010). An example of this is the considerable cost involved in covering playground surfaces with rubber to improve safety (estimated in the United Kingdom to have cost between £200 million and £300 million over a ten-year period) despite the likelihood of a child dying from a playground injury being one in 30 million. On the other hand, surfaces such as these may actually increase the likelihood of long arm fractures, when other surfacing materials are cheaper and equally (if not more) effective (Gill, 2007). As outlined in the discussion of risk earlier in this chapter, risk decisions should be based on weighing up the positive against the negative outcomes. Indeed, risk-management strategies that seek to find a more balanced approach appear to be more acceptable within the current regulatory context. For example, while section 167 of the National Law requires approved providers to ensure 'every reasonable precaution is taken to protect children from harm and from any hazard likely to cause injury . . . The National Law does not require services to eliminate all risk and challenge from children's play or environments' (ACECQA, 2016b, pp. 67–8).

As a means of providing a more balanced approach to managing risk in play, Ball, Gill and Spiegel (2008) developed the risk–benefit approach, which outlines two stages of the risk-management process: the policy framework; and risk–benefit assessment, which consists of the technical inspection and dynamic risk–benefit assessment.

Policy framework

The policy framework makes explicit the principles underpinning a risk–benefit assessment, and should reflect the need to take a balanced approach to responding to children's risk-taking and risks within the environment. The aim of the policy framework is to establish values, philosophy and understandings underlying a pedagogical approach that acknowledges the importance of opportunities for managed/calculated risk-taking with respect to children's play. It should provide an explicit rationale for supporting children's risk-taking in play, outlining the developmental benefits and learning opportunities and how educators will promote these. It also outlines how judgements are made in relation to potential risks in the environment and children's risk-taking behaviours—for example, explaining the measures taken to eliminate hazards and the strategies that have been adopted to ensure reasonable precautions have been taken to avoid injury (e.g. supervision and discussions with children about safety issues). The EYLF (DEEWR, 2009) and NQS (ACECQA, 2016a) can be referenced as promoting policy that supports risk-taking. For example, the NQS highlights the need for educators to 'plan to ensure that all areas used by children are effectively supervised, including when children are participating in high-risk activities' (ACECQA, 2016a, p. 68). This policy framework then sets the scene for, and is informed by, the risk–benefit assessment processes, including the technical inspection and dynamic risk–benefit assessment. Similar guidance is provided for playground safety management in schools, although the focus is primarily on the technical inspection aspect of the process (e.g. see NSW Department of Education, 2006 and Victorian Department of Education and Early Childhood Development, 2012).

Risk–benefit assessment

The risk–benefit assessment process involves two components: the technical inspection; and the dynamic risk–benefit assessment. The technical inspection involves the routine checking of equipment and the environment to identify and eliminate hazards (wear and tear, damage, and lack of cleanliness), and includes an indication of the relative risk in relation to the benefits as well as a schedule for regular repair and maintenance. The technical inspection also includes considerations in relation to setting up moveable equipment (see Chapter 6 for more information on issues to consider in relation to the technical inspection).

From a pedagogical perspective, the most important part of the assessment process is the dynamic risk–benefit assessment, as this relates to the decisions made in response to children's risk-taking as play unfolds. It includes educators' observations of children's play and decisions about potential support or interventions by the adults supervising children. A risky play situation for one child might be different from that of another, so a sound knowledge of individual children's dispositions, capabilities and patterns of risk-taking is essential for scaffolding them to take appropriate risks in play.

CONCLUSION

In early childhood education, there is a broad understanding that risk-taking contributes significantly to all aspects of children's physical, intellectual, social and emotional development, and that the ability to appraise risk accurately is an important life skill. This chapter has outlined a range of potential affordances in the outdoor environment that provide diverse opportunities for children's engagement in challenging physical play that invites children to take calculated risks to support their learning and development. However, there are challenges for educators in provisioning the outdoor environment and balancing the requirements for safety. Adopting a risk–benefit approach has been proposed as a means of achieving this balance to provide both a policy framework and pedagogical approach to supporting children in taking calculated risks that promote their emerging autonomy, interdependence, sense of agency and social and emotional wellbeing.

REFLECTION QUESTIONS

2.1   What are your own attitudes towards risk? Are you a risk-taker or a risk-avoider? How might your perceptions of risk impact on your response to children's risky play?

2.2   What opportunities do children have for challenging play where they can experience risk and the simultaneous emotions of exhilaration/fun and fear?

2.3   Are there gender differences in how you respond to children's risky play? Is risky play tolerated and encouraged more for boys than it is for girls? Are male educators more likely to support and encourage risky play?

2.4   Observe children in outdoor play. How do they have opportunities to actively move, try out new skills, practise them, take risks and explore how to use their bodies?

2.5   Do children have a variety of equipment, topographies and natural elements in the environment with which to test themselves? How can the environment be set up to provide opportunities for the development of problem-solving skills?

2.6   How can you create an illusion of risk in the environment, perhaps through play with heights or speed or play in secluded areas? What opportunities can you provide for children to push themselves further and extend their limits in an environment where the risks are obvious to the child?

2.7 What do you mean by keeping children safe? What restrictions do you place on children's play and are they always necessary? How do you support children to develop the skills to perceive, assess and minimise risks to their own and others' safety? How might you involve children in developing guidelines for safe practices in the outdoor environment?

2.8 Have you developed an outdoor play policy that includes the promotion of risky play? How do you involve colleagues, children and parents in its development and implementation?

RECOMMENDED RESOURCES

- Early Childhood Australia: www.earlychildhoodaustralia.org.au. This is the national peak body for early childhood. It provides a wide range of resources for educators relating to all aspects of early childhood practice. For specific examples relevant to risky play, refer to the following websites: www.earlychildhoodaustralia.org.au/nqsplp/e-learning-videos/observing-practice and www.earlychildhoodaustralia.org.au/nqsplp/e-learning-videos/talking-about-practice.

- International Play Association (IPA): http://ipaworld.org. IPA is an international non-government organisation and key advocate for children's play. IPA's purpose is to protect, preserve and promote the child's right to play as a fundamental human right. It provides a multidisciplinary and cross-sector forum for exchange and action.

- Play Australia: www.playaustralia.org.au. Play Australia promotes the value of play through resources, training programs and consultancy across public, school and early childhood education playspaces. Play Australia is the Australian sub-group of the International Play Association. Play Australia has developed *Getting the Balance Right*, which provides a guide for risk management as well as a ready reference for the AS 4685 Playground equipment Standard.

- Play England: www.playengland.org.uk. Play England aims to raise awareness about the importance of play. Its website has an extensive range of useful resources and research articles relating to the benefits and implementation of outdoor play, including a risk–benefit assessment form.

- Children and Nature Network: www.childrenandnature.org. The Children and Nature Network aims to connect all children, their families and communities to nature through innovative ideas, evidence-based resources and tools, broad-based collaboration and support of grassroots leadership.

REFERENCES

Australian Children's Education & Care Quality Authority (ACECQA) (2016a). *Guide to the National Quality Standard.* Retrieved 20 December 2016 from <files. acecqa.gov.au/files/National-Quality-Framework-Resources-Kit/NQF-Resource-03-Guide-to-NQS.pdf>.

——(2016b). *Guide to the Education and Care Services National Law and the Education and Care Services National Regulations 2011.* Retrieved 20 December 2016 from <files.acecqa.gov.au/files/National-Quality-Framework-Resources-Kit/NQF-Resource-02-Guide-to-ECS-Law-Regs.pdf>.

Australian Curriculum Assessment and Reporting Authority (ACARA) (2015). *Health and physical education: Sequence of content F–10.* Retrieved 31 October 2016 from <www.acara.edu.au/_resources/Health_and_Physical_Education_-_Sequence_of_content.pdf>.

——(n.d.). *Personal and social capability learning continuum.* Retrieved 31 October 2016 from <www.acara.edu.au/_resources/General_capabilities_-PSC_-_learning_continuum.pdf>.

Aven, T. & Renn, O. (2009). On risk defined as an event where the outcome is uncertain. *Risk Research, 12*(1), 1–11.

Ball, D.J. (2002). *Playgrounds: Risks, benefits and choices,* London: Middlesex University. Retrieved 19 December 2007 from <www.hse.gov.uk/research/crr_pdf/2002/crr02426.pdf>.

Ball, D.J., Gill, T. & Spiegel, B. (2008). *Managing risk in play provision: Implementation guide* (2nd edn). London: Play England. Retrieved 1 June 2015 from <www.playengland.org.uk/media/172644/managing-risk-in-play-provision.pdf>.

Boyer, T.W. (2006). The development of risk-taking: A multi-perspective review. *Developmental Review, 26,* 291–345.

Brussoni, M., Olsen, L.L., Pike, I. & Sleet, D. (2012). Risky play and children's safety: Balancing priorities for optimal child development. *International Journal of Environmental Research Public Health, 9,* 3134–8.

Chancellor, B. (2013). Primary school playgrounds: Features and management in

Victoria, Australia. *International Journal of Play, 2*(2), 63–75.

Christensen, P. & Mikkelsen, M. (2008). Jumping off and being careful: Children's strategies of risk management in everyday life. *Sociology of Health & Illness, 30*(1), 112–30.

Coleman, B. & Dyment, J. (2013). Factors that limit and enable preschool-aged children's physical activity on child care centre playgrounds. *Journal of Early Childhood Research, 11*(3), 203–21.

Department of Education Employment and Workplace Relations (DEEWR) (2009). *Belonging, being and becoming: The Early Years Learning Framework for Australia.* Retrieved 20 July 2009 from <www.coag.gov.au/coag_meeting_outcomes/2009-07-02/docs/early_years_learning_framework.pdf>.

Dyment, J. & Coleman, B. (2012). The intersection of physical activity opportunities and the role of early childhood educators during outdoor play: Perceptions and reality. *Australasian Journal of Early Childhood, 37*(1), 90–8.

Early Education (2012). *Development matters in the early years foundation stage (EYFS).* Retrieved 18 April 2016 from <www.early-education.org.uk/development-matters-early-years-foundation-stage-eyfs>.

Fenech, M., Sumsion, J. & Goodfellow, J. (2006). The regulatory environment in long day care: A 'double-edged sword' for early childhood professional practice. *Australian Journal of Early Childhood, 31*(3), 49–58.

Fjortoft, I. & Sageie, J. (2000). The natural environment as a playground for children: Landscape description and analysis of a natural playscape. *Landscape and Urban Planning, 48*(1/2), 83–97.

Gibson, J. (1979). *The ecological approach to visual perception.* Boston: Houghton-Mifflin.

Gill, T. (2007). *No fear: Growing up in a risk averse society.* London: Calouste Gulbenkian Foundation.

Greenfield, C. (2003). Outdoor play: The case for risks and challenges in children's learning and development. *Safekids News, 21*, 5.

Heft, H. (1988). Affordances of children's environments: A functional approach to environmental description. *Children's Environments Quarterly, 5*(3), 29–37.

Jambor, T. (1995). Coordinating the elusive playground triad: Managing children's risk-taking behavior, (while) facilitating optimal challenge opportunities, (within) a safe environment. Paper presented at the Playground Safety conference, Pennsylvania State University, Philadelphia, October.

Kelley, P., Hood, S. & Mayall, B. (1998). Children, parents and risk. *Health and Social Care in the Community, 6*(1), 16–24.

Kyttä, M. (2004). The extent of children's independent mobility and the number of actualized affordances as criteria for child-friendly environments. *Journal of Environmental Psychology, 24,* 179–98.

Little, H. (2006). Children's risk-taking behaviour: Implications for early childhood policy and practice. *International Journal of Early Years Education, 14*(2), 141–54.

—— (2010). Risk, challenge and safety in outdoor play: Pedagogical and regulatory tensions. *Asia-Pacific Journal of Research in Early Childhood Education, 4*(1), 3–24.

—— (2017). Promoting risk-taking and physically challenging play in Australian early childhood settings in a changing regulatory environment. *Journal of Early Childhood Research, 15*(1), 83–98.

Little, H. & Eager, D. (2010). Risk, challenge and safety: Implications for play quality and playground design. *European Early Childhood Education Research Journal, 18,* 497–513.

Little, H. & Wyver, S. (2008). Outdoor play: Does avoiding the risks reduce the benefits? *Australian Journal of Early Childhood, 33*(2), 33–40.

—— (2010). Individual differences in children's risk perception and appraisals in outdoor play environments. *International Journal of Early Years Education, 18*(4), 297–313.

Little, H., Wyver, S. & Gibson, F. (2011). The influence of play context and adult attitudes on young children's physical risk-taking during outdoor play. *European Early Childhood Education Research Journal, 19*(1), 113–31.

Madge, N. & Barker, J. (2007). *Risk and childhood.* London: Risk Commission. Retrieved 19 December 2007 from <www.rsariskcommission.org/blog/default.asps?PageId=650>.

Morrongiello, B.A., Corbett, M. & Brison, R.J. (2009). Identifying predictors of medically attended injuries to young children: Do child or parent behavioural attributes matter? *Injury Prevention, 15*(4), 220–5.

Morrongiello, B.A., Walpole, B. & Lasenby, J. (2007). Understanding children's injury-risk behavior: Wearing safety gear can lead to increased risk taking. *Accident Analysis and Prevention, 39,* 618–23.

Niehues, A., Bundy, A., Broom, A., Tranter, P., Ragen, J. & Engelen, L. (2013). Everyday uncertainties: Reframing perceptions of risk in outdoor free play. *Journal of Adventure Education and Outdoor Learning, 13*(3), 223–37.

New South Wales Department of Education. (2006). *Playing safe: Guidelines for the installation and maintenance of playground equipment in NSW government schools.* Retrieved 31 October 2016 from <www.kidsafensw.org/imagesdb/ wysiwyg/playingsafe1_1.pdf>.

Sandseter, E.B.H. (2007). Categorising risky play: How can we identify risk-taking in children's play? *European Early Childhood Education Research Journal, 15*(2), 237–52.

—— (2009a). Affordances for risky play in preschool: The importance of features in the play environment. *Early Childhood Education Journal, 36*(5), 439–46.

—— (2009b). Children's expressions of exhilaration and fear in risky play. *Contemporary Issues in Early Childhood, 10*(2), 92–106.

—— (2009c). Characteristics of risky play. *Journal of Adventure Education and Outdoor Learning, 9*(1), 3–21.

Smith, S.J. (1998). *Risk and our pedagogical relation to children: On the playground and beyond.* Albany, NY: State University of New York Press.

Standards Australia (2014). AS 4685 *Playground equipment. Part 1: General safety requirements and test methods.* Sydney: Standards Australia.

Stephenson, A. (1998). *Opening up the outdoors: A reappraisal of young children's outdoor experiences.* Unpublished Master of Education thesis, Victoria University of Wellington.

—— (2003). Physical risk-taking: Dangerous or endangered? *Early Years, 23*(1), 35–43.

Tovey, H. (2007). *Playing outdoors: Spaces and places, risk and challenge.* Maidenhead: Open University Press.

Victorian Department of Education and Early Childhood Development (2012). *Guidelines for school playgrounds: Playground safety management.* Retrieved 31 October 2016 from <www.education.vic.gov.au/Documents/school/principals/ infrastructure/schoolplaygroundguide.pdf>.

Waller, T. (2007). The trampoline tree and the swamp monster with 18 heads: Outdoor play in the foundation stage and foundation phase. *Education 3–13, 35*(4), 393–407.

Waters, J. & Begley, S. (2007). Supporting the development of risk-taking behaviours in the early years: An exploratory study. *Education 3–13, 35*(4), 365–77.

Wyver, S., Tranter, P., Naughton, G., Little, H., Sandseter, E.B. & Bundy, A. (2010). Ten ways to restrict children's freedom to play: The problem of surplus safety. *Contemporary Issues in Early Childhood, 11*(3), 263–77.

Chapter 3

Green outdoor environments
Settings for promoting children's health and wellbeing

Janet Dyment, Anne Bell and Monica Green

Around the world, children's outdoor environments, such as school grounds, early childhood education services, public playgrounds and backyards, are changing. Homogenous environments consisting primarily of asphalt and grass that are noted for being hot, hard and barren are being transformed or 'greened' into places designed to include a variety of natural elements, such as vegetable gardens, wetlands, trees, frog ponds, murals and butterfly gardens.

Internationally, a number of not-for-profit organisations support the process of greening children's outdoor environments. Organisations and programs such as Evergreen in Canada, the Centre for Ecoliteracy in the United States, Learnscapes in Australia, Movium in Sweden, the Ecoschools programs in South Africa and Learning Through Landscapes in the United Kingdom continue to grow in their profile and scope (see weblinks at the end of this chapter). These organisations provide guidance, funding and resources to administrators, teachers and parents who are interested in beginning the process of playground greening.

Evidence of the wide-ranging benefits of green outdoor environments for children is mounting. These benefits extend to children's environmental awareness; opportunities for learning and cognition; social, emotional and mental wellbeing; and safety and health (Dyment, 2005; Gill, 2014; Rosenow & Bailie, 2014). Green outdoor environments can thus be considered and developed as sites to enhance these various dimensions of children's lives. They also represent an opportunity for educators working in schools and early childhood education services to reach out and collaborate with people working in other related educational fields and movements—be it around issues of achievement, citizenship, peace, sustainability, safety or health.

Provocation

An emerging and exciting body of literature is exploring the relationship between outdoor learning environments and health promotion, particularly from a holistic health perspective (Dyment & Bell, 2008; Francesca, Elliott & Crighton, 2014; Moore & Cosco, 2014). School grounds and outdoor environments are often perceived as exclusive sites that privilege children's 'physical' movement. In this chapter, however, we are interested in examining the power and potential of green outdoor environments through a multi-faceted, settings-based health-promotion approach in schools and early childhood education services, which we argue expands the children's health and wellbeing discourse beyond the 'physical'. We propose that green outdoor environments are places that can unite, inform and support the interests of educators and children's health advocates. We begin the chapter with a general overview of recent thinking about health-promoting settings and green outdoor environments before considering how green outdoor environments can contribute to children's physical, mental, social and spiritual wellbeing.

The settings approach

There are several possible approaches to childhood health promotion which the World Health Organization (WHO) categorises as 'upstream', 'midstream' and 'downstream' (WHO, 2012, p. 17). The upstream or socio-ecological approach tackles the underlying determinants of health and social equity within a society. Such actions target food environments, physical activity environments and the broader socio-economic environment. Midstream or behavioural approaches aim to improve population-level dietary and physical activity patterns, and typically target the settings level where healthy eating and physical activity programs can be implemented. These settings include early childhood education services and schools. Downstream approaches typically are focused on individual healthcare interventions (WHO, 2012), such as immunisation programs or child health screening programs.

The notion of health promotion operating in a context beyond the individual has gained traction since the 1990s, and the emphasis has shifted to developing more holistic understandings of the complex social and ecological systems that underpin health. Whitelaw and colleagues (2001) identified the emergence of settings-based health-promotion activity as being one of the best developed forms of practice. In the settings approach, health promotion is reoriented from developing personal competencies towards creating healthy policies, reshaping environments to support health, and building partnerships and creating sustainable change through participation, empowerment and ownership of change throughout the setting (Dooris, 2009; Whitelaw et al., 2001). This locates public health action in the social, cultural and physical places in which people live, learn, work and play (WHO, 1986).

A setting is where people actively use and shape the environment; thus it is also where people can create or solve problems. Creating change (e.g. health promotion) requires capacity-building in the local setting *and* changes to the system in which that setting operates. Schools and early childhood education services are environments in which children spend significant portions of their lives, and thus present the potential for systems approaches to health promotion. The settings approach adopts a socio-ecological perspective, which explicitly recognises the contextual and environmental factors that influence health. Interventions therefore target the physical, organisational and social contexts in which people are found, not just the people contained in or defined by that setting (Poland, Krupa & McCall, 2009). The approach has been variously applied to schools, early childhood education services, hospitals, workplaces, neighbourhoods and cities.

Dooris (2009) identifies three key characteristics of the settings approach: an ecological model of health; a systems perspective; and a whole-system organisation development and change focus. In the ecological model, health is determined by a complex interplay of environmental, organisational and personal factors, largely determined outside of 'health services'. As Dooris explains, this represents changing focus from illness to salutogenesis (or the origins of health); from individuals to populations; and from a mechanistic and reductionist focus on single health issues, risk factors and linear causality to a more holistic view concerned with creating supportive contexts within the settings of people's lives. Within the ecological model, settings are viewed as dynamic, complex systems with inputs, throughputs, outputs and outcomes characterised by integration, interconnectedness, interrelationships and interdependencies between the different elements (Dooris, 2009).

The settings approach places its primary focus on introducing and managing change within the organisation, underpinned by values that include participation across the whole setting, empowerment, equity, partnership working and ensuring change is long lasting. As illustrated in Figure 3.1, Dooris (2009, p. 30) conceptualises this approach by highlighting the need to combine organisational development with high-visibility projects, to balance top-down commitment with bottom-up stakeholder engagement, and to ensure that initiatives are driven by both the public health and 'core business' agendas.

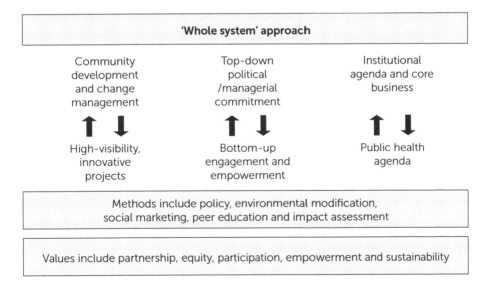

Figure 3.1 A model for understanding the healthy settings approach

Source: Adapted from Dooris (2009, p. 30).

The settings approach provides a comprehensive framework that encourages multi-stakeholder ownership of health. It allows connections among people, environments and behaviours to be explored, and it enables interrelationships between different people and among different health issues and initiatives to be recognised (Dooris, 2009).

The International Union for Health Promotion and Education (IUHPE, 2009) advocates whole-setting approaches to health promotion, in recognition that all aspects of a school and early childhood education community play an integral part in the promotion of children's health (Table 3.1). Schools and early childhood education services that are integrated, holistic and strategic are more likely to produce better health and education outcomes than those that are mainly information based and implemented only in the classroom (IUHPE, 2009). The six essential elements of a health-promoting setting are outlined in Table 3.2, based on the WHO's Ottawa Charter for Health Promotion (1986).

Table 3.1 Principles of a health-promoting setting

• Promotes the health and wellbeing of students	• Addresses the health and wellbeing issues of all school and early childhood education centre staff
• Enhances the learning outcomes of students	• Collaborates with parents and the local community
• Upholds social justice and equity concepts	• Integrates health into the setting's ongoing activities, curriculum and assessment standards
• Provides a safe and supportive environment	• Sets realistic goals built on accurate data and sound scientific evidence
• Involves student participation and empowerment	• Seeks continuous improvement through ongoing monitoring and evaluation
• Links health and education issues and systems	

Source: IUHPE (2009, p. 1).

Table 3.2 Essential elements of promoting health in educational settings

Elements	Explanation	Examples relevant to children's settings, such as schools and early childhood education centres
Healthy policies	Policies and practices that state expectations and set the scene for a consistent and sustainable whole-school/ service approach	• Provision of a school/service environment that promotes and normalises the drinking of water as the preferred drink • Policies that encourage physical activity as a normal part of every child's day • In early childhood education services, strong links to National Quality Standard (NQS) Quality Area 2, which points to the importance of 'healthy eating and physical activity being embedded in the program for children' (ACECQA, 2013, p. 44)
The physical environment	Buildings, grounds and equipment in and around the setting that enable healthy eating and physical activity	• Space for play outside and inside • Safe accessible drinking water availability • In early childhood education services, strong links to NQS Quality Area 3, which points to the importance of the physical environment being 'safe, suitable and providing a rich and diverse range of experiences that promote children's learning and development' (ACECQA, 2013, p. 78)
The social environment	Quality of relationships among staff, children, families and the broader community	• A whole-school/service approach • Involvement of families and the broader community in health activities • In early childhood education services, strong links to NQS Quality Area 6, which points to the importance of the developing 'collaborative partnerships with families and communities' (ACECQA, 2013, p. 139) • In early childhood education services, links to the Early Years Learning Framework (EYLF) in relation to Learning Outcome 2: 'Children are connected with and contribute to their world' (DEEWR, 2009, p. 25)

Table 3.2 Essential elements of promoting health in educational settings (cont.)

Elements	Explanation	Examples relevant to children's settings, such as schools and early childhood education centres
Individual health skills and action competencies	Formal and informal curriculum documents that allow children to gain age-related knowledge and skills that allow them to build competencies to improve their health	• In schools, links to the Australian Curriculum for primary students, especially within the Health and Physical Education learning area (ACARA, 2010) • In early childhood education services, links to the EYLF for preschool-aged children in relation to Learning Outcome 3: 'Children take increasing responsibility for their own health and physical wellbeing' (DEEWR, 2009, p. 32) • Links to relevant Australian dietary and physical activity guidelines
Community links	Connections between the school/service setting and children's families, as well as local community groups	• Identification of and collaboration with other initiatives working towards similar goals • In early childhood education services, links to the EYLF—for example, in relation to Learning Outcome 2: 'Children are connected with and contribute to their world' (DEEWR, 2009, p. 25) • In early childhood education services, strong links to NQS Quality Area 6, which points to the importance of developing 'collaborative partnerships with families and communities' (ACECQA, 2013, p. 139)
Health services	Other local, state or federal services with responsibility for children's health promotion	• Working in concert with government and private sector organisations working towards goals of healthy eating and physical activity—for example, oral health services

Source: WHO (1986).

While the intersection of green outdoor environments and their contribution to health promotion and the settings approach has received some attention, we believe that it merits much more. Green outdoor environments can affect all dimensions of children's health, and when thoughtfully designed can become an integral component of holistic settings-based approaches to promoting health in schools and early childhood education settings.

Dimensions of health

In our attempt to widen and disrupt the children's health and wellbeing discourse, the following section examines the broader literature pertaining to children's engagement with and interactions in outdoor environments via four key dimensions of health: physical health, social health, mental health and spiritual health.

Physical health

Green outdoor environments can result in many physical health benefits for young children, some of which are relatively straightforward. When pesticides are eliminated and shade is increased in school grounds or early childhood education centre playgrounds, for example, healthier settings are created by reducing children's exposure to harmful chemicals and ultraviolet radiation. With respect to both issues, medical research indicates that young children are a vulnerable population (Francesca, Elliott & Crighton, 2014). The provision of shade, for instance, is an important change to outdoor environments that makes it easier, and more likely, for children to protect themselves from the damaging impacts of ultraviolet radiation.

In addition to these obvious benefits, greening can also enhance physical health in more subtle ways. To appreciate these, however, we must address two common misconceptions about the design of outdoor environments. The first is the belief that the uniform wide-open spaces of conventional outdoor environments minimise physical risk and maximise children's safety because there is little that young children can fall down from, and little to block the sight lines of supervising adults (Wyver et al., 2010). From this perspective, it may be feared that green outdoor environments will increase the risk of injury—for example, by having young children fall from rocks or trees, slip into ponds, or get stung by insects attracted to the vegetation or compost. In addition, there may be concern that bushes, trees and other natural features will impair supervision.

While concerns about these risks are very real (often becoming barriers to encouraging children's play in outdoor environments), research into the contributions of children's outdoor interactions addresses this misconception. For example, a study of 45 schools in Toronto, Canada, indicates that green outdoor environments can actually calm the movement patterns of young children and soften play surfaces so that there are, in fact, fewer 'knock-and-bump' injuries (Dyment, 2005). With effective planning, vegetation can be placed and pruned so that adequate sight lines are maintained.

Other studies have reframed 'risk' in play settings, arguing that the sterile landscapes of conventional children's outdoor environments present a much greater risk than rocks and trees: the risk of depriving children of the quality and variety of experiences that are crucial to their healthy development (Little & Wyver, 2008; Sandseter, 2009). This risk is greatest for the growing numbers of children who have little access to the outdoors and/or natural environments (see also Chapter 2).

A second misconception about the design of outdoor environments pertaining to physical health is the belief that flat turf and asphalt provide ideal surfaces for burning off excess energy, and are therefore best suited to promoting physical activity (Evans & Pellegrini, 1997). Again, recent studies offer a more balanced perspective. They indicate that physical activity is best supported in outdoor environments comprising a diversity of landscape features that respond to a wide variety of young children's interests and capabilities (Dyment, Bell & Lucas, 2009; Moore & Cosco, 2014). A Canada-wide survey of 59 elementary schools suggested that greening school grounds diversifies children's play repertoire and creates opportunities for boys and girls of all ages, interests and abilities to be more physically active (Bell & Dyment, 2006). Complementing the rule-bound, competitive games supported by asphalt and turf playing fields, greened areas in children's outdoor environments invite children to jump, climb, dig, lift, rake, build, role-play and generally get moving in ways that nurture all aspects of their health and development. Of particular significance is the potential to encourage moderate and light levels of physical activity by increasing the range of enjoyable, non-competitive, imagination-based, open-ended forms of play in green outdoor environments.

Another physical health benefit offered by green outdoor environments is the opportunity to promote better nutrition through children's participation in food gardening. Rates of obesity are rising among children in Australia, Canada, the United States and other industrialised nations, with significant physical, mental and social health impacts (WHO, 2016). Health officials are therefore striving to improve dietary behaviours, and are calling upon schools and early childhood education services to support healthy eating choices. While attention is focused on the food choices offered in school canteens and early childhood education services, food gardening offers a complementary means of supporting nutrition programs through the design and use of outdoor environments. By planting, tending, harvesting and eating a variety of vegetables and fruits, children can gain hands-on knowledge about nutritious food and its production. Incorporating a vegetable garden into health programing can thus have a positive effect on children's eating preferences, habits and nutrition knowledge (Gibbs et al., 2013).

Many of these considerations underpin the Australian Curriculum's Health and Physical Education learning area, which can be identified in the Personal, Social and Community Health and Movement and Physical Activity Content Descriptors (ACARA, 2010). Similar themes inform *Belonging, Being and Becoming: The Early Years Learning Framework for Australia* (EYLF) (DEEWR, 2009), specifically Key Learning Outcome 3: 'Children have a strong sense of wellbeing', supported by the over-arching themes 'Children become strong in their social and emotional wellbeing' and 'Children take increasing responsibility for their own health and physical wellbeing'. We recognise these collective curriculum frameworks as pedagogically influential in assisting educators to engage children effectively in all aspects of physical health and wellbeing.

Social health

Green outdoor environments are important settings for social learning and development (Maller, 2009). Through their design and culture, they influence social behaviours and relationships. Green outdoor environments have an important role to play in enhancing social health by providing a more diverse environment that responds better to the needs and interests of more children, and by creating opportunities for children, staff and parents to work together towards shared goals. In so doing, green outdoor environments promote social inclusion and equality, and can foster greater civility, cooperation and communication among children and between children and adults.

In her influential work on children and school ground design, Wendy Titman (1994) found a positive correlation between the conditions of the school ground and the behaviours and attitudes of children. She revealed how school grounds, in themselves, function as a 'hidden curriculum' and a 'form of mass communication' with a 'vocabulary and grammar' of their own (pp. 16–17). Children in her study considered school grounds to be inextricably connected to the school buildings, and believed that those who were responsible for the design of the school ground 'made it like that' for a reason (p. 57). Thus, when school grounds failed to meet the needs of children, thereby making time in the school ground unenjoyable, they believed that this was a conscious decision by people in positions of authority, who did not care.

Building on the work of Titman (1994), others have examined the relationships between the design of outdoor environments, play opportunities, and social hierarchies and interactions. American researcher Ann Barbour (1999) compared play behaviours on two school grounds: one that primarily provided opportunities for physical play, and another that provided for a diversity of play opportunities. At schools that only provided opportunities for active and physical play, social hierarchies were established through these means, and children with low physical competence or desires were often socially excluded. Conversely, at schools where diverse play opportunities were afforded, students who were less physically competent could still engage in types of play that were more aligned with their abilities and interests.

Conventional outdoor environments, by their design, provide a limited range of play opportunities that privilege certain individuals. Expanses of pavement and manicured grass offer opportunities primarily for large-group, competitive and rule-bound games. They satisfy some children, but provide few choices for those who prefer to play in smaller groups, who do not wish or are not able to compete, or who prefer more open-ended or creative kinds of play. Research suggests, for example, that conventional playgrounds cater only to a portion of the population—primarily boys, older students and students with high physical competence, who tend to dominate large, open spaces and play equipment (Dyment, 2005). In contrast, green outdoor environments present the possibility of alternative and more inclusive approaches that deal with these issues, largely by satisfying the desires and needs of a wider variety of children.

Gardening activities in particular seem to provide ongoing opportunities to build positive relationships among children, staff and parents, which is a key element in establishing a healthy school culture (Maller, 2009). Some have argued that these benefits can be even more dramatic if children are involved in the full process of greening; from planning and design to implementation and maintenance (Green, 2014). In such cases, children typically have opportunities to work with a range of individuals from both within and outside the school or early childhood education centre. They are able to share interests, values and time with other children, teachers, parents and community members, as they work towards common goals. They also learn important social life skills, such as teamwork, cooperation and persistence.

Because greening projects tend to encourage broad community involvement, the social benefits can extend beyond the immediate school or early childhood education centre, affecting the social health of the broader community (Maller, 2005). Greening outdoor environments provides a process and a place where people can meet, make friends and build a sense of community and purpose. As projects evolve, and outdoor spaces become greener and more inviting, they embody the effort, care and vision of those involved, sending a powerful message to the broader community (of course, if projects are untended or abandoned, the opposite is also true). According to an Australian study, students who were involved in greening initiatives felt a greater sense of commitment to and from the broader school community, as well as more links with other schools, parents and the local community (Maller, 2005).

Mental health

It has long been acknowledged across a range of cultures that plants, gardens and gardening can have positive impacts on the mental health and wellbeing of humans (Maller & Townsend, 2005). A basic premise is that contact with the natural world can provide relief from stress. Much of this research has been conducted with adults, although there is evidence of similar benefits for children. For example, Wells and Evans (2003) found that the presence of natural elements moderated the impacts of stressful life events on children aged from 6 through 12 years who lived in a rural setting. They discussed the policy and design implications of their findings, noting that 'natural areas closer to housing and schools are essential features in an effort to foster resilience of children and perhaps to promote their healthy development' (p. 327). This assertion is particularly relevant for health-promoting schools and the green outdoor environment movement. Stressful events negatively influence children's disposition for learning, rendering them less able to concentrate, overly anxious and lacking in self-esteem (Chawla et al., 2014; Wells & Evans, 2003). If nature can play a restorative role, then potentially it can also enhance children's ability to learn in early childhood education and school settings.

Indeed, research indicates that contact with nature supports attentional functioning, and can enhance human effectiveness and make life's demands seem more manageable. A study focusing on children (ages 7–12) with Attention Deficit Disorder (ADD) examined the relationship between children's exposure to nature through leisure activities and their attentional functioning (Faber-Taylor, Kuo & Sullivan, 2001). Parents were surveyed regarding their child's attentional functioning after activities in several settings. Results indicated that children with ADD function better than usual after activities in green settings. Further, the 'greener' a child's play area, the less severe their attention deficit symptoms tend to be. Thus contact with nature may benefit a population of children who desperately need attentional support.

Other studies also point to the ways that green outdoor environments support children's mental health. A recent study in the United States demonstrated that green school grounds were seen as 'havens' for children that allowed them to escape stress and to focus and build competence (Chawla et al., 2014). Another United States study in an early childhood education service also lends support to the relationship between green outdoor environments and mental health of children by specifically exploring how natural environments promote self-determination (Kochanowski & Carr, 2014). The authors found that play in nature encouraged children to demonstrate choice-making, problem-solving, self-regulation and engagement.

Spiritual health

Although spiritual health is recognised within the health-promoting settings movement, it is not easily defined or discussed. For our purposes here, we turn to a recent conceptualisation of spiritual health offered by Schein (2014, p. 78), who defines spiritual wellbeing/health for children as:

> A system of children's deep connections leading first to self-awareness, and later to the nurturing of basic and complex dispositions ignited by moments of wonderment, awe, joy, and inner peace that develops into the prosocial personality traits of caring, kindness, empathy, and reverence. The system requires love and attachment.

In light of this definition, it makes sense to consider how green outdoor environments can foster wonder, awe and joy, which in turn might generate caring, kind and empathetic traits in children. A common purpose of green outdoor environments is to create a place for other life in schools or early childhood education services where children will have regular ongoing opportunities for interaction with plants and animals, and for understanding and experiencing themselves as interconnected with the whole. As they listen or watch for birds, follow animal tracks or look for caterpillars or ladybugs, children can become attuned to the comings and goings of other beings and to their purposeful existence. As they plant seeds, fill bird feeders or mulch trees, they assume a nurturing role and develop a sense of relationship and intimacy with a living world in which they can actively participate. Gardening in particular can provide an opportunity to deal with losses and failures, and to experience the responsiveness of plants to care and nurturing.

A study in Toronto, Canada, reveals that these potential benefits are being realised widely in green outdoor environments (Dyment, 2005). Questionnaire respondents indicated that students were more likely to explore widely (90 per cent), to learn about their local environment (91 per cent) and to have a greater sense of wonder and curiosity (92 per cent) after their school ground had been greened. Over 90 per cent of respondents also indicated that student environmental awareness and stewardship had increased on the green school ground.

As environmental awareness and stewardship increase, there is reason to believe that young people's sense of hope and commitment to their local environment and to the living world around them will also be enhanced. Through hands-on involvement with the human and natural communities of which they are a part, children learn that barren patches of pavement and manicured grass can successfully be transformed into diverse and welcoming places that better respond to their own needs as well as those of other living beings. Depending on their level of involvement in the greening project, they can also learn that they have a right to participate in decisions that affect their quality of life (see the UN Convention on the Rights of Children, United Nations Treaty Collection, 1990). Research shows that, when given the opportunity, young children are willing participants in opportunities to critically appraise outdoor spaces, and reimagine new possibilities through collaborative processes that support their 'greening' ideas (Green, 2014). As this particular study highlights, when fully involved in the greening process, young children can acquire skills related to democracy, participation and citizenship that they can potentially carry forward into adulthood (see also Chapter 8).

Ultimately, green outdoor environments can help to nurture a deeper sense of purpose and meaning. Gardening, working and playing with plants allow children to participate in life processes and to foster a sense of identity and belonging, which are important priorities highlighted in the EYLF (DEEWR, 2009).

Implications

In our role as academics familiar with the literature that supports teaching and learning in green outdoor environments, we find the evidence base across the four dimensions of health areas to be comprehensive, convincing and compelling. In our role as researchers who have studied the impacts of greening initiatives in Australia and Canada, our research endeavours and associated findings lend strong support to the ideas presented in this chapter. Equally importantly, in our role as teacher educators and practition-ers, we have worked with and alongside children, teachers and community members in transforming and sustaining outdoor environments around the world. Our personal experiences add further credence to the conten-tion that green outdoor environments have an important role to play in the health of children. Overwhelmingly, in all our roles—as academics, researchers, teacher educators and practitioners—we witness these settings as valuable contexts for cultivating children's sense of ownership, dwelling and belonging. One of the many ways to develop this sense of stewardship is through proactive processes that invite children to inhabit their local places through embodied and experiential opportunities. Taken to the next level, these experiences support and encourage children's ecological, personal and social understandings of the world, and provide a gateway into their comprehension of, and commitment to, the places that sustain ongoing human health and wellbeing.

The relationship between the potential of green outdoor environments, health, health promotion and what actually happens in school grounds and early childhood education services remains complex. Despite the discussed benefits of green outdoor environments on children's health, anecdotal evidence suggests that parents, teachers and the wider community often continue to question the validity of teaching and learning within these sites. Thus experiences in green outdoor environments can be viewed as less valid than those that occur in conventional educational contexts. Sadly, in schools (less so in early childhood education services), both formal and informal outdoor experiences can still be perceived by many as 'filling in time' or as a 'break' (Malone & Tranter, 2003, p. 289) from the 'real' learning that takes place within the confines of indoor spaces (Skamp & Bergmann, 2001, p. 349). Inherent in these concerns is the ever-increasing culture of inspection and accountability in schools, including the implementation of standardised testing and national curriculum frameworks that tend to reinforce decontex-tualised practices.

Such perspectives point to the need for greater support to enable pre-service teachers, practising teachers and early childhood educators in schools and early childhood education services to understand the contributions of green outdoor environments for children's health. In the Australian context, we recognise the critical role and contribution of current curriculum policy and directives—for example, the Australian Curriculum (ACARA, 2010), the EYLF (DEEWR, 2009) and the National Quality Standard (ACECQA, 2013)—as frameworks that can support professional judgement and practice in facilitating children's learning about physical health and wellbeing. We view these frameworks as valuable in guiding educators to deliver diverse aspects of health and wellbeing in the unique and local outdoor places children inhabit.

Globally, children, primary teachers, early childhood educators, parents, administrators and communities are creating and utilising green playgrounds and other local outdoor environments as pedagogical sites that support the development of children's ecological, personal and social understandings of the world. We believe that the future of the green outdoor environment movement is viable, thriving and rich with potential.

CONCLUSION

It is widely recognised that health promotion must extend beyond interventions that target individual behaviour to a more comprehensive and ecological model that addresses the settings where people live, work and play. With regard to children's health specifically, this chapter has provided strong evidence that green outdoor environments clearly represent an important site for intervention that influences children's physical, mental, social and spiritual health.

REFLECTION QUESTIONS

3.1   Consider a school or early childhood education service with which you are familiar and evaluate it in light of the IUHPE's guidelines (refer to Table 3.1):

a. Does it adopt a 'settings' approach to health promotion? If yes, what does this look like? If no, what are the barriers that prevent this approach from being taken?

b. Does the outdoor environment help to work towards delivering the IUHPE's principles of a health-promoting setting? Which principles in particular are enabled through a well-designed green outdoor environment?

3.2   Audit your own context in relation to the World Health Organization's Ottawa Charter for Health Promotion (Table 3.2). Which elements for promoting health in educational settings are targeted in your context? Which elements might deserve more focus and attention? What are the barriers and enablers to working on each element?

3.3   What other interventions/approaches, beyond the physical environment, could be used to promote health in early childhood education services and primary schools?

3.4   Assess whether and how your context supports the linkages between outdoor environments and the four dimensions of health profiled in this chapter. What is the evidence to support your claims? How might these relationships be strengthened?

RECOMMENDED RESOURCES

Organisations that support greening children's outdoor environments
- Evergreen: www.evergreen.ca
- Learning Through Landscapes: www.ltl.org.uk
- Ecoschools: www.ecoschools.global
- Stephanie Alexander's Kitchen Garden Foundation: www.kitchengardenfoundation.org.au

Policies, recommendations and guidelines
- Australian Health Promoting Schools Association: www.ahpsa.org.au
- Ottawa Charter for Health Promotion: www.who.int/healthpromotion/conferences/previous/ottawa/en/index4.html
- The National Physical Activity Recommendations for Children in Australia (birth to 5 and 5 to 12 years): www.health.gov.au/internet/main/publishing.nsf/content/health-pubhlth-strateg-phys-act-guidelines
- Blueprint for an Active Australia: http://heartfoundation.org.au/for-professionals/physical-activity
- Achieving Health Promoting Schools: Guidelines for promoting health in schools: www.dhhs.tas.gov.au/__data/assets/pdf_file/0011/115895/guidelines_for_health_promoting_schools1.pdf

REFERENCES

Australian Children's Education and Care Quality Authority (ACECQA) (2013). *National Quality Framework*. Retrieved 20 December 2016 from <www.acecqa.gov.au/national-quality-framework>.

Australian Curriculum Assessment and Reporting Authority (ACARA) (2010). *The Australian Curriculum*. Retrieved 1 October 2016 from <www.australiancurriculum.edu.au>.

Barbour, A.C. (1999). The impact of playground design on the play behaviours of children with differing levels of physical competence. *Early Childhood Research Quarterly, 14*(1), 75–98.

Bell, A.C., & Dyment, J.E. (2006). *Grounds for action: Promoting physical activity through school ground greening in Canada*. Retrieved 5 May 2007 from <www.evergreen.ca/en/lg/lg-resources.html>.

Chawla, L., Keena, K., Pevec, I. & Stanley, E. (2014). Green schoolyards as havens from stress and resources for resilience in childhood and adolescence. *Health and Place, 28*, 1–13.

Department of Education, Employment and Workplace Relations (DEEWR) (2009). *Belonging, being and becoming: The Early Years Learning Framework for Australia*. Canberra: Commonwealth of Australia.

Dooris, M. (2009). Holistic and sustainable health improvement: The contribution of the settings-based approach to health promotion. *Perspectives in Public Health, 129*(1), 29–36.

Dyment, J.E. (2005). *Gaining ground: The power and potential of green school grounds in the Toronto District School Board*. Retrieved 6 January 2006 from <www.evergreen.ca/en/lg/lg-resources.html>.

Dyment, J.E. & Bell, A.C. (2008). Grounds for health: The intersection of green school grounds and health promoting schools. *Environmental Education Research, 14*(1), 77–90.

Dyment, J.E., Bell, A.C. & Lucas, A.J. (2009). The relationship between school ground design and intensity of physical activity. *Children's Geographies, 7*(3), 261–7.

Evans, J. & Pellegrini, A. (1997). Surplus energy theory: An enduring but inadequate justification for school breaktime. *Educational Review, 49*(3), 229–36.

Faber-Taylor, A., Kuo, F.E. & Sullivan, W.C. (2001). Coping with ADD: The surprising connection to green play settings. *Environment and Behaviour, 33*(1), 54–77.

Francesca, S.C., Elliott, S.J. & Crighton, E.J. (2014). Protecting our children: A scan of Canadian and international children's environmental health best practices. *Children, Youth and Environments, 24*(3), 102–52.

Gibbs, L., Staiger, P.K., Johnson, B., Block, K., Macfarlane, S., Gold, L., . . . Ukoumunne, O. (2013). Expanding children's food experiences: The impact of a school-based kitchen garden program. *Journal of Nutrition Education and Behavior, 45*(2), 137–46.

Gill, T. (2014). The benefits of children's engagement with nature: A systematic literature review. *Children, Youth and Environments, 24*(2), 10–34.

Green, M. (2014). Transformational design literacies: Children as active place-makers. *Children's Geographies, 12*(2), 189–204.

International Union for Health Promotion and Education (IUHPE) (2009). *Achieving health promoting schools: Guidelines for promoting health in schools.* Cedex, France: IUHPE.

Kochanowski, L. & Carr, V. (2014). Nature playscapes as contexts for fostering self-determination. *Children, Youth and Environments, 24*(2), 146–67.

Little, H. & Wyver, S. (2008). Outdoor play: Does avoiding the risks reduce the benefits? *Australian Journal of Early Childhood, 33*(2), 33–40.

Maller, C. (2005). Hands on contact with nature in primary schools as a catalyst for developing a sense of community and cultivating mental health and wellbeing. *Journal of the Victorian Association of Environmental Education, 28*(3), 16–21.

—— (2009). Promoting children's mental, emotional and social health through contact with nature: A model. *Health Education, 109*(6), 522–43.

Maller, C. & Townsend, M. (2005). Children's mental health and wellbeing and hands-on contact with nature. *The International Journal of Learning, 12*, 1447–540.

Malone, K. & Tranter, P.J. (2003). School grounds as sites for learning: Making the most of environmental opportunities. *Environmental Education Research, 9*(3), 283–303.

Moore, R.C. & Cosco, N. (2014). Growing up green: Naturalization as a health promotion strategy in early childhood outdoor learning environments. *Children, Youth and Environments, 24*(2), 168–91.

Poland, B., Krupa, G. & McCall, D. (2009). Settings for health promotion: An analytic framework to guide intervention design and implementation. *Health Promotion Practice, 10*(4), 505–16.

Rosenow, N. & Bailie, P. (2014). Greening early childhood education. *Children, Youth and Environments, 24*(2), 1–9.

Sandseter, E.B.H. (2009). Characteristics of risky play. *Journal of Adventure Education and Outdoor Learning, 9*(1), 3–21.

Schein, D. (2014). Nature's role in children's spiritual development. *Children, Youth and Environments, 24*(2), 78–101.

Skamp, K. & Bergmann, I. (2001). Facilitating learnscape development, maintenance and use: Teachers' perceptions and self-reported practice. *Environmental Education Research, 7*(4), 333–58.

Titman, W. (1994). *Special places, special people: The hidden curriculum of schoolgrounds.* Woking: Surrey, World Wildlife Fund, UK.

United Nations Treaty Collection (1990). *Convention on the Rights of the Child.* Retrieved 10 February 2017 from <https://treaties.un.org/Pages/Home.aspx>.

Wells, N.M. & Evans, G.W. (2003). Nearby nature: A buffer of life stress among rural school children. *Environment and Behaviour, 35*(3), 311–30.

Whitelaw, S., Baxendale, A., Bryce, C., MacHardy, L., Young, I. & Witney, E. (2001). 'Settings' based health promotion: A review. *Health Promotion International, 16*(4), 339–53.

World Health Organization (1986). *Ottawa Charter for Health Promotion.* Ottawa: World Health Organization.

—— (2012). *Population-based approaches to childhood obesity prevention.* Geneva: World Health Organization.

—— (2016). *Report on the Commission on Ending Childhood Obesity.* Geneva: World Health Organization.

Wyver, S., Tranter, P., Naughton, G., Little, H., Sandseter, E.B.H. & Bundy, A. (2010). Ten ways to restrict children's freedom to play: The problem of surplus safety. *Contemporary Issues in Early Childhood, 11*(3), 263–77.

Chapter 4

Caring for the environment
Towards sustainable futures

Julie Davis

This chapter begins with the notion that the sustainability concerns confronting humanity—indeed, all species and habitats on the planet—require urgent attention. Past approaches to early childhood environmental education have rested mainly with children playing *in* nature and learning *about* nature. I argue that, while important, such opportunities are not enough to address issues such as climate change, biodiversity losses, ongoing water shortages and impending energy disruptions—all major environmental trends that appear to be worsening (Watts et al., 2017). Nothing short of transformative early education that places social change and empowerment at the core of sustainability learning is necessary. This chapter expands on this argument, citing international studies where early childhood educators have put such approaches into action with successful outcomes.

Provocation

Young people today face considerable challenges in creating bright futures for themselves, with many deeply affected emotionally by the dystopian images presented in multiple forms of media (Australian Psychological Association, 2017; Gidley, 2017). Every generation has its challenges—in the 1960s and 1970s, nuclear proliferation and war were major concerns for youth. Fifty years or more on, concerns about war are just as prevalent—perhaps even more so given the ongoing conflicts and new forms of war and terror facing humanity—while the range of issues impacting on our lives seem to be increasing rather than decreasing. Teaching our children and young people how to create healthy, peaceful and sustainable futures, and preparing them to be thinkers and actors for sustainability, are arguably the major challenges for future generations and are the focus of this chapter.

The Earth and its peoples are facing multiple, complex challenges; we cannot continue as we are. Nature's ability to provide essential ecosystem services to stabilise world climate systems; maintain water quality; ameliorate increasing chemical loads on plants, animals, humans, soils and air; support secure food production; supply energy needs; moderate environmental impacts; and ensure social harmony and equity is seriously compromised (Hamilton, 2017; McMichael, 1993). Current rates of resource consumption by the global human population are unsustainable for both human and non-human species, and for future generations—especially if we consider that the global population will approach 9.6 billion humans around 2050 (UN Department of Economic and Social Affairs, 2015), rising from just over 1.2 billion at the turn of the twentieth century.

Undeniably, these challenges require urgent attention. Education—especially early childhood education—has a key role to play here, as it is in the early years that the foundations are laid for how we live, learn, belong and relate. Past approaches to early childhood education in the outdoors/nature have rested mainly with children playing *in* nature and learning *about* nature, with an unstated belief that such experiences will lead to caring for nature and natural environments in later life. In this chapter, I argue that, while important, such nature-based opportunities are simply not enough to address today's pressing environmental and sustainability issues.

As Inoue (2014), a Japanese expert in early childhood education for sustainability (ECEfS), argues, while there is a long tradition of nature-based activities in Japan, where children have been learning about the natural world and have been encouraged to have nature-based outdoor play in their lives for centuries, 'simply conducting the same kinds of nature-based activities that children have engaged in in the past will not facilitate the development of attitudes, knowledge and skills necessary for building a sustainable society' (p. 90). This chapter is based around this key idea. The text is also framed around the idea that nothing short of transformative early education, which places social change and empowerment at the core of learning, is necessary to create both short- and long-term futures that are healthy, just and sustainable. To provoke readers to seriously consider these viewpoints, the chapter draws on recent national and international reports and articles, and cites international case studies where early childhood educators have successfully put transformative early education for sustainability into action.

Identifying the sustainability problem

> **Sustainability:** A concept that incorporates all dimensions of living—social, economic, political economic and environmental.

First, it is timely to outline in more detail what these environmental and sustainability challenges are, and what they mean for children. For example, the overwhelming consensus is that climate change is real and accelerating, described eloquently as a 'catastrophe in slow motion' (Pierrehumbert, 2006). Key impacts of climate change include increasing extreme weather events, such as floods, droughts and heatwaves—and, of course, Australia is not immune (Research Australia, 2007). For example, 2015 recorded the hottest temperatures since records began, while the first months of 2016 demonstrated that those records were again broken (Bureau of Meteorology, 2016). In 2016 and again in 2017, the Great Barrier Reef saw massive coral bleaching, widely considered to be the result of warming temperatures from the immediate effects of El Niño weather patterns compounded by longer term climate warming (Australian Institute of Marine Science, 2016). In Tasmania, there is real concern about the regrowth of buttonbush ecosystems after the 2015–16 extreme drought and fires (Bowman, 2016). Some scientists are declaring that such extreme weather is a warning of potential ecosystem collapse (Huete & Ma, 2016), with stark consequences for ecosystems, individual species and human beings. This is a cause for concern as farms and crops, for example, can be thought of as agricultural ecosystems and are highly sensitive to climate variability. This means that the ability to maintain adequate livestock and crop production is being seriously challenged in many parts of the world. In India, for example, where the late arrival of the monsoon season in 2013, 2014 and 2015 caused extreme temperatures and severe drought followed by massive flooding, climate change impacts are not some future prospect but are already happening (Loo, Billa & Singh, 2015). A similar situation occurred in Papua New Guinea, where 87 per cent of the population of 7.3 million live outside urban centres and most are subsistence farmers. The 'food bowl' of Papua New Guinea, centred on the Highlands region north of Port Moresby, has been severely impacted as the El Niño-driven drought that started in 2014 affected two million people (Bourke, 2015). As drought struck, the effects have rippled through the economy—one of the poorest per capita countries on the planet (International Monetary Fund, 2015); food prices skyrocketed, food supplies dried up and some communities were living on famine foodstuffs, such as ferns and unripe bananas. There has also been large-scale migration, especially to Port Moresby—a city with poor infrastructure and inadequate housing supplies, as people search for work or short-term cash, and city workers—many already under financial pressure—send money back to their villages so families can buy food to survive (Clark, 2016). While the mass migration of refugees from war-torn areas of the Middle East has alarmed and challenged us over the last couple of years, similar waves of climate change refugees in the future cannot be dismissed (UNHCR, 2016).

Children and sustainability

While we should all have concerns for our own vulnerability in relation to climate change, the stark reality is that children—those currently in kindergartens, preschools and schools, our children and grandchildren—will bear the worst impacts of climate change and unsustainability. Professor Tony McMichael of the Australian National University, who was part of the Nobel-prize-winning Intergovernmental Panel on Climate Change, has commented that the rapidly escalating impact of climate change on the natural environment is casting an enormous shadow over the health of future generations (Research Australia, 2007). This view is echoed by a growing number of scientific reports, Australian and international, which link human and child health and wellbeing to unsustainability, and climate change in particular. In fact, the health and medical professions have been taking a lead in alerting human populations to the health implications of a warmer planet. These reports, citing the latest research over the last decade, include:

- *Healthy Planet, Places and People* (Research Australia, 2007)
- *Our Climate, Our Children, Our Responsibility* (UNICEF UK, 2008)
- *Feeling the Heat: Child survival in a changing climate* (Save the Children, 2009)
- *The Challenges of Climate Change: Children on the front line* (UNICEF, 2014)
- *No Time for Games: Children's health and climate change* (Doctors for the Environment, 2015)
- *Health and Climate Change: Policy responses to protect public health* (Lancet Commission, 2015).

Many reports, position statements and research papers recognise that children are particularly vulnerable to the impacts of climate change, especially in terms of their health and wellbeing, because their behaviours expose them to increased risks, their bodies respond with greater vulnerability to harms, and they are dependent on others (Research Australia, 2007; Save the Children, 2009). Specifically, medical research (e.g. see Xu et al., 2014) shows a link between excessive heat and childhood emergency department attendances for conditions such as diarrhoea, asthma, gastroenteritis and electrolyte imbalances. There is evidence that extreme exposure to heat during pregnancy is related to premature births (US National Institutes of Health, 2016). Flooding and severe storms can have comprehensive health effects on children, causing injury, drowning, hypothermia and electrocution. Malnutrition related to food insecurity is a high risk, and there is growing evidence of climate change impacts and disaster impacts on children's mental health as they struggle with disruption and, particularly among some older age groups, a sense of hopelessness about the future (Farrant, Armstrong & Albrecht, 2012).

Diseases carried by mosquitoes, such as dengue fever, malaria and Zika virus (Gatherer & Kohl, 2014)—with its devastating microcephaly effects—are on the increase as temperatures rise (Shuman, 2010), and are particularly hitting the most vulnerable: those babies conceived in the favelas of Rio de Janeiro in Brazil, for example.

Sustainability: A rights issue

The disproportionate impact of climate change on children and future generations makes unsustainability a children's rights issue. The 1989 United Nations Convention on the Rights of the Child (UNCRC), an international human rights treaty that grants all children and young people a comprehensive set of rights, has key principles that can be related specifically to climate change and sustainability. These include that children and young people (up to 18 years) have the right to life, survival and development; that they should have their views respected; and that primary consideration be given to the child's best interests in all matters affecting them. As noted, climate change is already having an impact of children's life chances, survival and development prospects, and thus must fall within our consideration of children's rights. Understandably, however, this rights focus is human-centred, and I argue elsewhere (Davis, 2014) that the UNCRC, by and of itself, is an inadequate vehicle for addressing issues of climate change and sustainability. Instead, I argue that we need a common world view of rights (Taylor & Guigni, 2012) that is focused less on individual rights, and more on our shared common interests, not just with each other but also with future generations, non-human species, landscapes and earthly elements, such as water and air. If we have this comprehensive view of rights, then it changes fundamentally how we practise early education.

Even though it is a cliché, children *are* the future; however, it is not fair, just or equitable to leave the issues of unsustainability to children to solve at some future time. Further delays simply add to accumulating problems, meaning that the imperative of learning to live sustainably must start as soon as possible. Everyone has a part to play in education for sustainability, which has been recognised as a crucial investment in transitioning to sustainability with a key role in guiding the changes required to reduce consumption to sustainable levels and empowering people for change (UNESCO, 2009). Rickinson, Lundholm and Hopwood (2009, p. 106) state that education and learning should be viewed from a life-course perspective, allowing us 'to think about what we know and what we need to know about environmental learning during infancy, childhood, adolescence, adulthood, middle age, retirement and old age'. With this in mind, it is imperative that all education institutions—from early childhood centres, schools and community education, through to colleges and universities—provide effective ways to educate communities about concepts of sustainability and environmental responsibility, through student learning and via their larger societal connections (Adlong & Dietsch, 2015; Poland, Dooris & Haluza-Delay, 2011).

How are early educators working with transformative early childhood education for sustainability?

Education for sustainability (EfS): Transformative education that equips learners, educators and systems with the knowledge, skills, values and ways of thinking to achieve social and economic prosperity, equality and responsible, active citizenship while restoring and enhancing the health of the living systems upon which all living beings depend.

Early childhood education for sustainability (ECEfS): The natural starting point of EfS that goes beyond nature play and learning; it emphasises the agentic capacities of children to shape the world in which they live, in ways that are healthy, just and sustainable.

Education for sustainability (EfS) is no longer a 'greenie' fringe movement of education. It is an issue increasingly being taken up by architects, town planners, the insurance and finance industries—indeed, by people and professions from all walks of life who understand that climate change has the potential to impact everyone and everything (Australian Academy of Technological Sciences and Engineering, 2010). Leaders of major religions have also endorsed the urgent need to address climate change—for example, in his 2015 encyclical *Laudato Si: Care for our common home* (Vatican, 2015), Pope Francis called for action 'here and now' to tackle climate change and halt the unprecedented destruction of ecosystems for the sake of life and future generations, and for humans to see the climate as a common good.

The Gothenburg Recommendations on Education for Sustainable Development (Davis et al., 2008) identify early childhood as a 'natural starting point' for all ongoing education for sustainability. Early childhood education for sustainability (ECEfS) is a newly emerging area in early childhood education globally, and Australians are at the forefront as advocates, educators, teacher educators and researchers. We are in the fortunate position where our key national curriculum frameworks, the Early Years Learning Framework (EYLF) (DEEWR, 2009) and National Quality Standard (NQS) (ACECQA, 2011) for the before-school sector, and the Australian Curriculum (ACARA, 2015) for the school sector, offer support for sustainability and EfS, although such support cannot be taken for granted. In the EYLF, for example, a key outcome is that children 'show respect for their environment', which is evidenced by children, among other things, developing 'an awareness of the impact of human activity on environments and the interdependence of living things' (p. 29). The NQS (ACECQA, 2011) supports 'sustainable practices' through Quality Area 3.3, which requires that children's education and care services take an 'active role in caring for their environment and contribute to a sustainable future' by embedding sustainable practices in their operations and supporting children 'to become environmentally responsible and show respect for the environment'. For the school sector, sustainability is a cross-disciplinary strand in the Australian Curriculum, to be embedded across all school subjects.

As a result of the leadership of the pioneers in ECEfS, and the support of the afore-mentioned curriculum initiatives, there is now a growing list of first-class exemplars of children and teachers in early childhood education centres, kindergartens, childcare centres, preschools and schools engaged in EfS activities (Davis, 2015). While these have predominantly been about the environmental aspects of sustainability, such as water education, energy reduction, recycling and growing gardens, increasingly educators and children are turning to investigations that explore the socio-economic pillars as well, discussing issues such as poverty, support for refugee families and the strengthening of Aboriginal and Torres Strait Islander communities. Further, there is evidence that these early lessons in learning for sustainability are helping to reshape adult actions around sustainability issues, and that some children and their parents have influenced school actions and learning once the children have moved into formal schooling (Vaealiki & Mackey, 2008).

Some people may think it is inappropriate to 'burden' young children with sustainability issues. I agree—indeed, I would go so far as to say that it is unethical to expose children to doom and gloom scenarios. No one should be turning young children into worriers or warriors. The form of EfS being promoted in Australia offers positive education, where young children are not only supported to be heard and have a voice, but recognised as thinkers and problem-solvers learning to 'make a difference' (see Chapter 8 for more on children's agency in action).

Examples of ECEfS in practice

The following examples offer illustrations of how early childhood education services are embedding sustainability.

The project approach

Despite different contexts, the project approach (Katz & Chard, 2000) has been found to work well in both Australian and Korean early childhood education settings. The project approach has been championed mainly in primary schools, but increasingly has found its way into preschool settings, at least since the 1990s. The project offers opportunities for deep and wide learning, with plenty of time given to explore ideas and for children to act for sustainability.

A project usually has three phases:
1. getting the project started
2. project in progress
3. concluding the project (Ji & Stuhmcke, 2014, p. 160).

The project approach emphasises the role of children as co-constructionists, together with teachers and parents, of a project. What is significant about these projects is that they focus on sustainability issues.

Case study 1: The project approach in Australia and Korea

In Stuhmcke's Australian example, a class of 22 children aged between 3.5 and 4.5 years investigated local environmental issues and, armed with this knowledge, initiated sustainability projects within their kindergarten and wider community. In particular, the children created a book that was designed to convey their new environmental awareness to family members. As a result of their children's adoption of the role of change-agent, parents were inspired to embrace sustainable practices, including amending shopping habits to reduce the use of plastic bags and building possum boxes for the kindergarten (Ji & Stuhmcke, 2014, p. 162).

In Ji's Korean example, a class of 23 children aged 5 years investigated the wildlife and plants of the Musim Stream, a well-known local waterway. As a result of their investigations, the children became aware of the negative impacts of poaching and a polluted water supply on resident otters. Among other methods of investigation, the children employed information and communication technologies (ICTs) to learn more about otters, watching video clips on the internet to understand their characteristics and habits. In order to improve community awareness regarding the otters' plight, the children submitted a proposal to their City Hall to include otters within the current biotope map for the stream and also held an educational event within a local park (Ji & Stuhmcke, 2014, pp. 166–8).

In both examples, the educators applied a *transformative* project approach (Stuhmcke, 2012) that encouraged the children to do more than merely learn about environmental/sustainability issues. Instead, they were actively engaged in changing the situation. For instance, in Stuhmcke's Australian example, children actively promoted recycling practices among local businesses and consumers by making and then distributing pro-recycling posters, while in Ji's Korean example, children publicly campaigned for the protection of the stream and its wildlife, and interacted with their local communities and city politicians to raise awareness.

Read Ji and Stuhmcke (2014) for more details about these two projects.

Ji's example illustrates that the use of ICTs in ECEfS can be a beneficial mix that counters the notion that nature play is antithetical to children's use of technologies, and is somehow 'better' or more 'authentic' or more 'natural' for children. This is a false dichotomy (Fauville, Lantz-Andersson & Säljö, 2014; Lloyd, 2015). Even though it is estimated that three-quarters of British children now spend less time outside than prison inmates (Carrington, 2016), and that screen time is partly to blame, the reality is that screen time—regardless of size and location, and monitored by adults or not—is an everyday reality for children. Smedley (2016), for example, argues that the right technology might actually encourage more children to play outdoors. He offers the example of Hybrid Play, a Spanish start-up that uses augmented reality to transform playgrounds into video games. Children meet a robot companion on their smartphone and the program registers the movement of children as they play. Another example is the Lil' Monkey climbing frame that comes with an app containing a monkey character that suggests different games that children can play at different levels of difficulty. The manufacturer emphasises that the technology should enhance children's outdoor play, not be the driver of it, and as education campaigner Sir Ken Robinson notes, technology 'offers huge opportunities to inform and inspire children's sense of adventure and appetite for outdoor play' (Smedley, 2016). Even in a forest kindergarten in Sweden, I have witnessed the productive and purposeful use of ICT to enhance learning, with teachers and children using tablets to record information and events and to search on the internet when an interesting plant or animal incited curiosity. GPS is also employed to allow parents to locate their children in the forest before the end of the kindy session if needed.

School-based EfS

In many parts of the world, there are a range of initiatives, organisations and programs in schools that promote EfS. These include Enviroschools in New Zealand; the Green School Project in China; Global Green's Green Schools in the United States; the Environment and Schools Initiatives (ENSI) Eco-Schools; and the Foundation for Environmental Education's (FEE) Eco-Schools, the largest internationally coordinated effort. In Australia, the Sustainable Schools initiative has been a strong force for EfS, although in recent times it has been somewhat contentious, resulting in funding cuts and a lack of support from government departments. Nevertheless, the idea of Sustainable Schools lives on in many school communities.

Closely allied with such Sustainable Schools initiatives—and sharing many of the same participatory goals, purposes, and curriculum and pedagogical approaches (Davis & Cooke, 2007)—is the Health Promoting Schools (HPS) initiative. Indeed, these two movements could usefully be converged in order to create green and healthy schools (Davis & Cooke, 2007; Dyment and Bell, 2008; see also Chapter 3). Boon and colleagues (2011, p. 1) refer to the integration of schools, climate and health promotion as 'a vital alliance' for addressing and ameliorating the impacts of climate disasters on children and vulnerable populations.

A key characteristic of most of these programs and initiatives is that they use a whole-school or systems approach to embedding sustainability. That is, they work not only through a formal curriculum that promotes empowerment and the ability to take action and generate change, but also through alignment with good environmental management, the design and effective use of healthy physical and social environments—both indoors and outdoors—and partnerships with parents and the wider community.

Case study 2: Harrington Park Public School and Ashgrove State School

Harrington Park Public School in New South Wales became the first Australian school to be registered as an Eco School in 2014. Harrington Park has implemented a number of sustainability-driven programs that aim to reduce its negative impact on the environment, and encourage students to take action and make decisions to improve sustainability. These programs have a global and local focus. All Harrington Park students participate in environmental campaigns, such as National Tree Planting Day and Earth Hour, and the school has created a student-led group to promote environmental awareness in the school and its community. The school is home to worm farms and compost bins that are fed by the fruit scraps of students and staff, a 'food forest' with over 30 fruit trees, a community herb garden, a raised vegetable garden, a large chicken coop and a native garden with a frog pond. The school recycles paper, captures rainwater in its water tanks and generates its own electricity (Harrington Park Public School, 2016). These environmental management projects encourage students to develop an understanding of the interrelatedness of human activities and the natural environment.

Ashgrove State School in Brisbane is another example of a school that has embraced sustainability and health promotion as part of the school curriculum and management plan. In 1992, the Ashgrove school community commenced the Ashgrove Healthy School Environment Project, a long-term plan for the development of a healthier school environment. The project initially found its form in the redevelopment of its degraded playground area for the school's youngest children, which led to a greener, shadier and more interesting space for playing and learning (Davis & Cooke, 1998). Building on these earlier achievements, the school has embraced a number of health and environmental projects, including the recent installation of a Stephanie Alexander Kitchen Garden (SAKG). The SAKG is an Australia-wide curriculum project that teaches students to grow, produce and then use this produce to cook tasty and healthy meals (www.ashgrovess.eq.edu.au). The SAKG aligns with the outdoor and action learning principles of education for sustainability, enabling primary students to form a deeper understanding of the natural world and how they can make changes for the better.

Schools like Harrington Park Public School and Ashgrove State School offer examples of how we can engage children in health promotion and sustainability in a fun and informative way, which in turn affords them the knowledge, skills and values to make contributions to sustainable futures.

CONCLUSION

EfS is so much more than nature play, and while this *is* important, it is not enough to shape sustainable lifestyles or create sustainable communities. Support children to be active and informed citizens. Engage them in thinking, problem-solving and acting around environmental and sustainability topics. It is our responsibility as parents, grandparents, citizens and educators of the future generation of Australian and global citizens to do our best to leave the world a better place—or, at least, no worse a place—for the future. Children have the right to sustainable futures and to be deeply involved in making and shaping the futures we want.

REFLECTION QUESTIONS

4.1   EfS is more than environmental management; however, it is important to support renewable energy initiatives, reduce your centre's carbon footprint, save water and reduce waste. What aspects of your environmental management practices need overhaul?

4.2   Recognise that ICT is not nature play's rival. They can both be excellent tools for teaching about sustainability. How can ICT be used to enhance children's inquiry through nature play to support learning and teaching about sustainability?

4.3   Encourage children and adults to think critically about the connections between nature, environment, people and sustainability. Can you see a place for learning about Aboriginal and Torres Strait Islander, Confucian, Muslim and alternative worldviews that more overtly make connections between place, people and planet?

4.4   Be active in your early childhood education centre and local community. Support and strengthen sustainability and environmental education programs and initiatives. What are the local groups and networks in your area that support sustainability and EfS initiatives?

4.5   Be an informed citizen. Don't be swayed by loud sceptics and climate deniers. What reputable scientific and educational sources can you identify to bolster arguments for your sustainability initiatives?

RECOMMENDED RESOURCES

Below are some key resources for further reading on sustainability in early childhood education:

Davis, J. (edn.) (2015). *Young children and the environment: Early learning for sustainability* (2nd edn). Melbourne: Cambridge University Press.

Elliott, S. (2014). *Sustainability and the Early Years Learning Framework*. Sydney: Pademelon Press.

Lang, J. (2007). *How to succeed with education for sustainability.* Melbourne: Curriculum Corporation.

Sneddon, S. & Pettit, A. (2016). *Sustainability in action in early childhood settings.* Blairgowrie: Teaching Solutions.

The following early childhood environment/sustainability education networks have emerged in Australia. These networks recently formed the Australia–Aotearoa Alliance for Early Childhood Education for Sustainability to work together to amplify advocacy and outreach for ECEfS:

- Queensland Early Childhood Sustainability Network
- New South Wales Early Childhood Environmental Education Network
- Environmental Education in Early Childhood (Victoria)
- Early Education for Sustainability South Australia
- Sustainability Learning Centre (Tasmania).

REFERENCES

Adlong, W. & Dietsch, E. (2015). Nursing and climate change: An emerging connection. *Collegian: The Australian journal of nursing practice, scholarship and research, 22*(1), 19–24.

Australian Academy of Technological Sciences and Engineering (2010). *Climate change and the urban environment: Managing our urban areas in a changing climate.* Retrieved 28 March 2017 from <https://atse.org.au/Documents/Publications/Reports/Climate%20Change/Climate%20Change%20and%20the%20Urban%20Environment%202009.pdf>.

Australian Children's Education and Care Quality Authority (ACECQA) (2011). *National Quality Standard.* Retrieved 20 December 2016 from <www.acecqa.gov.au/national-quality-framework/the-national-quality-standard>.

Australian Curriculum, Assessment & Reporting Authority (ACARA) (2015). *Australian National Curriculum.* Retrieved 31 October 2016 from <www.acara. edu.au/curriculum/curriculum.html>.

Australian Institute of Marine Science (2016). *Coral bleaching events.* Retrieved 28 March 2017 from <www.aims.gov.au/docs/research/climate-change/coral-bleaching/bleaching-events.html>.

Australian Psychological Association (2017). *Climate change—what you can do.* Retrieved 28 March 2017 from <www.psychology.org.au/publications/tip_sheets/climate>.

Boon, H., Brown, L., Clark, B., Pagliano, P., Tsey, K. & Usher, K. 2011. Schools, climate change and health promotion: A vital alliance. *Health Promotion Journal of Australia, 22,* S68–71.

Bourke, R. (2015). As Papua New Guinea faces worsening drought, a past disaster could save lives. *The Conversation,* 26 August. Retrieved 28 August 2015 from <https://theconversation.com/as-papua-new-guinea-faces-worsening-drought-a-past-disaster-could-save-lives-46390>.

Bowman, D. (2016). Fires in Tasmania's ancient forests are a warning for all of us. *The Conversation,* 29 January. Retrieved 31 January 2016 from <https://theconversation.com/fires-in-tasmanias-ancient-forests-are-a-warning-for-all-of-us-53806>.

Bureau of Meteorology (2016). *Australia in April 2016.* Retrieved 28 March 2017 from <www.bom.gov.au/climate/current/month/aus/summary.shtml>.

Carrington, D. (2016). Three-quarters of UK children spend less time outdoors than prison inmates—survey. *The Guardian,* 26 March. Retrieved 23 March 2017 from <www.theguardian.com/environment/2016/mar/25/three-quarters-of-uk-children-spend-less-time-outdoors-than-prison-inmates-survey>.

Clark, M. (2016). PNG's food bowl is all but empty as drought affects 2 million people. *Sydney Morning Herald,* 13 February. Retrieved 28 March 2017 from <www.smh. com.au/world/pngs-food-bowl-is-all-but-empty-as-drought-affects-2-million-people-20160204-gmlixh.html>.

Davis, J.M. (2014). Examining early childhood education through the lens of education for sustainability: Revisioning rights. In J.M. Davis & S. Elliot (eds), *Research in early childhood education for sustainability: International perspectives and provocations* (pp. 21–37). New York: Routledge.

—— (ed.) (2015). *Young children and the environment: Early learning for sustainability* (2nd edn). Melbourne: Cambridge University Press.

Davis, J.M. & Cooke, S.M. (1998). Parents as partners for educational change: The Ashgrove healthy school environment project. In B. Atweh, S. Kemmis & P. Weekes (eds), *Action research in practice: Partnerships for social justice in education* (pp. 59–85). New York: Routledge.

—— (2007). Educating for a healthy, sustainable world: An argument for integrating health promoting schools and sustainable schools. *Health Promotion International*, 22(4), 346–53.

Davis, J.M., Engdahl, I., Otieno, L., Pramling Samuelsson, I., Siraj-Blatchford, J. & Valladh, P. (2008). *The Gothenburg recommendations on education for sustainable development*. Gothenburg, Sweden: Swedish International Centre for Education for Sustainable Development (SWEDESD), Chalmers University & Gothenburg University.

Department of Education, Employment and Workplace Relations (DEEWR) (2009). *Belonging, being and becoming: The Early Years Learning Framework for Australia*. Retrieved 1 May 2016 from <https://docs.education.gov.au/system/files/doc/other/belonging_being_and_becoming_the_early_years_learning_framework_for_australia.pdf>.

Doctors for the Environment (2015). *No time for games: Children's health and climate change*. Retrieved 28 March 2017 from <http://dea.org.au/news/article/report-no-time-for-games-childrens-health-and-climate-change1>.

Dyment, J.E. & Bell, A.C. (2008). Grounds for movement: Green school grounds as sites for promoting physical activity. *Health Education Research*, 23(6), 952–62.

Farrant, B., Armstrong, F. & Albrecht, G. (2012). Future under threat: climate change and children's health. *The Conversation*, 9 October. Retrieved 29 March 2017 from <http://theconversation.com/future-under-threat-climate-change-and-childrens-health-9750>.

Fauville, G., Lantz-Andersson, A. & Säljö, R. (2014). ICT tools in environmental education: Reviewing two newcomers to schools. *Environmental Education Research*, 20(2), 248–83.

Gatherer, D. & Kohl, A. (2014). Zika virus: A previously slow pandemic spreads rapidly through the Americas. *Journal of General Virology*, 97, 269–73.

Gidley, J. (2017) *The future: A very short introduction*. Oxford: Oxford University Press.

Hamilton, C. (2017). *Defiant earth: The fate of humans in the Anthropocene.* Sydney: Allen & Unwin.

Harrington Park Public School (2016). *Information booklet.* Retrieved 30 May 2016 from <www.harringtnp-p.schools.nsw.edu.au/documents/37831044/37837641/ Information%20Booklet%202016.pdf>.

Huete, A. & Ma, X. (2016). Rising extreme weather warns of ecosystem collapse: Study. *The Conversation,* 18 February. Retrieved 28 March 2017 from <http:// theconversation.com/rising-extreme-weather-warns-of-ecosystem-collapse-study-54898>.

Inoue, M. (2014). Perspectives on early childhood environmental education in Japan: Rethinking for a sustainable society. In J.M. Davis & S. Elliott (eds), *Research in early childhood education for sustainability: International perspectives and provocations* (pp. 79–98). New York: Routledge.

International Monetary Fund (2015). Poorest Countries by GDP (nominal) per capita. *Statistics Times. International Monetary Fund World Economic Outlook, October.* Retrieved 28 March 2017 from <statisticstimes.com/economy/poorest-countries-by-gdp-capita.php>.

Ji, O. & Stuhmcke, S.M. (2014). The project approach in early childhood education for sustainability: Exemplars from Korea and Australia. In J.M. Davis & S. Elliott (eds), *Research in early childhood education for sustainability: International perspectives and provocations* (pp. 158–79). New York: Routledge.

Katz, L.G. & Chard, S.C. (2000). *Engaging children's minds: The project approach* (2nd edn). Stamford, CT: Ablex.

Lancet Commission (2015). *Health and climate change: Policy responses to protect public health.* Retrieved 28 November 2015 from <www.thelancet.com/ commissions/climate-change-2015>.

Lloyd, M. (2015). The world is getting flatter: ICT and education for sustainability in the early years. In J.M. Davis (ed.), *Young children and the environment: Early education for sustainability* (2nd edn, pp. 145–61). Melbourne: Cambridge University Press.

Loo, Y., Billa L. & Singh, A. (2015). Effect of climate change on seasonal monsoon in Asia and its impact on the variability of monsoon rainfall in Southeast Asia. *Geoscience Frontiers, 6,* 817–23.

McMichael, A.J. (1993). *Planetary overload: Global environmental change and human health.* Cambridge: Cambridge University Press.

Pierrehumbert, R.T. (2006). Climate change: A catastrophe in slow motion. *Chicago Journal of International Law, 6*(2), 1–24.

Poland, B., Dooris, M. & Haluza-Delay, R. (2011). Securing 'supportive environments' for health in the face of ecosystem collapse: Meeting the triple threat with a sociology of creative transformation. *Health Promotion International, 26,* ii, 202–15.

Research Australia (2007). *Healthy planet, places and people.* Retrieved 28 November 2016 from <http://aries.mq.edu.au/publications/other/HealthyPlanet.pdf>.

Rickinson, M., Lundholm, C. & Hopwood, N. (2009). *Environmental learning: Insights from research into the student experience.* Amsterdam: Springer Verlag.

Save the Children (2009). *Feeling the heat: Child survival in a changing climate.* Retrieved 28 November 2015 from <www.savethechildren.org.uk/resources/online-library/feeling-the-heat-child-survival-in-a-changing-climate>.

Shuman, E. (2010). Global climate change and infectious diseases. *New England Journal of Medicine, 362,* 1061–3.

Smedley, T. (2016). Swings, slides and iPads: The gaming companies targeting kids' outdoor play. *The Guardian*, 11 April. Retrieved 17 September 2016 from <www.theguardian.com/sustainable-business/2016/apr/11/ipads-playground-gaming-companies-targeting-kids-outdoor-play>.

Stuhmcke, S.M. (2012). *Children as change agents for sustainability: An action research case study in a kindergarten.* PhD thesis, QUT, Brisbane. Retrieved 28 March 2017 from <eprints.qut.edu.au/61005/1/Sharon_Stuhmcke_Thesis.pdf>.

Taylor, A. & Guigni, M. (2012). Common Worlds: Reconceptualising inclusion in early childhood communities. *Contemporary Issues in Early Childhood, 13*(2), 108-19.

United Nations Department of Economic and Social Affairs (2015). *Revision of world population prospects 2015.* Retrieved 28 March 2017 from <http://esa.un.org/unpd/wpp>.

United Nations Educational, Scientific and Cultural Organization (UNESCO) (2009). *Bonn Declaration.* UNESCO World Conference on Education for Sustainable Development. Retrieved 28 March 2017 from <www.esd-worldconference-2009.org/fileadmin/download/ESD2009_BonnDeclaration.pdf>.

United Nations High Commissioner of Refugees (UNHCR) (2016). *Climate change and disasters.* Retrieved 28 March 2017 from <www.unhcr.org/climate-change-and-disasters.html>.

United Nations Children's Fund (UNICEF) (1989). *United Nations Convention on the Rights of the Child.* Retrieved 11 March 2015 from <www.unicef.org/crc>.

—— (2014). *The challenges of climate change: Children on the front line.* Retrieved 28 March 2017 from <www.unicef-irc.org/publications/pdf/ccc_final_2014.pdf>.

UNICEF United Kingdon (2008). *Our climate, our children, our responsibility: The implications of climate change for the world's children.* Retrieved 17 September 2016 from <www.unicef.org.uk/Documents/Publications/climate-change.pdf>.

United States National Institutes of Health (2016). *Extreme temperatures could increase preterm birth risk.* Retrieved 28 March 2017 from <www.nih.gov/news-events/news-releases/extreme-temperatures-could-increase-preterm-birth-risk>.

Vaealiki, S. & Mackey, G. (2008). Ripples of action: Strengthening environmental competency in an early childhood centre. *Early Childhood Folio, 12,* 7–11.

Vatican (2015). *Laudato si: Care for our common home.* Promulgated by Pope Francis. Vatican City. Retrieved 11 November 2015 from <w2.vatican.va/content/francesco/en/encyclicals/documents/papa-francesco_20150524_enciclica-laudato-si.html>.

Watts, N., Adger, N., Ayeb-Karlsson, S., Bai, Y., Byass, P., Campbell-Lendrum, D., . . . Costello, A. (2017). The Lancet countdown: Tracking progress on health and climate change. *The Lancet, 389*(10074), 1151–64.

Xu, Z., Hu W., Su H., Turner L.R., Ye X., Wang J. & Tong S. (2014). Extreme temperatures and paediatric emergency department admissions. *Journal of Epidemiology and Community Health, 68*(4), 304–11.

Chapter 5

Birds and babies
A meeting of species

Janet Robertson, Meredith Chan and Karen Fong

Outdoor playspaces for children aged from birth to 2 years provide rich opportunities to connect with the environment. Children do this in company with friends and connected adults, who are knowledgeable about the place, its creatures and its elements, and open to the surprises and gifts it offers the program and children's affections. This chapter offers narratives of young children's engagement with the beyond-human world, a world in which other species live parallel, equally important lives, interconnected with humans and vice versa (Haraway, 2007).

All three authors are early childhood teachers. Janet Robertson is the outdoor teacher, while Meredith Chan and Karen Fong are teachers in the infants room. We will refer to ourselves throughout the chapter as Janet, Meredith and Karen. These chronological narratives were distilled by Janet from the reflective programs Karen and Meredith wrote and displayed for families to read at the end of each day throughout 2015. The three authors collaborated daily, reflecting on the information gathered as well as their pedagogies and future directions. These reflections and those written within the program guided the curriculum, providing a catalyst for further intentional teaching. Each reflection included a written page, two or three anecdotal observations and, as narratives, these were punctuated by quotes and references to either *Belonging, Being and Becoming: The Early Years Learning Framework for Australia* (EYLF) (DEEWR, 2009) or pertinent statements from educational theory or other relevant disciplines. The complex process of reflecting on pedagogy must be informed by many sources, of which the EYLF is one. Rather than only working within the confines of the EYLF Learning Outcomes (DEEWR, 2009), we considered the outcomes to be embedded in our daily pedagogy, and to be drawn from sound early childhood knowledge. We frequently referenced more specialised knowledge, depending on the curriculum context and children's learning—for instance, other-than-human theory (Haraway, 2007). This focus of thinking beyond the EYLF created a learning environment for the three of us as we explored anthropomorphism, social geography and ornithology, generated by the infants' engagement with the wild birds in the garden.

Furthermore, we intentionally included the children's voices in the daily reflections, even though at times, with such young infants, spoken language was emerging. This honoured their various communications and highlights how capable they are. It is also our intention to give teachers a voice in this chapter, giving us agency and power to tell directly of the pedagogy of teaching and listening. Too often, teachers' voices are silenced in texts that tell of education.

Meredith and Karen team-teach with two other staff, Jessie and Sudha, and a group of twelve children aged from 6 to 25 months at Mia Mia Child and Family Study Centre in the Department of Educational Studies, Macquarie University, Sydney, Australia. This is a long daycare program. The children have access to the playground every day; the centre, including the playground, is situated on the leafy urban campus of the university. The playground offers children chances to run, play, shout, dig in the sandpit, clamber on the climbing structures, construct with blocks, potter about and garden—in essence, to do everything children do outside. This small garden playspace is where the infants learn to sit, crawl, walk, balance, stand on tiptoes and hold hands with a friend. The program is constructed so that children are offered challenge, serenity, rituals and relationships in every space.

This chapter highlights the children's connection with the co-inhabitants of this place. 'We all come from some place, we all live in some place. Our identity and our very sense of authenticity, it seems, are inextricably bound up with the places we claim as "ours"' (Gentry, 2002, cited in Wattchow & Brown, 2011). This theory of place shapes our thinking; the uniqueness of our place drives our curriculum and is prominent in our philosophy. As Wattchow and Brown state, 'places are not simply locations or abstract concepts, rather they are sites of lived experiences and meaning making' (2011, n.p.). The notion that pedagogy can be crafted from place is described by Somerville and colleagues (2011, p. 1):

> We explore how one might come to know oneself differently by focusing not on one's individualised self whose identity is constructed in its separation from others and from place, but on oneself in relation to those others, including human, non-human and earth others, who make up the places we live in.

In conceptualising the embodied *im-placement* to place and identity, Merleau-Ponty (2002, p. xxiii) discusses that 'we witness every minute the miracle of related experience, and yet nobody knows better than we do how this miracle is worked, for we *are* ourselves this network of relationships'.

From the outset, the other-than-human species (Haraway, 2007) that occupy the campus and playground made an impact on the program.

The birds, wheeling and swooping, calling fearlessly and rearing their young around us; the ducks with their ducklings wandering through en route to the creek; the cute but feral cats and rabbits shyly dashing about; the insect life buzzing, creeping and burrowing; and the slow, charming gastropods leaving their shimmering trails intrigued all from the beginning. A flock of white cockatoos make the campus home. They are raucous, gregarious and easily recognised, and are integral to our curriculum.

Reading through the 2015 daily reflections and the children's discoveries and experiences, it is clear that both children and staff embraced any connections with those with whom they shared the place. The following narratives are arranged chronologically, interspersed with direct quotes, interpretations and references.

The narratives

The first extract, dated 5 February, was written several weeks into the school year and Ann (12 months) was settling in, becoming familiar with new significant others from the security of her pram. Karen wrote that Daisy (19 months) was the bird enthusiast:

> A plane flew over. The sound of its engine caught our attention as Vicky (15 months), Daisy, Fred (13 months) and Ann looked up, and in that moment the aeroplane's shadow passed over us. 'Oh!' Vicky commented, pointing up to the sky. 'Noisy,' Daisy followed. 'Er?' Ann asked. Fred waved to the plane as it flew further away. They returned to their sand play. Shortly after, a cockatoo perched itself on the branch of a tree and squawked. Daisy, announcing 'Bird!', acknowledged the cockatoo's presence. Vicky, Ann and Fred looked up. 'Where? We heard the cockatoo but we can't see it,' I commented. 'Er?' Ann asked, eagerly scanning the trees. 'There!' Daisy pointed. 'Er?' Ann asked again. Daisy hurried to her aid and shifted the pram so that Ann could see the cockatoo. 'Ah!' Ann cheered, seeing the white feathers behind the gum leaves. 'Yay, we found it!' I said. Vicky clapped and wriggled her hips. Her energetic dance made Fred laugh as he continued to put the spoon in his mouth. Young children are observant

and constantly curious about everything in their surroundings, as Ann Pelo (2013, p. 68) notes, 'Knowing one place intimately makes possible knowledge of other place: we become adept at paying attention, we are attuned to the marvellous and beautiful.'

The rain is always a vital element in our program. Sydney's hot and sticky summer felt as though it would last forever, and the rain was a welcome relief:

> The shower on a humid morning was ideal as Vicky, Eva (16 months), Ann, Ian (25 months) and Daisy stood with Karen on the verandah and watched it gush down. 'Oh oh!' Vicky gasped pointing up to the grey clouds. The cockatoos, galahs and rainbow lorikeets screeched and squawked from the treetops, relishing the downpour. 'Birds!' Daisy announced. Their presence was irresistible, adding to the sound of rain falling. Shortly after, the children noticed traces of rain in our garden. 'There there,' said Vicky, pointing into the drain. Eva followed as they listened closely to raindrops echoing inside its cavernous hollow. Ian chuckled as he found a puddle of water nearby and with a heavy foot he made a splash. 'There!' said Daisy, noticing the rain drenching our garden bench. She patted her hands on it and studied the water transferring to her skin. The opportunity to witness the changes in our natural environment is a blessing every day.

These intimate and detailed (Pelo, 2013) experiences within our place reflect children's first understandings of the water cycle. Learning to appreciate and delight in rain, or indeed falling in love with it, is a visceral learning, a beginning step in caring for the Earth. Australia is one of the driest continents on the planet, so coming to grips with the impact of rain, the changes it brings and the dependency of all creatures on it is a lesson one is never too young to learn. The birds caterwauling and playing in the rain offer no greater image of the preciousness of rain.

On 5 March, the sensations of sound and air captivated two of the youngest children. Children think about the world with their whole bodies (Stolz, 2014), and it is for us to notice what is an invisible influence on their learning and give it the gravitas it deserves. Sound and air movement are with us at all times, a part of the soundscape and airscape of this place, and as the children learn to accommodate these sensations, identify them and layer them into their ways of being, we need to be cognisant of their occurrence. Knowing the place, the place becomes known to them:

> Fred (13 months) looked up when he heard the aeroplane fly over. 'Ah . . .' he called out. He returned to the green lid he had found until Zara (10 months) joined him at the table. Zara energetically tapped the table. Fred stopped and observed her. In reply, he tapped the table as well. Together they reached and manipulated the objects on the table with strategies such as tapping, tasting and transferring. A gush of wind blew over us. 'Oh . . .' said Fred. They both stood still and felt the breeze brush past. Shortly after the wind returned and this time Zara turned around and chuckled as she caught the wind with an open mouth. The chilling sensation brought on fits of laughter while Fred raised his arm up and touched it with his fingertips. What observant infants they are, clearly expressing 'wonder and interest in their environments' (DEEWR, 2009, p. 34).

On 6 March, Daisy's ornithological interest was clearly scaffolded with the provision of a book. We know that children crave and need the words for the things and beings that make up their world (Pelo, 2013). It is part of our philosophy and pedagogy that children deserve to be involved in the complex and dynamic curriculum the natural world offers them:

> The visit of a kookaburra drew much delight from Daisy, Vicky and Sonia (23 months) as they squealed and pointed in excitement. 'There! Kooka, kooka!' exclaimed Daisy to Karen, remembering it from the books she has been reading the whole week. 'Ka ka ka ka,' Vicky dramatised, perhaps encouraging the kookaburra to make its famous call for all to hear. The kookaburra flapped its wings and took off and the children chorused 'ohhh' in dismay. It landed on a tree nearby and Sonia and Daisy rushed over to the fence to check on it. 'Kookaburra, kookaburra,' Daisy assured her friends that it was still close by. Jessie brought out *The Field Guide to the Birds of Australia* (Pizzey, 1982) and Daisy recollected the page in which she had spotted the kookaburra, once again going over it in detail.

What a serendipitous moment it was that a kookaburra visited us this morning, just when we had been marvelling at the illustrations of the birds the day before. In this way we assisted the children to 'resource their own learning through connecting with people, place, technologies and natural and processed materials' (DEEWR, 2009, p. 34).

In a day peppered with connections, Meredith wrote:

> Later in the morning, Karen made another discovery inside. A goat moth was resting on the door near the gate. Once again, Daisy, Sonia and Vicky raced over to gawk at the moth that was similar to the one they saw on the verandah yesterday. Noticing that the moth was very still, Sonia suggested that it might be asleep and reminded everyone to be quiet with a 'Shhh'. 'Sleeping,' Daisy nodded, agreeing with Sonia's idea. 'Is the moth asleep? Shall we sing it a song?' I asked. 'Twinkle,' Daisy replied. 'Hao,' ['okay' in Mandarin] Sonia said with a nod. The girls did the actions to the song, staring intently at the moth and ensuring that it could hear their serenade. Just at that moment, Karen called out from outside, 'Oh look, there's another moth here!' And the children were off in their moth-watching quest. This time it was a brown leaf-shaped moth resting on the staff room door. The glass door was helpful as they were able to examine the underside of the moth without needing to touch it. What a privilege it is to learn more about the world they live in, put a name to each creature and attune their senses to appreciate the beautiful wonders of nature, because 'Every child deserves to know the pulsing, cycling life of the Earth through simple intimacies and daily encounters' (Pelo, 2013, p. 44).

Here children engage in anthropomorphic ideas, in this instance attributing a love of music to the moth. Rather than disabuse children of these notions, the pedagogy capitalises on them, strengthening the children's engagement, making the relationship tender and reciprocal.

On 12 March, Daisy, once again reading *The Field Guide to the Birds of Australia* (Pizzey, 1982), had become familiar with books as a source of knowledge. The set of birds she knows, and can identify, is used to create a sub-set, including an unknown, but hauntingly familiar species. Karen wrote:

Daisy exclaimed when she saw her favourite bird, the kookaburra, 'There, kookababa!', sharing her finding with Sonia and myself. Turning the page, it was Sonia's turn to point out the picture of the duck amongst the other birds, remembering them from the walk we had last year. As they continued looking at the book together, they identified the birds they were familiar with that have visited our garden. Daisy and Sonia examined the galah, cockatoo and other ducks closely and admired the different colours. Noticing the similarities between the white and black cockatoos, they paused at the page and differentiated between the colours. 'White, black, white cockatoo,' Daisy analysed and Sonia followed the movement of Daisy's finger between both birds. Revisiting their interest in the birds with the new book reinforced the children's understanding of the different types of birds, and increased their awareness of the details in their appearance. Names are important, as Pelo (2013, p. 107) notes: 'When we hold in common the names of the places where we live, and the names of the beings that live with us, we can speak together of our life in these places with these creatures.'

We know the shape of a cockatoo is distinctive, and in field guides species are grouped, but Daisy's discovery of the black cockatoo, and her explanation of her findings to Sonia was indicative of her cognitive investment in understanding cockatoos. Daisy, our expert, brought passion and knowledge to the group, while Vicky was the avian spotter, with a keen eye for the bird's whereabouts. They complemented each other's abilities; without each other, the total sum of their understandings would be diminished.

It is 23 March and Tom (12 months) shows how attuned children are to their surroundings, and his determination to communicate this to others is apparent. The reader can see below the infection of bird enthusiasts, and the interest in birds is not Daisy's' alone. Karen wrote:

'Ehh ehh!' Tom exclaimed loudly and pointed upwards. 'What is it, Tom? What are you looking at?' I asked. 'Ehhhhh!' he replied more loudly this time, as he sat bolt upright, still pointing with a fixed gaze and eager to share his findings. Curious to see what Tom was trying to show us, Daisy and Sonia looked in the same direction. 'Oh there, bird!' Daisy cried out, catching sight of what Tom was looking at. 'Oh yes, you're right. It's a cockatoo perched on the balcony over there,' I reaffirmed. The children stared for a good few minutes, managing the tricky task of maintaining an upward gaze and balancing their bodies at the same time. 'Aahh!' Tom announced as the cockatoo flew away and Daisy confirmed that it was now 'gone'. The intrigue with the birds in our environment continues as the children remembered their usual resting places and they have developed a keen eye in spotting them among the trees or within the building, exploring 'relationships with other living and non-living things' (DEEWR, 2009, p. 29).

The plumage of our creatures is also a source of curriculum. A few days later, on 31 March, some feathers were discovered. Karen wrote:

'Oh look, Vicky, feathers up there. Please, Karen?' Daisy asked. Daisy held the feathers and offered one to Vicky. The girls giggled when they brushed the feathers against their cheeks. 'Is it tickling you?' Karen asked. 'Tickling me!' Daisy answered. Vicky wriggled her body and laughed. 'No birds, no cockatoo,' Daisy noticed as she stood on the verandah. She was right: outside was quiet for a moment until a few noisy miner birds flew over. 'Oh noisy bird!' Daisy named. 'Yes the noisy miner,' Karen replied. 'Noisy,' Vicky followed, holding her ear. 'Cockatoo . . . Come!' said Daisy, 'Come,' pleaded Vicky. No sign of the cockatoos was evident. Instead, Karen offered the children the book, *A Brush with Birds: Australian Bird Art from the National Library of Australia* (National Library of Australia, 2008). Together, they studied the painting of the Australian birds. 'There, cockatoo!' Daisy noticed. Vicky smiled and brushed the feather over the page. Daisy followed. 'More?' Daisy asked. 'What should we find next?' Karen asked. 'Um . . . Kookaburra,' she said. 'Burra,' said Vicky. Their research continued and together they noticed the magpies, rosellas and kookaburras. How admirable it is to see children making deep connections with the environment.

The induction of a future ornithologist continued as, on 2 April, Karen witnessed dramatic games:

Daisy retrieved the cockatoo and kookaburra puppets from the basket. 'Good morning,' she began, and carried them to the morning tea table. 'Say good morning, cockatoo, kookaburra. Kiss?' she asked. Zara (11 months), Vicky and Karen greeted the puppets. Vicky and Daisy laughed at this notion. 'Goodbye,' Daisy said, animating the puppet's response. 'Book up there, please,' she asked Sudha. Sudha sat with Daisy and Vicky as the girls revisited the bird book they had been investigating. 'There, there,' Vicky pointed, and found the picture of the cockatoo for Daisy. Daisy manipulated the puppet and made it dance on the page. Zara heard the girls' delight and crawled over to look at the book. She crawled onto it and stopped when Vicky gasped, 'Oh no.' 'I think she wants to show us the picture. You're right, we don't sit on books,' Sudha commented. Vicky nodded as Zara tapped on an illustration and then reversed off. 'That's an owl,' Daisy named for Zara. 'Owl!' Vicky followed. Zara listened and looked at both girls. She chuckled as she hurried her crawl towards the mirrors. A community of learners is constant and exists in everyday moments; children certainly are 'curious and enthusiastic participants in their learning' (DEEWR, 2009, p. 34).

Zara's curiosity, piqued by their merriment in the puppet joke and her welcome inclusion in their information-gathering meant she too was able to indicate her delight in our feathered companions. Daisy's work with the puppets, giving them a human voice, added porosity to the borders between human and other-than-human.

Towards the end of April, it is raining again and Jessie, a staff member, celebrates its bounty:

The rain was irresistible this morning. Vicky and Daisy hurried with the sparkly material draped over their shoulders as they dashed towards the fence. 'Rain, rain!' Daisy called out. 'Rain!' Vicky followed. They reached out with their palms. 'Rain!' they marvelled and studied the drops against their skin. 'It's beautiful, isn't it?' Jessie commented. 'Beautiful,' Daisy followed. Vicky chuckled as she licked it off her hand while some tickled her nose. 'Oh!' she gasped, wriggling her wet nose. The girls are right; it is like magic to catch raindrops.

In June, the winter breezes offered another aural opportunity:

> The loud rustling of the leaves from a sudden gust of wind caught Amy's (20 months) and Ben's (28 months) attention. They climbed into the cubbyhouse and observed the movement of the trees, mesmerised by their fluid song and dance. 'Wind, wind,' explained Ben continuously as he pointed out the reason for the movement to Amy and Karen. Amy spent a good few minutes surveying the environment and making sense of this phenomenon. The children are constantly in awe of nature and derive much sensorial pleasure from it.

For Ben and Amy, knowing where to go to experience the breeze is a signal that they hold knowledge about this landscape. This embodied knowledge, of wind on skin, coupled with knowledge of place thus creates a shortcut for children to make sense of the world.

It isn't just moths and birds that capture the children's attention. On 2 July, a lizard surprised them all:

> A sudden squeal of delight echoed in the playground as Charles (26 months) and Sonia announced there was a 'lizard!' Its unpredictable movements caused uncertainty as they couldn't decide where to stand. 'We can sit and watch,' Karen suggested. In a circle, Eva, Vicky, Charles and Sonia stopped to observe with caution. The baby lizard froze in motion, with us waiting in anticipation. Sonia called out, 'Lizard!' The reptile turned a little and caused a startled reaction. 'Oh no, it moved!' Charles described. Eva and Sonia shuffled backwards and continued to observe. 'The lizard is okay, it turned because it heard you talk,' I explained. 'It's okay, Eva. It's okay, Sonia,' Vicky reassured her friends. The girls listened and moved back a little more. They looked at each other and cackled in recognition of each other's nervousness. We sat and observed in awe until Charles questioned, 'Where is it going?' 'I'm not sure,' I replied. 'Oh . . . ' Sonia marvelled. The children continued to be still and gathered the information they needed to understand the baby lizard lived in the cracks of our walls. Listening to children enables us to hear their narratives, adding to the understanding that 'natural history knowledge is not just the accumulation

of facts, but also the layering of stories in which personal experience, social interactions and locality together give both order and meaning to nature' (Brookes, 2002, p. 77).

Later in the year, as the days shortened, encounters with the birds changed. On 31 July, Ashleigh (a relief teacher) observed:

> It is shared knowledge between the children that at dusk, the cockatoos squawk and make their presence known as they prepare to roost for the night. Ian, Vicky, Eunu (11 months), Connie (17 months) and Daniel (31 months) raced to the wooden bench. Together they pointed and announced that the cockatoos had arrived. 'Where?' we asked. 'Coc, coc,' Ian pointed. 'Cockatoos there!' Vicky followed. Just as the children predicted, the cockatoos were perched on the verandah railing on the third level. Daniel chuckled with glee as he hurried to show Ashleigh what we had found. 'Oh yes, I can hear them,' Ashleigh answered. Daniel smiled as he returned to the bench and suddenly held his ears when more cockatoos arrived. To our surprise, a raven flew by and landed near them, followed by another that sat on our tree. Eunu hurried to point out this other raven and gained his friends' attention. For half an hour, we watched and listened in awe as the cockatoos and ravens prepared for the night to arrive. Children are keen observers and curious about all the happenings in their world.

Time—time to help children notice twilight falling, to sense the crisp air, to observe and hear creatures prepare for the night—is no accident at Mia Mia. We value our place in this place, and create opportunities to simply live in wonder. We build memories for children; this place is their memory palace (Lyndon & Moore, 1994).

We caught up with Tom on 28 September, now steady on his feet and keen to move about:

> 'Oh! Look what I found!' exclaimed Jessie in the sandpit. 'A feather, wow, a white feather,' she continued. Michael (30 months) and Tom hurried over, taking big strides in the sand. 'Oh look, the wind is blowing it, ooooh,' Jessie narrated. Michael peered more closely at the wispy

feather, waiting for the wind to move it again. 'Would you like to blow the feather instead?' Jessie invited when there was no gust of wind. He pursed his lips slightly and started aiming his breath at the feather, giving a small grin when the feather started dancing along. Motivated by this, he started blowing more forcefully and his grin widened as he saw the feather's increasing movement. Tom was keen to blow on the feather and waited for his turn. He chuckled in amusement, delighted that he was able to contribute to the feather's movement and mirrored Michael's repeated attempts to master a stronger breath. The children continued to monitor the feather's whereabouts, following it as the wind picked up and moved it along. These 'simple intimacies and daily encounters' (Pelo, 2013, p. 44) of the wonders of nature never fail to intrigue the children and deepen their sense of curiosity and amazement.

The year cycles along, and the seasons change. The wattle trees are laden with seeds, and the cockatoos feast on them. So attuned are the children that they can correct adults who incorrectly identify bird calls! Karen wrote of one such moment:

> 'Oh I can hear the kookaburra outside,' Cassy (another staff member) commented. 'Oh . . . There cocky,' Ann said, naming the caller. Ann was right as she recognised the squawk of a cockatoo. 'I heard about some cockatoos eating in a tree near your garden, can you show me where?' Cassy continued. 'There!' Vicky and Ann pointed out. Together they led the way to the path behind the garden. Just as they children anticipated, five cockatoos were feeding in a wattle tree. Jay (16 months), Fred, Connie (17 months) and Eunu joined in when suddenly they sensed the sweeping sound of a cockatoo as it flew over. The children looked up and followed it until it sat on the wattle branch. More cockatoos entered the garden as they travelled between the balcony upstairs and the tree nearby. Sheer delight echoed in this space as the children admired the cockatoos showing their way of living. How fortunate to witness this in our everyday ritual!

The weather is warmer; it's 10 November. The visible traces the cockies have left behind are treasured:

Amy and Jay heard a cockatoo fly above. They remembered where the cockatoos had been and made their way towards the wattle tree, waiting for further signs of cockatoos. 'Are they here?' Jessie asked. Amy and Jay peered through the fence and waited. Jay sounded out the call of a cockatoo and waited a little more. 'Oh look!' Amy marvelled as she held the feather of a cockatoo in her hands. 'Yes, look at the feathers here,' Jessie commented. Amy continued to search for feathers and on this hunt they came across a raven's feather. The black and silky texture was irresistible. Amy joined in and admired it with us as she ran the tip of finger along it. 'Yes, it's beautiful,' Jessie continued. 'Oh wow!' said Amy. 'Wow,' Lena (17 months) followed. What beautiful connections the children have made with the cockatoos as they begin to understand their belonging among the trees in our back garden, gathering knowledge of an 'intrigue with nature itself and the diversity of textures, sights, sounds, smells, tastes and living entities that nature provides' (Lekies & Berry, 2013, p. 79).

These feathers kept on giving, as on 17 November:

Amy and Vicky stopped suddenly when they noticed the smallest feather from a raven sitting on the ground. 'Karen, look!' they called. 'What's that?' Vicky asked. 'Oh!' Amy gasped. Our investigators were unsure of whether they could pick it up; instead they waited for my affirmation. 'Oh yes, now I see it. It's a feather,' Karen commented. 'Oh . . .' Amy marvelled. Vicky carried the feather and noticed a similarity. 'Look, look! It's the same . . . See?' she announced and matched it to the large raven feather sitting on our bench. Alice (20 months) joined in and observed this new finding. 'The same. See, Alice?' Vicky continued. Alice made comparisons and smiled as she recognised it as well. Together these scientists gathered new insights into the ravens and cockatoos that live with us every day. What a treasure it is to think and share new meanings with another.

It is now 3 December, the weather is hot and the days outside are languorous:

Revisiting their usual morning routine of checking the balcony above for cockatoos, both Sarah (16 months) and Eunu dashed to the gate to have a look. 'Ehhh, ehhh,' exclaimed Sarah, pointing and informing Sudha where to look. Eunu fixed his gaze upwards admiring the cockatoo lineup with which he had become so familiar. The birds have become synonymous with the outdoor playground and the children have now become accustomed to searching for them as soon as they go outside.

Later in December, we met Ben again, with a group of budding meteorologists:

Ben, Vicky and Amy waited by the gate and observed me setting up the sandpit. 'I wonder if it's going to rain?' Karen thought out loud. Amy looked up to the sky and pondered, 'Um . . . No rain!' she announced as she held out her hand to sense any raindrops. 'Um, Karen? The clouds are moving now,' Vicky noticed. 'Wow . . . ' Ben marvelled. Together the children transformed into meteorologists and studied the weather change. 'See . . . The clouds are moving,' Vicky noticed again. 'All gone,' Amy followed. 'No more,' Ben added. The clouds parted above and to their surprise the sun was bright. 'Look! Sun!' Amy cheered. 'Yes, Amy, the sun is out now,' Vicky celebrated. They reached out and caught the glimmer of the sun against their skin. 'Mmm . . . It's a warm day, Karen,' Vicky added. 'Mmm . . . Hot today,' said Amy. 'Hot,' Ben blew. 'Okay, hat now please, Karen, um for me, Amy and Ben,' Vicky instructed. It is important to appreciate the children's keen interest in understanding the complexities of science in daily life.

CONCLUSION

Learning to listen to the voice of the land, hearing and seeing how it can assist you in teaching children, and yourselves, to belong, be and become is one we need to embrace (Robertson, 2012, p. 23).

The concept of biophilia, a love for the Earth and all living creatures (Wilson, 1984) is central to our teaching at Mia Mia. We cannot leave young children's encounters with rain, birds, trees, wind and place to chance. In this chapter, the intentional recognition and extension of these elements, and provision for them to take their rightful place in the curriculum were illustrated.

The magic of these encounters deserves to be treated with a light hand, a mindful, thoughtful inclusion within the daily events of young infants' lives. It is our hope that, armed with this delight, these infants will care for this place and the Earth more broadly in their later years. As Louv (2010) maintains, environmental education must teach children hope, not despair. But for their here and now, to be given time and companionship to be a part of the startling wonders of the playground is our aim. The identity of place, and of those within it, simultaneously creates and is created by place. As Brookes (2002, p. 81) notes, 'Knowing the place becomes knowing the self.'

REFLECTION QUESTIONS

5.1   What potential role do wild or domesticated animals play in early childhood curricula?

5.2   Is the wellbeing of animals prioritised within a curriculum or are they just another resource?

5.3   What role does nature play in the curriculum for children under 3 years of age? What would it look like in other educational settings?

5.4   What is the pedagogical role of the teacher when reflecting about their engagement with the outdoor curriculum?

5.5   What is your vision for an outdoor infant curriculum? What values and priorities would you identify?

REFERENCES

Bone, J. (2013). The animals as the fourth educator: A literature review of animals and young children in pedagogical relationships. *Australasian Journal of Early Childhood, 38*(2), 57–64.

Brookes, A. (2002). Lost in the Australian bush: Outdoor education as curriculum. *Journal of Curriculum Studies, 34*(4), 405–25.

Department of Education, Employment and Workplace Relations (DEEWR). (2009). *Belonging, being and becoming: The Early Years Learning Framework for Australia.* Retrieved 30 October 2016 from <https://docs.education.gov.au/system/files/doc/other/belonging_being_and_becoming_the_early_years_learning_framework_for_australia.pdf>.

Haraway, D. (2007). *When species meet.* Minneapolis, MN: University of Minnesota Press.

Lekies, K. & Berry, T. (2013). Everyone needs a rock: Collecting items for nature in childhood. *Children Youth and Environments, 23*(3), 66–88.

Louv, R. (2010). *Last child in the woods: Saving our children from nature deficit disorder.* London: Atlantic Books.

Lyndon, V.D. & Moore, C. (1994). *Chambers for a memory palace.* London: MIT Press.

Merleau-Ponty, M. (2002). *Phenomenology of perception.* Trans. C. Smith. London: Routledge.

National Library of Australia (2008). *A brush with birds: Australian bird art from the National Library of Australia.* Canberra: National Library of Australia.

Pelo, A. (2013). *The goodness of rain: Developing an ecological identity in young children.* Redmond, WA: Exchange Press.

Pizzey, G. (1982). *A field guide to the birds of Australia.* Sydney: Collins.

Robertson, J. (2012). Who needs a forest? *Rattler,* December, 20–4.

Somerville, M., Davies, B., Power, K., Gannon, S. & de Carteret, P. (2011). *Place pedagogy change.* Rotterdam: Sense.

Stolz, S.A. (2014). Embodied learning. *Educational Philosophy and Theory, 47*(5), 474–87.

Wattchow, B. & Brown, M. (2011). *A pedagogy of place: Outdoor education for a changing world.* Melbourne: Monash University Publishing. Retrieved 14 October 2016 from <books.publishing.monash.edu/apps/bookworm/view/A+Pedagogy+of+Place/131/pp100003.xhtml>.

Wilson, E.O. (1984). *Biophilia.* Cambridge, MA: Harvard University Press.

Part 2

Designing and planning for outdoor learning

Chapter 6

Planning outdoor learning environments

Mary Jeavons

Outdoor play has many benefits for children. It promotes physical activity, exploration and inquiry, and creates a connection to the natural world. Yet not all outdoor environments are created equal. The benefits and value of any given environment will depend greatly on how well that environment has been planned and organised.

Four main factors stand out as the most critical:

- the qualities or characteristics of these spaces to suit the needs of babies and young children
- the organisation of space into smaller activity areas, and how these relate to one another
- the amount and distribution of space per child
- the management/amenity/utilities that support the wellbeing of the users and effective functioning of the physical environment.

Ultimately, the overall amount and distribution of outdoor space influence the success of all other factors.

This chapter explores these factors in more detail, and outlines a simple process for planning an outdoor play environment in supervised centres for the education and care of preschool-aged children. It builds on a philosophy that values outdoor play, nature and children's engagement with natural environments. It is based on the assumptions that children are competent learners capable of directing their own play, and that the physical environment has an influence on children's behaviour (DEEWR, 2009).

Most importantly, quality outdoor play 'means more than play equipment' (Herrington et al., n.d., p. 8).

> **Provocation**
>
> Think of some different contexts that might affect the specific outdoor activities that should be provided in a children's centre. How should the design respond, for example, to an inner-city long day care centre versus a centre for Aboriginal children in a remote settlement versus a sessional kindergarten in a country town?

Outline of a planning process

When planning an outdoor play environment, many factors need to be considered. The steps are similar whether the project is a new centre, an existing centre in need of a redesign or a small area requiring a facelift.

When a playspace is on a rooftop or over a suspended slab, the same principles apply, but much more attention must be paid to the engineering of the slab, and the load-bearing potential to support sand and soil. These are essential, but very heavy, components of an outdoor playspace. Spaces on rooftops require specialist input from day one.

For existing outdoor spaces, the process involves some observations and diagnostics of how the space currently functions. Sometimes they don't work effectively, but it is difficult to pinpoint the exact reason. Consider whether any of the following points apply:

- The space is too small.
- There is not enough to do outdoors.
- The qualities of the space do not engage children.
- Children don't have enough time to settle and engage deeply in activities.
- Children running or riding bikes are disturbing other activities or preventing children engaging in quieter/more sedentary activities.
- Spaces are too single purpose—that is, not adaptable/open-ended, or they are dominated by fixed play equipment that cannot easily be adapted.
- The space is too open and bland.

- Loose materials spill into one another and onto other surfaces.
- Children move sand and dirt around the space and the place is perceived as messy and dirty.

These issues can be addressed in the planning process outlined below.

Starting out: The first steps

The following steps are important starting points for any project.

1. Consult key stakeholders:
   - Consult stakeholders: educators, children, directors, families, management; gather and sift ideas and priorities.
   - Settle on the philosophy of outdoor play and learning—the qualities and characteristics that are preferred.
2. Establish a budget:
   - Establish what funds and resources are available now and whether some elements can be staged for the future.
   - Establish what technical/professional input will be required (e.g. landscape architect and structural/civil engineer) and plan fees into the budget.
3. Review the existing conditions:
   - Obtain an accurate plan of the site (a contour and feature plan, or site survey).
   - Investigate the particular characteristics of the individual site, including drainage issues and how to protect existing trees.
   - If the space is on a rooftop or suspended slab, seek specialist/engineering input.
   - Steep slopes, odd-shaped fence lines and small spaces need more careful planning.
   - If the playspace is existing, analyse how well it functions, and the causes of any underlying problems.
4. Refine the brief:
   - Establish the priority activities and functional zones that are needed.
   - Research the size, location and ideal relationship between the main functional zones.

Further considerations for site planning are considered in later sections of the chapter. The following section provides an overview of some key factors to consider in relation to the provision of diverse playspaces.

Outdoor activity zones: A 'shopping list' with design implications

The first step in planning is the preparation of a basic list of the outdoor play activities and functions that are required. This 'shopping list' becomes part of the design brief for the outdoors.

Examples of various activity types are described below, including:

- broad types of activities that have similar characteristics
- general considerations affecting these activities
- some examples of specific activities that loosely fit within that category
- simple design tips for these outdoor activities, to help make them fit for purpose.

The design of the outdoor play environment should respond to constraints and local conditions, and provide the kinds of outdoor experiences that local children require. For example, there are many ways in which the outdoor environment can encourage children to use their bodies physically, and these all have different design requirements. A centre catering to children who live in high-rise apartments may choose different priorities from a rural centre whose children habitually ride bikes and climb trees in their own backyards.

Spaces for physical activity

Children engage in physical activity in many different ways. Educators can use the outdoor play environment to encourage children to use their bodies, take on and master progressive challenges, and develop physical, social, sensory and psychological skills. Many different parts of the outdoor play-space contribute to this development, each with slightly different purposes and design considerations.

The speed and height of activities are determining factors, as these affect children's safety, how they impact on others, where these activities should be located and what kinds of surfaces are necessary. Where children of a wide range of ages use the same space, care must be taken to protect babies and toddlers from hazardous situations while providing suitable challenges for older children. Address the following physical activities early in the process as they need the largest amounts of relatively flat unencumbered space.

High-conflict/fast-moving activities

These activities might be located in open, multi-purpose areas, but swings and bikes are included here too.

Open, multi-purpose activity areas

A large, open area is useful for a variety of purposes, including running and ball games, picnics, group games and gatherings (see Figure 6.1).

It needs to be relatively flat and, ideally, surfaced with living turf/lawn, but grass will be difficult to maintain for intensively used areas.

Ideally, it will have a varying degree of enclosure—some open boundaries where other activities can flow onto the open area, and some sections separated by vegetation, a low fence or a structure that can help to protect adjacent activities from disturbance.

Figure 6.1 An open, grassed area adjacent to the climbing area provides a large, central and multi-purpose zone.

Source: Author's collection.

Bike riding

Bikes provide opportunities for unique and valuable physical development, and for risk-taking (see Chapter 2), as well as excellent opportunities for social interaction.

Fast-moving bikes affect everything in their path, and very small outdoor spaces might not be able to accommodate bike play. Bikes need to be managed carefully, and do not need to be in use at all times. Set careful rules about their use.

To minimise the disturbance of others, a bike route should ideally not encircle the whole yard, affecting everything within it. Select a route to ride bikes that only utilises one section of the space. Add value and complexity by adding dramatic play opportunities along the way (changeable rather than permanent). Ideally, design in a basic route with optional branches with slopes and bumps to extend skills when children are ready.

Swings

Swings offer multiple benefits for children: soothing, therapeutic rocking; wildly swinging movement and challenge; a vantage point from which to observe the social environment; and important kinaesthetic sensory development. Swing frames should have removable, changeable components, such as different seat types, ladders and knotted ropes, and these require storage.

Hazardous if located in the wrong place, swings must be placed where children do not have to run past them for any reason.

Swings need an impact-absorbing surface and an adequately sized impact zone (see Chapter 7). They are often located on the edge of a larger climbing area, and can use the same surface. Locate a swing where a staff member pushing a child can also supervise the main playspace.

High climbing, hanging, agility and sliding

It is important to provide opportunities for children to develop their climbing skills and confidence. Chapter 2 provides a detailed analysis of risky play, including climbing.

Trees provide excellent opportunities for promoting not only physical skill but also cognitive development (Elliott, 2015), encouraging decision-making and mastery of unevenly spaced branches. The suitability of individual trees and the surface underneath them needs to be assessed.

Fixed structures (maximum height 1800 millimetres) provide opportunities for climbing, hanging from the arms and sliding. Structures need to remain adaptable to a wide variety of play purposes. Moveable equipment (maximum height 1500 millimetres) can be adjusted for different age and skill levels. A combination of fixed and moveable equipment may be ideal if space allows. Planks and moveable equipment need storage close to the climbing area.

All play equipment above 600 millimetres in height needs an impact-absorbing surface, with a large and flat enough space (impact zone) for climbing and sliding equipment. The selection of impact-absorbing surfaces depends on local availability of materials, environmental and aesthetic factors, as well as practicalities such as the slope of the site, the cost and maintenance requirements.

The open running area and the climbing area are likely to be the largest spaces within the outdoor environment. Ideally, these will be located close to each other, so equipment less than 600 millimetres in height can extend into an adjacent flat surface (see Chapter 7).

Jumping/balancing

Balancing and jumping activities are very important for the development of balance and strength, and are especially crucial for bone health in children. Specific challenges can be set up to encourage children to jump, for example, from varying heights. These should take place on the impact-absorbing surfaces provided for climbing activities.

Incidental design elements, such as low retaining edges, changes in level, bumpy terrain, slopes and steps, all provide children with opportunities to test their skills as they move around a space. Every opportunity to turn a utilitarian item into something playful or with interesting detail will add small progressive challenges and value into a space.

Upper body movement

Opportunities for digging in sand and dirt; for shovelling autumn leaves or compost into a wheelbarrow and moving these around; for lifting loose materials and outdoor blocks all contribute to children's strength, fitness, skills and understanding about the physical properties of materials.

Playspaces need to offer loose materials for pushing, pulling, carrying and digging, routes for barrowing, and places to store wheelbarrows, tools and equipment. Refer also to the section below on sand.

Loose spaces for creative, sensory and messy play

Children need to engage with their world directly with their own hands as they evolve their creative/sensory imaginative/dramatic play over time (Dowdell, Gray & Malone, 2011). They need:

- an environment that is somewhat negotiable, adaptable and loose
- opportunities to create, build and collect
- suitable spaces to use materials.

These characteristics can be challenging for adults. What is exciting and full of possibilities to some people is messy, unattractive and out of the comfort zone of others. Loose, creative environments can be orderly but creative at one end of the spectrum, and chaotic and cluttered at the other. It is important to openly discuss this matter with educators and parents to seek an optimal way to meet children's needs, so adults are comfortable with the approach taken. Loose materials can be well managed, contained and even hidden from view if that is necessary. Outdoor environments must include spaces that encourage exploration, where children can use various materials in their play and not be disturbed by others running through. As well as providing suitable time and space, educators need to keep up a supply of loose play materials and the associated access to storage that will be required.

Issues that are important to think about here are:

- connections
- protection/location out of traffic flow
- containment
- storage.

Connections between materials and spaces

The combination of loose materials and suitable settings in which to use them offers children what Gibson (1977) describes as 'affordances'. These are clues in the environment that indicate possibilities for action. For example, children may take sand from the sandpit, and see an opportunity at the other end of a playspace where they want to use the sand for a purpose such as mixing or cooking. Sometimes this is both perplexing and challenging to adults, who view this as messy and wasteful of the sand. The design has inadvertently set up opportunities perceived by children who make connections between activity areas that adults had not anticipated. The solution requires setting up the right connections/relationships between sand and these other opportunities (see Chapters 2 and 12 for further discussions on affordances). There are many typical ways in which early childhood centres provide for creative/sensory play with loose materials, and each has its own considerations. These are explored below.

Sand

Sand is a valuable and versatile play material, considered a fundamental in most centres. Sand should be fine in texture and have sufficient clay content to enable moulding and construction, but should not set hard.

Children of different ages use sand in many and varying ways: for pure sensory exploration; basic pouring and mixing; creative/cognitive purposes; and as a medium in complex social/dramatic play.

In order to add complexity to the play, sand needs:

- water
- natural materials, such as leaves, flowers and twigs
- digging tools
- toys, such as trucks and excavators
- containers, PVC pipes, pots and pans
- a dramatic play setting in which to frame the sand play.

Two sandpits linked by a small path will enable transporting sand from one to the other.

Sand kitchens/open cubbies

A purpose-built deck or bench, log, flat rock, open cubby or platform close to the sandpit (ideally forming one edge) provides a place to mix, 'cook' and use sand for dramatic, creative/sensory play. Children connect this play into their broader games, linked to other parts of the outdoor environment. Small social spaces, nooks under weepy shrubs, cubbies and the like have potential to connect with this play, and ideally could be located nearby to prevent carried sand from spreading too far.

Sand should ideally be located:

- away from doors
- down a slope, rather than at the top
- where it is not disturbed by foot traffic or cut through by fast-moving children
- close to a water supply
- close to storage, for containers, toys and tools
- close to a sand kitchen, open cubby, platform or nook
- close to a garden with a plentiful supply of pickable flowers, leaves, gumnuts, pods and so on
- where it is protected from wind
- where it can be drained.

Sand play is vulnerable to disturbance and running through, and ideally is protected by a partial backdrop, such as a hedge, fence, low screen, wall or other element, along part of its boundary; otherwise the space feels too exposed on all sides. Scale affects how we feel, and different scaled spaces suit different people and different activities (Greenman, 1988). Partial physical containment helps to reduce the scale of the space, which is more suited to this kind of play. Ensure that adults can still supervise the space. Because children play in sand for extended time periods, good summer shade is vital, but winter sun is also valuable.

Managing spillage

Spilled sand possibly causes the most headaches of all materials, when poorly located. A raised edge encourages use as a work bench, which causes spillage, and the edge prevents the sand from ever being swept back. Sand pits should not be placed in a mulched/tan bark area without a wide path or other barrier separating the two materials, which will inevitably become mixed. Benches, planks, rocks or logs intended as working surfaces for moulding and play are best located in the centre so the sand spills back into the sandpit rather than over the edge.

One of the few ways to contain sand is to set the sand down below the surrounding levels (see Figure 6.2). This requires good drainage. A wide paved path on at least one side of a sandpit, with the sand below this, provides easy access for children with a disability and contains the sand by this sweepable edge.

Figure 6.2 One of the few ways to contain sand is to set the sand down below the surrounding levels.

Source: Author's collection.

Loose soil/digging patches

Soft, loose soil (ideally a sandy loam where available) provides a different type of experience from sand and should be provided in a separate location to avoid the sand and soil from mixing. Like sand, soil or dirt needs to be contained and should be located out of a foot traffic zone, and downslope from buildings. Storage is required for spades, small trucks, containers and so on. Digging patches need a water supply. Older children often use steel spades when digging so the dirt patch ideally should allow enough room for a few children to work alongside each other safely. As some adults find digging patches unattractive (possibly without understanding their value), a less prominent position may be ideal. Digging patches need to be loosened up by adults periodically if the soil is prone to set hard; otherwise they will remain unused.

Creek beds

Creek beds are popular in playspaces. They embody a range of ideas, and they can be designed in many ways, from formal, sealed concreted or pebble-lined creeks for flowing water to dry gravelly beds between mounds or edges of rocks.

The benefit of the creek idea is that it is frequently an open-ended setting where children can scratch in the loose surface, drive their little trucks, build dramatic role-play games, or explore a natural environment, depending upon their interests.

A creek is a useful design theme within a space, and can be used to link other smaller areas. Bridges, plantings and varying stream bed widths can add complexity and visual interest. Loose pebbles, sand, gravel and water can all be contained within the creek (see Figure 6.3). The edges can be formed by a swale, mounds, low flat boulders, logs or any combination along its length.

Figure 6.3 A creek bed can include both sealed and loose surfaces.

Source: Author's collection.

Dramatic play opportunities along the stream, such as a boat, a cubby, a low deck or a jetty, all have potential to add complexity to this play setting.

Ideally, creeks should be:

- placed where the natural landform would form a creek or drainage way, to look realistic
- set below the surrounding surface
- well drained, as water must not be able to lie in the creek bed between supervised play sessions.

If a concrete base is proposed, take care with the finish along the edges. Erosion and wear can expose the raw concrete underside.

Water

Water is an important medium for play, either for combining with other materials, such as sand or soil, or for its own sensory potential. Purpose-provided water play can be expensive where water is scarce, and where pumps and filters need to be installed.

As a minimum, it is recommended that taps be located close to key areas, such as sandpits, gardens and digging patches. Sustainable water use can be monitored by educators. Hand pumps for water play provide excellent opportunities for both water play and social interaction/communication. Maintenance of these can be ongoing and demanding of resources. Where no other options are feasible, a simple hose, a garden spray and troughs for water play still provide excellent play value.

Consider the following carefully:

- children's safety to avoid risks of drowning, and slipping
- availability of adequate water supply and its sustainability
- possibilities of capturing water from roofs and tanks, and the health/hygiene regulations that apply locally
- capabilities for and costs of maintaining any infrastructure
- drainage and disposal of the water after use.

Programmable spaces for art and block building

It is useful to have a variety of spaces where children can build and create, and where educators can set up and program activities.

Outdoor blocks and crates are valuable for children's building, either as an end in itself or to create a setting for other games. Troughs, work benches, tables and easels with art materials also provide for children's creative expression through a variety of media. Water taps or troughs nearby are useful for cleaning up.

The ideal space for a variety of creative pursuits is one that is paved, relatively sheltered and protected from foot traffic/bikes. The area should be approximately 3 square metres in size and be located near storage. Flat decks and pavement are ideal, though it is also a good challenge to build on uneven surfaces.

Verandahs

Generous shady verandahs can be ideal for setting up creative activities. They should ideally be a minimum of 3 metres wide, with limited numbers of doors, and with a larger space at one end purposely provided for activities. When too many doors open onto a narrow verandah, it ceases to be a useful playspace and is reduced to a thoroughfare.

Gardens as a supply of loose play materials

Well thought-out gardens and planting provide useful play materials that children can appropriate for their play.
- Select plants that are tough and suited to their environment, and preferably include indigenous species.
- Deliberately select plants for their sensory qualities and the potential of leaves, pods, seeds, bark and flowers to become play materials.
- Avoid plants that produce just one or two single flowers, but choose those with prolific flowers and practise ethical picking.
- Locate plants where they will not be trampled, or fence them off from foot traffic.
- Locate them close to spaces where they can add creative value—close to sand, digging patches, cubbies or art areas.
- Provide adequate water and drainage.
- Avoid poisonous species, limb dropping trees and plants that produce allergens, irritants, very sharp spikes or choking hazards (especially in spaces for babies and toddlers).

Productive gardens

Productive gardens—those growing herbs, vegetables and fruit—provide children with endless learning opportunities. Effective gardens can be created in a very wide range of ways, from tiny pots, to planting into hay bales and raised planters, through to formal vegetable gardens and orchards.

Apart from the satisfaction of observing edible produce emerge from a seed, tuber, cutting or seedling, these gardens attract bugs and wildlife to observe; they offer sensory and aesthetic value; and they provide constant change and delight. Composting vegetable waste from the early childhood education centre connects children to the cycles of decomposition, thus producing soil nutrients essential for plant life.

The design of suitable gardens depends upon the local climate and the type of plants, but the following considerations usually apply:

- Choose a location where there is sufficient sun.
- Ensure there is a suitable growing medium/soil.
- Ensure an adequate water supply.
- Provide adequate drainage.
- Choose a location where the garden can't be trampled.

Select fast-growing vegetables to provide quick results. Where educators are not confident gardeners, assistance could be sourced from grandparents, volunteers or professionals to help with training and garden maintenance.

Spaces and props for dramatic play/role-play

Children seek out suitably scaled spaces and suitable props for a variety of dramatic play/role-play activities. This kind of play enables children to play out different roles and to reflect on events that happen in their lives, and is fundamental to the development of social skills, empathy, creativity, imagination and language (Drown & Christensen, 2014).

Many items that adults add to playgrounds (with the best of intentions) remain unused or under-used because they limit children's play rather than extend it. These include prescriptive themed play equipment, many play panel products, murals, over-designed cubbies, play houses with fully designed plastic kitchens and many toys. These items may be useful in playspaces where children just make a quick visit, but they offer poor play value in the long term, where children spend extended hours in the space. There is an important difference, for example, between a child-built, constantly evolving cubby and a factory-produced one.

The ideal outdoor environment provides:

- spaces at a variety of scales, with varying degrees of enclosure
- the potential to adapt a space
- access to the props children need
- protection for other children running through
- time for the play to develop.

Some examples of particular settings suited to this kind of play are included below. There are many others, including low platforms, decks and play equipment.

Intimate-sized spaces

An ideal outdoor playspace is not completely open and bare, but includes spaces of various sizes and scales. Plantings, light screens or low fences, hedges and any barrier or material that provides a sense of enclosure while allowing opportunities for supervision are ideal.

The shape of these spaces, and where they are located, will affect the play behaviour:

- Small circular spaces or nooks of less than a few metres across (ideally even smaller) will invite a range of dramatic play options, especially if materials such as tree stumps, low rocks and other moveable elements can be introduced and changed.
- Linear 'runways' between plantings invite movement, and can be used to join up the other dramatic play nooks.

Built cubbies

Some thoughts on how to increase the play value from built cubbies are offered below.

- The size, including the height, should ideally be fairly intimate. A space approximately 1.8 square metres in size invites a few children at a time and is large enough for a child in a wheelchair to turn around.
- Spaces with fully enclosed walls and a door that can close will limit the

connection of the cubby play with external spaces, are difficult to supervise and can be used to exclude children. These cubbies can be enhanced by:
- removing the door
- removing at least half a wall and capping the half wall with a shop counter
- adding benches, niches and shelves.
- The addition of a stage, deck or verandah extends the play outside (see Figure 6.4).
- Some hooks or options to connect fabric, a curtain and props make it easy to adapt further.
- A location next to a different sort of small-scale space, such as under a weeping bush or the under-deck space beneath play equipment, extends the play and adds additional value.
- Cubbies connect well with sand play areas, especially if they are set on a deck from which sand can be directly swept back into the sandpit.
- This kind of play is ideally protected from fast-moving activities.
- Small cubby spaces can be set up by educators and children using loose materials and minimal permanent fixtures. Outdoor blocks, furniture, moveable play equipment and vegetation can be adapted by draping fabric, placing floor coverings, and bringing in dress-ups, cushions and toys.
- Use planting, gardens and trees to define small-scale spaces.

Figure 6.4 Adding this deck, and opening up the walls, enhanced the play value of this cubby.

Source: Mishka Nansi.

Gathering/seating/social spaces

It is useful to provide a gathering/multi-purpose space outdoors that can be used for a variety of purposes, including group activities, social gatherings, eating and celebrations (see Figure 6.5). These spaces can act as a focal point for the whole outdoor space. They should not be over-designed, as this can limit their usefulness. They should be:

- larger than the small, intimate, dramatic playspaces discussed previously
- designed to avoid general foot traffic passing through them
- accessible by wheelchair
- semi-enclosed, shaded, easily supervised and comfortable.

Figure 6.5 An example of a central gathering space

Source: Author's collection.

Conclusion: Site planning

The information above has outlined many key issues that need to be considered when planning an outdoor space. Using this information, it is necessary to place these in relation to the site itself, and also in relation to each other. This chapter concludes with a summary of these steps.

Undertake preliminary steps

- Establish the rough size required for the main functional zones.
- Sketch these to scale on a plan. This initially can be done just as a simple bubble of roughly the right size.
- Set out the 'big picture' of what activity could go where (especially in relation to the building, playroom doors and bathrooms).

Plan the ideal relationships between spaces and activities

- Connect activities that relate well to each other.
- Separate other spaces in order to minimise conflicts—for example, between running children and quiet play.

Consider how people will move through the space

- Plan access/circulation for children and adults with disabilities, emergency egress and maintenance.
- Plan a hierarchy of paths: some for easy, safe movement; others for play and exploration.

Resolve site levels

These will have a major impact on how the space functions and need to be considered from the beginning.

Consider surfaces and placement of loose materials

- Consider whether living turf will be feasible and where it should be located (in relation to foot traffic, sun and shade).
- Decide which surfaces need to be paved (e.g. all-weather paths, gathering spaces).
- Work out where to place surfaces that are loose (such as sand, soil, water, mulch and gardens).

Develop the details: Add layers, qualities and characteristics

All other design elements and details are added and refined once the 'big' parameters above are established.

There are many ways in which the philosophy of a children's centre can permeate the design of the outdoor environment. The choices of materials, the presence and condition of planting, the availability of loose elements, and the possibilities for change and adaptation are all reflections of the philosophy of the centre community.

These are variables that need to be identified from the outset, and as the design progresses from vague bubbles and ideas to something that can be built, the qualities and characteristics need to be progressively discussed, refined, reviewed, costed and recorded on the plans.

Review the design and the budget

Each of the decisions that have been made will have an up-front cost implication as well as longer-term management commitments, so the budgets need to be refined and confirmed as the process unfolds.

Repeat as required

Sometimes all of this needs to be done a few times, or even many times, to get it right. This is okay. It is a lot cheaper to change a design while it is still on paper than after it is built.

REFLECTION QUESTIONS

6.1   Reflect on how fragile elements, such as plants, could be positioned in a busy children's centre in such a way that they contribute to children's experience of nature but are not damaged by children's movement through the space.

6.2   How could a small space accommodate fast-moving activities, such as bike riding, while protecting quieter, more reflective activities?

6.3   How can loose materials, such as sand, soil and mulch, best be placed within a space, and in relation to one another, to avoid spillage and mixing?

6.4   How would you set up a playspace to provide adequate challenge for 4- and 5-year-olds in a space shared with younger children?

REFERENCES

Department of Education Employment and Workplace Relations (DEEWR) (2009). *Belonging, being and becoming: The Early Years Learning Framework for Australia.* Retrieved 20 July 2009 from <www.coag.gov.au/coag_meeting_outcomes/2009-07-02/docs/early_years_learning_framework.pdf>.

Dowdell, K., Gray, T. & Malone, K. (2011). Nature and its influence on children's outdoor play. *Australian Journal of Outdoor Education, 15*(2), 24–35.

Drown, K. & Christensen, K. (2014). Dramatic play affordances of natural and manufactured outdoor settings for preschool-aged children. *Children, Youth and Environments, 24*(2), 53–77.

Elliott, S. (2015). Children in the natural world. In J. Davis (ed.), *Young children and the environment: Early education for sustainability* (2nd edn, pp. 32–59). Melbourne: Cambridge University Press.

Gibson, J.J. (1977). The theory of affordances. In R. Shaw & J. Bransford (eds), *Perceiving, acting, and knowing: Toward an ecological psychology* (pp. 67–82). Hillsdale, NJ: Lawrence Erlbaum.

Greenman, J. (1988). *Caring spaces, learning places: Children's environments that work*. Redmond, WA: Exchange Press.

Herrington, S., Lesmeister, C. Nicholls, J. & Stefiuk, K. (n.d.). *7Cs: An informational guide for young children's outdoor playspaces*. Victoria, BC: Consortium for Health, Intervention, Learning and Development (CHILD). Retrieved 26 February 2017 from <www.wstcoast.org/playspaces/outsidecriteria/7Cs.pdf>.

Chapter 7

Application of standards and regulations to early years outdoor playspaces

Mary Jeavons, Sharon Jameson and Sue Elliott

All outdoor playspaces, play equipment and surfaces in Australia, including public playgrounds, school playgrounds and supervised early childhood services, need to comply with a suite of Australian Standards for Playground Equipment and Surfacing (full details and references are listed at the end of this chapter). In educational settings, these Playground Standards offer a basis for effective and sound decision-making processes by educators regarding outdoor play equipment and overall playspace arrangement and management. The Playground Standards are devised from a range of safety, technical and anthropometric data, and draw on international precedents to promote playspaces that offer challenge and risk, but also promote safe play environments for children.

In addition, early childhood services regulated under the early childhood National Quality Framework (NQF) (ACECQA, 2013b) must also meet the requirements of the National Quality Standard (NQS) (ACECQA, 2013a) and National Law and Regulations. Some aspects of the NQS specifically guide the provision of outdoor playspaces, notably Quality Area 3 (ACECQA, 2013a). These documents aim to raise quality and drive continuous improvement and consistency in early childhood education and care services, including school-age care.

This chapter provides insights into the rationale for national Playground Standards and what they mean, then explores the Playground Standards and their application to early childhood settings with illustrative examples.

The intent is to identify how benefit/risk analysis can be supported by the national Playground Standards and to facilitate comprehensive understandings of early years outdoor playspaces.

Provocation

The issue of risk-taking in childhood, and the role of safety standards has come under increased scrutiny and debate all over the world in recent years. The Australian media frequently have drawn attention to the problem of 'helicopter parents' and 'cotton-wool kids'—children living in environments protected from any kind of perceived risk by over-protective parents. Many outdoor playspaces in the early childhood and school sector reflect this conservative approach—not only to risk-taking and challenge, but also in relation to messy play, loose elements and children engaging hands-on with the natural environment.

In a 2016 newspaper article on risky play, Associate Professor David Eager, Chair of the Standards Australia Playground Equipment Committee, was quoted: 'children who are exposed to too little challenge often take inappropriate risks, where the chance of injury is high, because they lack the ability to judge the level of risk and the strategies and skills to tackle it effectively' (Baker, 2016). However, the pendulum is now swinging in both Australia and overseas, and there is an increasing recognition of the importance of providing play environments where children can take on more challenges (see Chapter 2).

These changes in thinking are reflected in the recent revisions to the Australian Playground Standards (AS4685 Part 1 revised in 2014; and Part 0 in 2017), which have increased the maximum fall heights allowed for fixed play equipment in all settings; relaxed the surfacing rules for elements under 600 millimetres fall height; allowed somewhat more flexibility in design; and recognised that natural play elements provide acceptable variations, and inherent challenges and risks.

The Playground Standards are built on the premise that their purpose is to reduce the frequency and severity of injury in outdoor playspaces. They are not designed to prevent cuts, bruises and broken bones. The underlying philosophy is that risk and challenge are essential to children's healthy growth and development.

This chapter briefly introduces and explains some of the key points covered in the Australian Playground Standards AS4685 Part 0–6 and 11, for Playground Equipment and Surfacing (Standards Australia, 2014). These Playground Standards cover the development, installation, inspection, maintenance and operation of playground equipment; general safety requirements; and specific requirements for swings, slides, cableways (such as flying foxes), carousels and rocking equipment (such as seesaws). In addition, AS4422 (2016) specifically addresses playground surfacing, including specifications, requirements and test methods (Standards Australia, 2016).

These standards contain specific clauses that are applicable to supervised education and care settings (SECS), a category that includes early childhood services regulated under the NQF and children's services not captured under the NQF, such as occasional care services.

The special SECS clauses do not apply to general school playspaces (unless the school has a regulated early childhood service within its grounds, in which case the SECS clauses only apply to the area within its fenced playspace). The special clauses for SECS allow a little more flexibility in the rules. They recognise that these services are staffed by qualified early childhood educators, whose supervision and judgement are safety provisions.

We do not assume that educators and approved providers of SECS are familiar with the intricacies and technical specification requirements of the Playground Standards (Standards Australia, 2014). This chapter aims to provide readers with sufficient information to enable them to create safe, challenging and dynamic outdoor learning spaces for promoting children's learning and development, and to support educators in meeting the early childhood education NQS (ACECQA, 2013a). The chapter also focuses on some important aspects around the development and maintenance of outdoor learning environments not directly covered by the Playground Standards.

The following pages are framed around these key questions:

- What are safety standards and regulations and why are they important?
- What are common safety issues in early years outdoor playspaces?
- What is the role of professionally informed judgement?
- How are educators creating safe, challenging and dynamic learning spaces?

What are safety standards and regulations and why are they important?

Australian Standards generally are published documents setting out specifications and procedures designed to ensure products, services and systems are safe, reliable and consistently perform the way they are intended to. They establish a minimum set of requirements defining quality and safety criteria. Australian Standards are voluntary documents that are developed by consensus and, because of their rigour, many Australian Standards are adopted into legislation to become mandatory (Standards Australia, 2016).

The Playground Standards have been developed by technical, business, government and user representatives, and academic experts who come together to debate how playground safety standards are developed and applied. The Playground Standards are evidence based, using the latest international research and data. Where possible, they have been aligned with international standards, with some modifications for the Australian context—for example, to promote playground longevity despite long-term exposure to the Australian climate, including high levels of UV radiation.

The NQF (ACECQA, 2013a), which was introduced in 2012, also saw a shift away from the more highly regulated and prescriptive requirements that previously had been enshrined in state legislation. This shift recognises that educators are skilled practitioners who are able to exercise professional judgement to support the provision of dynamic outdoor learning environments based on 'best practice'. *Belonging, Being and Becoming: The Early Years Learning Framework for Australia* (DEEWR, 2009) highlights the importance of children experiencing risk-taking, challenge and exploration with nature in outdoor learning environments.

Further, the current Education and Care Services National Regulations (ACECQA, 2013a) prescribe very few requirements in relation to outdoor playspaces. The regulations stipulate minimum space requirements, shade and fencing, the importance of designing the premises to facilitate supervision, and the need to provide opportunities for children to explore and experience natural environments. These regulations are not overly prescriptive. For example, there is no stipulated fence height; however, Regulation 104 of the Education and Care Services National Regulations requires that the service premises are 'enclosed by a fence or barrier that is of a height and design that children preschool or under cannot go through, over or under it' (NSW Council Parliamentary Office, 2014, p. 65). Also, in accordance with Regulation 114, shade requirements need to be adequate 'to protect children from overexposure to ultraviolet radiation from the sun' (NSW Council Parliamentary Office, 2014, p. 68). Shade provision requirements for a service in Tasmania may be very different from those for a service in Central Australia. What constitutes adequate shade depends on the design of the building, the amount of UV radiation exposure in particular geographical locations and how the area is intended to be utilised. This will be explored later in this chapter when common safety issues are considered.

Standards Australia: The nation's peak non-government standards body that facilitates and manages the development and maintenance of Australian Standards and resources, including handbooks, guides and technical reports.

Australian Standards for Playground Equipment and Surfacing: A set of safety standards developed by industry experts, which specify the minimum recommended safety requirements for the design, installation and maintenance of playground equipment and surfacing.

Education and Care National Regulations: Regulations that set out minimum operational requirements for most education and care services, which are regulated under the National Law. The regulations are organised around each of the seven quality areas of the NQS (ACECQA, 2013a).

Supervised education and care settings (SECS): Defined playspaces used by an education and care service or children's service for children under school age, which are supervised by educators (AS 4685 Part 1 2014).

Hazard: Possible sources of harm. These will vary according to context and specific circumstances. Informed judgements about hazards determine whether they are acceptable or desirable because of their potential benefits, or require action, such as removal or modification (Ball, Gill & Spiegal, 2014).

Risk: Generally indicates the probability or chance of an adverse or negative outcome. In playground risk-management, risk includes both consideration of the potential severity of any adverse outcome and the probability of a severe outcome occurring (Ball, Gill & Spiegal, 2014).

What are the common safety issues in early years outdoor playspaces?

This following section explains some of the fundamental safety issues that apply to outdoor play as outlined in AS4685 Part 1, 2014 (Standards Australia, 2014). Even though it is not expected that all educators will be familiar with the whole of the Playground Standards documents, it is important to understand the basic principles and their application to SECS and schools. This knowledge informs educators' decision-making practice, so they can enable children to safely extend their capabilities, and discuss what is suitable and acceptable with parents, other staff members and management.

The most common safety issues that the Playground Standards aim to prevent are:

- impact injuries caused by falls, forced movement and collisions
- entrapment, crush injuries and strangulation
- sharp protrusions.

There are other safety issues, such as solar radiation, that are mentioned only briefly in the Playground Standards, and there are many other safety issues, such as toxicity in the environment, drowning and bio-hazards, that are not the focus of these documents.

> **Moveable equipment:** Purpose-built manufactured equipment used in supervised settings (e.g. SECS and schools) that is not permanently fixed in place and can be adjusted and moved by educators on a regular basis to vary play opportunities.
>
> **Moving equipment/forced movement:** Equipment where the structure itself is securely anchored, but the equipment has moving parts (such as a swing, carousel or rocker), which cause or enable the user to move. Note that a slide is fixed equipment, upon which the user moves.
>
> **Impact-absorbing surface/softfall:** Playground surface or surfacing materials that have shock-absorbing properties and are designed to reduce the risk of head and other serious injury.
>
> **Free height of fall:** The maximum height from which children can fall. It is measured from the height of the highest standing point or foothold (for climbing equipment) and from the seat or hold point for equipment on which the user sits (i.e. a swing) or hangs (i.e. a monkey bar) (Standards Australia, 2014).

The heights from which children can fall

As outlined in AS4685 Part 1, these vary, depending upon:

- the type of equipment, and whether it is fixed, moveable or moving, and
- the nature of the surface onto which children might fall.

Table 7.1 shows the maximum height (free height of fall) for various situations in SECS. Note that these are different from the requirements for public playgrounds and schools. It is important to note that these heights are a maximum, and educators need to exercise their judgement as to when children are ready for these heights. The value of flexible, adaptable equipment is that educators can adjust the height of challenging equipment as the year progresses, and as children develop and practise their skills with increasing proficiency.

Table 7.1 Maximum height (free height of fall) for various situations in SECS

Type of equipment (or other play element)	Maximum free height of fall	Surface required	Example
Fixed	1800 mm	Impact-absorbing	
Moveable	1500 mm	Impact-absorbing	
Moving	Varies depending upon the item	Impact-absorbing	

Source: Standard Australia (2014); illustrations by Mary Jeavons.

What kinds of surfaces are suitable under equipment?

Impact-absorbing ground surfaces are required in areas where children climb, to minimise the severity of injuries if they do happen to fall. These materials are also often referred to as softfall materials. A wide variety of materials can be used for this purpose, each with its inherent benefits and problems. A combination of materials is sometimes desirable, and centres/schools need to find practical, affordable materials that suit their context, philosophy and pedagogy. The Playground Standard applying specifically to surfacing, AS 4422:2016 Playground surfacing—specifications, requirements and test method, describe these materials in more detail. Broadly, they fall into two categories: loose or sheet-type ground surfaces/softfall.

Loose materials include:

- various forms of softfall mulch, which may be either shredded timber or bark ('tan bark'). This needs to be installed at a minimum depth of 300 millimetres to provide an adequate cushioning effect.
- sand, which for the purposes of impact absorption needs to have a low clay content and not be the type of sand that packs down hard with rain or compaction by foot traffic.

All loose materials need to be of adequate depth, contained, well drained, topped up and raked over regularly to remain clean and effective. The types of loose softfall vary in availability around Australia. Note that they also offer the benefits of adding another loose play material into a playspace.

Sheet products also come in a variety of styles, including:

- wet-pour rubber with a cushioning underlay
- rubber tiles of various types
- synthetic grass carpet with a cushioning underlay.

It should be noted that none of these sheet products is effective without the cushioning underlay, and they are also ineffective if they clog up with sand or debris. They do offer the advantage of providing durable surfaces and easy access within a fall zone for children with mobility aids, and mats can be useful to prevent erosion in high-use areas, such as under a swing or at the end of a slide. Many of these sheet products can become excessively hot when exposed to the sun, and are expensive to repair and replace.

What are the dimensions of these softfall surfaces?

The extent of the area that needs to be covered with an impact-absorbing material is called the *impact area* in the AS4685 (Standards Australia, 2014) documents (see Table 7.2). This is commonly referred to as the *fall zone*.

- For both fixed and moveable equipment between 600 millimetres and 1500 millimetres in height, a 1500 millimetre-wide impact area (fall zone) is required. All moveable equipment set up by educators requires this surrounding impact area.
- For fixed equipment between 1500 millimetres and 1800 millimetres in height, a 1700 millimetre-wide impact area (fall zone) is required.

Adherence to the basic dimensions for safe impact areas around play equipment (see Table 7.2) has important implications not only for providers, planners and designers, but also for educators. This is discussed further below.

Site planning to minimise safety concerns

Many safety issues arise from poor site planning, poor layout and design of the outdoor spaces, and an overall lack of space (see Chapter 6). Today, many early childhood services are constructed on small sites built to minimum standards for outdoor playspace provision (7 square metres per child, irrespective of age). This has implications for both children and educators. Swings are often one casualty of smaller spaces. Another is that it becomes difficult to adequately challenge children in the outdoor environment. Setting up varying arrangements of climbing equipment without compromising on fall zones can be very difficult where there is inadequate space, especially in centres with large numbers of mixed-age children.

- Outdoor spaces need to be fully considered when the building is first being planned for the site.
- Climbing spaces less than 8–10 metres wide in any direction inevitably provide limited challenge and variety for changing the equipment arrangement (considering that fall zones take up at least 1500 millimetres on all sides of most equipment).
- Any space intended for climbing that is less than 5 or 6 metres wide has virtually no potential to safely set up adequately varying or challenging physical activities.

Table 7.2 Fall heights and extent of impact-absorbing surface required for various situations in SECS

Fall heights	Extent of impact-absorbing surface required	Example
Between 1500 mm and 1800 mm in height	1700 mm in all directions around the equipment	
Between 600 mm and 1500 mm in height	1500 mm in all directions around the equipment • Where the equipment (such as a low plank) is less than 600 mm high at one end, the educator can judge whether the full impact area is required. • For slippery, narrow or challenging items where balancing is difficult, it may still be advisable to position these within an adequate impact area.	
Moving equipment or items with forced movement	• Each type of equipment has its own requirements. • For swings, the impact area depends upon the height of the swing bearings; this is frequently around 1800 mm in early childhood centres.	

Source: Standards Australia (2014); illustrations by Mary Jeavons.

The more difficult the outdoor space, the more educators will need to exercise their care, creativity and judgement in order to achieve the regular change and progressive challenge children need.

Restricted spaces with lots of edges make it difficult to arrange moveable equipment safely and in a way that progressively challenges children (see Figure 7.1). It is more efficient to have one larger space with an impact-attenuating surface than two or more smaller spaces.

Figure 7.1 Restricted spaces with lots of edges make it difficult to arrange moveable equipment safely and in a way that progressively challenges children.

Source: Mary Jeavons.

To minimise general safety problems related to surfaces:
- Position swings in their own space, where children won't run across their path.
- Select a space for the climbing area that is large enough for the softfall surface under the equipment plus the required fall zones, with room to extend the arrangement of moveable equipment in a variety of directions if possible.
- It is generally preferable to limit the amount of fixed climbing equipment in favour of moveable equipment.
- Where fixed climbing equipment is installed, ensure that the structure also provides rungs to enable the connection of planks, trestles and so on to extend the play. Much fixed equipment does not provide this capability, and is limited in its value to children.
- Ensure that an adequately sized softfall surface is provided in the right place to enable this extension of the moveable equipment.
- Consolidate softfall surfaces into one usefully sized space rather than two or more smaller spaces, to reduce the 'edge effect' of a fall zone for each space.
- Avoid cluttering up a climbing space with shade sail posts or verandah poles in the softfall zone.
- Position sandpits away from paths to avoid sand spills that may create slip hazards.
- Ideally, sand should be set down below the general level of the surroundings, so that it can be swept back in.
- Overhanging trees need to be managed to avoid providing a foothold near fences.

Setting up moveable equipment to minimise safety problems

Educators need to use their judgement when setting up moveable elements within a playspace. The following points provide a guide:
- Place moveable climbing and other equipment away from perimeter fences, rocks/boulders or similar large objects and pathways or high-traffic areas.
- Check the stability of moveable equipment before children use it and each time it is repositioned.

- When arranging moveable play equipment, check that the placement does not create spaces that cause entrapment or crush points between the parts of the equipment.
- Incorporate adequate shade and various types of shade over the moveable equipment and minimise reflective surfaces, such as white painted walls, nearby (refer to www.sunsmart.com.au).

What is the role of professionally informed judgement?

The Playground Standards are not mandatory; however, they provide a valuable guide not just for manufacturers and designers, but also educators. They should not, however, be used in isolation. Educators are well placed to make informed professional judgements about children's safety and the best ways to utilise their outdoor environments based on their experience and knowledge of children's learning and development. Educators need to take into account the uniqueness of their setting, children's abilities and group dynamics when planning and developing the outdoor learning environment, and when actively working with children in the environment.

Quality Area 1: Educational program and practice in the NQS (ACECQA, 2013a) requires educators to critically reflect on children's learning and development, both as individuals and in groups to implement the program. An effective outdoor learning environment with one group of children one day, may not work with the same group of children the next. While it is often not possible to change some elements of the learning environment, such as fixed equipment, the environment should be open and flexible enough for educators to add loose parts and other equipment to extend on and reflect children's interests and abilities. Common moveable equipment, including trestles, jouncing boards, cleated planks, balancing beams, play cubes, ropes and portable slides, can provide an effective way to add interest and challenge.

For example, where a group of children are very capable and able climbers, and need opportunities to extend their skills, educators can adjust moveable equipment to higher levels to enable a suitable degree of challenge for this group (see Figure 7.2). The educator needs to check the surface and the impact area around the higher equipment, and may need to supervise it more intently than other outdoor areas. They use their knowledge of each child's development to adjust the intensity of supervision each child may require. In a space shared by other age groups, the educator's use their judgement to limit access by younger or less skilled children to this set-up of challenging equipment, and might dismantle it after the session.

The weather also needs to be considered when setting up the outdoor learning environment. For example, on a very hot day, rubber surfacing may present a burn hazard to children, requiring equipment to be set-up in more shaded environments. Equipment may need to be relocated during the day, depending on the availability of shade. Also, mapping the shade coverage at midday in summer can provide an instructive guide for the placement of equipment and lead to further strategic planting of shade trees or creepers to improve the availability of shaded play areas.

Figure 7.2 An example of educator judgement used to rearrange equipment and extend children's climbing skills

Source: Mishka Nansi.

Tree climbing can offer a level of risk and challenge to children, providing opportunities for children to use problem-solving skills and their upper body strength in a way that is not possible with traditional fixed equipment. Tree climbing is sometimes referred to as 'cognitive climbing' because trees offer inherently challenging and unique climbing opportunities. Educators may choose to designate a specific tree as a 'climbing tree' after assessing the tree for its suitability. A good climbing tree needs to have strong branches and low-level branching to facilitate accessibility. Some services indicate by the placement of a line/tape on the tree the maximum height to which children can climb; others choose to invite children to conduct their own risk assessment and decide how high it is safe for them to climb. Some children may be developmentally unable to undertake an accurate risk assessment of their skills and abilities, and in those circumstances educators will need to use their professional judgement to determine whether they place limits on individual children or undertake closer supervision when these children engage in more risky play (see Chapter 2). Integral to facilitating tree climbing is the need to discuss with children main-taining three points of contact to promote safe climbing. This relates to the potential issue of intersecting branches that form an upright U or V shape, as these may present a head and neck entrapment hazard.

Maintenance: What are day-to-day operational aspects of promoting safety?

Before children use an outdoor playspace each day, educators need to briefly carry out a visual inspection to ensure that the space is in good condition and suitable for children's use. The intensity of the check depends upon the location of the centre/school and whether there has been vandalism or an unusual weather event, such as a storm, but should include the following:

- Check that the perimeter/fenceline is intact and has not been damaged or vandalised.
- Check for any objects that may have been thrown over or through the fence, such as glass, litter or syringes.
- Rake over sand and loose surfaces to check for fouling by animals, glass or other hazards (and missing toys).

- Sweep up loose sand and debris, especially on paths.
- Check for broken limbs dropped from trees.
- Check that all structures are in good condition and have not been damaged in any way.
- Check that no bolts have become loose on structures; inspect pigtail hooks on swings for wear and looseness.
- Check that loose softfall surfaces are at least 200 millimetres deep and are not contaminated by debris.
- Check that drainage pits are not overflowing and taps and pipes have not leaked.

A regular, more detailed inspection should also be carried out periodically to check for more substantial defects, such as structural problems, excessive wear and material failure, subsidence or failure of surfaces and drainage problems. This should be carried out by competent contractors. A detailed checklist is provided in AS4685 Part 0.

How are educators creating safe, challenging and dynamic learning spaces?

The following two case studies offer examples of how early childhood education services are developing engaging and challenging spaces for children.

Case study 1: Madge Sexton Kindergarten, South Australia

Madge Sexton Kindergarten is one of 20 Department for Education and Child Development (DECD) preschools with outdoor learning areas that are being redeveloped as part of a $6 million project being undertaken by the South Australian Government. The 20 preschools will act as demonstration sites, supporting other education and care services to actively engage children, families and the local community in connecting with nature.

The service already had an enviable outdoor learning environment with lots of natural elements, but the preschool identified that, as competent and capable learners, the children needed to have more opportunities to challenge and develop their physical skills and competencies, and experience risk.

The first stage of the project was the development of a concept plan. The preschool had a strong commitment to listening to both the children's and the community's voice in the design and redevelopment of the outdoor space. A community development coordinator, who is based at a nearby children's centre, supported the preschool's development of a consultation plan and worked closely with the preschool to ensure that the area was accessible and available to the community 'after hours'.

Kidsafe SA assessed the outdoor play area prior to completion to ensure that fixed equipment met Australian Playground and Equipment Standards (Standards Australia, 2014) and that the environment was safe from hazards. Educators also completed risk–benefit assessments on more challenging pieces of equipment—such as the slide, which is surrounded by natural rocks.

The service now has huge granite boulders with bowls dug out of them that can be used as mortars for use with pestles. A sensory fence sits alongside these installations, which enables children to use plants and loose materials in their play. Another addition is the planning of an outdoor fruit orchard, which the service intends to use in conjunction with its already established vegetable garden. The addition of loose parts, such as sticks and branches, increases choice and diversity in children's play scenarios.

Educators state that the area is now used differently, with the environment being the provocation for children's learning and there being a decreased reliance on educators setting up the environment. Educators have noted an increase in children's risk-taking and a growing confidence in negotiation and climbing large boulders and navigating a rope bridge. Children have increased the amount of time they play outdoors, and educators have noticed an increase in the variety and type of children's play and levels of engagement. The use of loose parts is not restricted to any particular area, and can be used throughout the service.

Further information on the DECD's Preschool Outdoor Learning Project, including documentaries on the development of the first five sites and concept plans, can be found on the department's website at <earlyyears.sa.edu.au>.

Case study 2: Boroondara Preschool, Victoria

Boroondara Preschool is located in an inner urban area of Melbourne, and offers sessional programs for 3- and 4-year-olds. It has a well-established outdoor play area, which includes extensive planting, artistic elements (such as mosaics and hand prints), a large sandpit with a bridge, a vegetable garden and a dry creek bed with three large rock shards and stones. The space also includes what was a much-loved climbing tree, with lower branches that offered challenge and risk-management opportunities. One aspect missing from the outdoor space was a shelter to facilitate dramatic play or offer weather protection from sun, wind and rain when needed.

A timber shelter with a sloping roof and partly open sides was installed near the climbing tree—but perhaps too near, as children readily recognised they could climb the tree as usual, and then clamber onto the roof of the timber shelter. This posed an unacceptable safety hazard. Resolution of this safety issue was not to remove the shelter or tree, but to communicate that this was no longer a climbing tree. The communication approaches employed were verbal and in context with children, but the space beneath the tree was also modified. Where there had once been tanbark softfall clearly communicating a good place to climb, the under-tree landscape was planted to create a small garden bed with a rock edging. The garden bed and rock edging were obvious visual cues for the children that the tree was no longer a safe place to climb.

This example illustrates how spaces and equipment fixtures can be rearranged with unexpected, and potentially hazardous, consequences. Once realised, the actions to modify the hazard were based on professionally informed judgements. The communication approach to mitigate the hazard was multifaceted and, importantly, promoted children being knowledgeable about their own risk-management and able to 'read' landscapes for visual cues about safety. Such cues are explicit—far more so than the under-cushioning of synthetic surfacing, which may or may not be present. Both children and adults cannot see the under-cushioning of synthetic surfaces, and thus are unable to undertake their own risk-assessments in situ. Further information can be found on the Booroondara Preschool's website at https://boroondarapreschool.wordpress.com.

CONCLUSION

This chapter has offered a starting point and practical guide for educators seeking to create safe but challenging and inviting outdoor playspaces. It provides a unique focus on balancing risk and safety, an essential aspect to consider when facilitating possibilities for outdoor play. While standards and regulations apply, there is a significant role for educators to make informed professional decisions in each outdoor learning context relevant to the children, families and other educators.

REFLECTION QUESTIONS

7.1   Draw and review an outdoor playspace where your practicum was undertaken. Are any changes advisable or suggested considering the points raised in this chapter?

7.2   Review an outdoor play equipment catalogue online. What, if any, purchase would you make and on what basis?

7.3   Relate a scenario from your practicum to illustrate best practice and informed professional judgement about safety.

7.4   Offer an example of the factors that need to be to considered in how you might make a professional decision about the safety or otherwise of a specific piece of equipment or a small arrangement of equipment.

7.5   Reflect on how you could create challenge for children in small spaces.

7.6   Consider how upper body strength might be promoted. What options might be implemented?

7.7   Collate photographs of safety aspects from various playspaces and discuss as a group how the Australian Playground Standards might apply.

7.8   Visit a public playground and identify the ongoing maintenance aspects required to promote safety.

7.9   Use tape measures, chalk, sand and/or string outdoors to map out the various free heights of fall and fall zones around hypothetical fixed or moveable equipment, so you become familiar with the scales involved. Consider how these measures relate to your own body as a readily accessible benchmark in practice—for example, is 600 millimetres your knee, or is it higher or lower?

7.10   Practise determining the compass points in an outdoor playspace and then predicting and mapping shade patterns over the day and/or year.

RECOMMENDED RESOURCES

- Kidsafe: www.kidsafe.com.au and www.kidsafensw.org. Kidsafe is a non-government, not-for-profit organisation that is regarded as a leader in injury prevention. There is a Kidsafe in each state and territory of Australia. Kidsafe offers information and an advisory service regarding the safety of children in and around the home and community. Kidsafe also operates a playground advisory service in some states, which can provide information and support on playground design and safety, and publishes a number of resources to support safe play in outdoor learning environments.
- South Australia Department for Education and Child Development: www.decd.sa.gov.au. The department has some useful resources to assist services in the design and development of outdoor learning environments, including an Education Risk–Benefit Assessment Template and a Preschool Outdoor Learning Area Design Guide. You will also find documentaries on the first five sites involved in the Preschool Outdoor Learning Project.
- International School Grounds Alliance (ISGA): www.international schoolgrounds.org. A global network of organisations and professionals working to enrich children's learning and play by improving the way school grounds are designed and used. The resource section of the website includes a number of videos showcasing innovative school grounds around the world.

Australian Standards for Playground Equipment and Surfacing
- AS4685—Part 0 2017: Development, installation, inspection and operation
- AS4685.1.2014: General safety requirements and test methods
- AS4685.2.2014: Additional specific safety requirements and test methods for swings
- AS4685.3.2014: Additional specific safety requirements and test methods for slides
- AS4685.4.2014: Additional specific safety requirements and test methods for cableways
- AS4685.5.2014: Additional specific safety requirements and test methods for carousels
- AS4685.6.2014: Additional specific safety requirements and test methods for rocking equipment

- AS4685—Part 11 2014: Additional specific safety requirements and test methods for spatial networks
- AS4422 2016: Playground surfacing: Specifications, requirements and test method

REFERENCES

Australian Children's Education and Care Quality Authority (ACECQA) (2013a). *Guide to the National Standard.* Retrieved 20 December 2016 from <files.acecqa. gov.au/files/National-Quality-Framework-Resources-Kit/NQF03-Guide-to-NQS-130902.pdf>.

——(2013b). *Guide to the National Quality Framework.* Retrieved 20 December 2016 from <files.acecqa.gov.au/files/National-Quality-Framework-Resources-Kit/ NQF01-Guide-to-the-NQF-130902.pdf>.

Baker, J. (2016). Cuts and bruises are just what kids need. *Sunday Mail,* 17 January.

Ball, D., Gill, T. & Spiegal, B. (2014). *Play safety forum: Risk–benefit assessment form.* Edinburgh: Play England, Play Scotland, Play Wales and Play Board Northern Ireland.

Department of Education, Employment and Workplace Relations (DEEWR) (2009). *Belonging, being and becoming: The Early Years Learning Framework for Australia.* Canberra: DEEWR.

New South Wales Council Parliamentary Office (2014). *Education and Care Services National Regulations.* Sydney: NSW Council Parliamentary Office.

Standards Australia (2014). *Australian Playground Standards AS 4685 2014 Part 0–6 and 11, for Playground Equipment and Surfacing.* Sydney: Standards Australia.

——(2017). *Australian Playground Standards AS 4685 2016 Part 0: Development, Installation, Inspection and Operation.* Sydney: Standards Australia. Retrieved 5 November 2016 from <www.standards.org.au/OurOrganisation/Documents/ Developing%20Australian%20Standards.pdf>.

Part 3
Children's voices

Chapter 8

Strengthening children's agency in outdoor learning environments

Glynne Mackey

Children have the opportunity to explore what it means to live and learn in a society where we value citizenship, agency and democratic process, and where children have the freedom to make decisions about where and how to play. This chapter will follow four themes to illustrate how agency is practised and strengthened: agency in the natural world, the social world, the democratic world and the Indigenous world. We value opportunities for children to experience outdoor playspaces that allow them to explore; however, there are elements in the environment that must be respected and protected. These elements have an authority that guides the way we respond and often restricts the actions we can take.

> **Provocation**
>
> The right to the freedom to congregate and be with family and friends is a concept we all value; however, adults often limit children in where they can do this. Over-protection risks children becoming disengaged from community life, the natural landscape and its cultural significance (Young & Cutter-Mackenzie, 2014). Michael Sandel (2009) has written that access to public spaces allows for diverse groups of people to come together in a common place, often to share, be with family and friends, meet others and explore what

the area has to offer. These opportunities to come together, build community and develop feelings of belonging make them significant in the development of agency and democracy. In accordance with Article 29 of the United Nations Convention on the Rights of the Child (UNCRC), children have the right to learn how to live responsibly 'in a free society, in the spirit of understanding, peace, and tolerance' (Office of the United Nations High Commissioner for Human Rights, 1989).

This chapter will refer to research to help us understand more about how outdoor experiences for children have deep significance in confirming their sense of agency and maintaining the peaceful and democratic foundations of our communities.

International early childhood research in sustainability is providing evidence of young children's demonstration of their agency by making a difference and influencing others (Ärlemalm-Hagsér & Davis, 2014; Clark, 2005; Mackey, 2014). This is excellent news as adults, at times, can dismiss the contribution of our youngest citizens as being fanciful and unscientific in its conception. Their contribution must now be taken seriously, as children are citizens of today with a valuable and unique perspective on life (Hayward, 2012; James & Prout, 1997). It is therefore important that early childhood settings support children in making a meaningful contribution that gives genuine affirmation for sound thinking and positive action (Mackey, 2012).

Importance of 'agency' in early childhood

Embracing pedagogies that move beyond the centre's four walls and into the outdoors gives young children less restriction in their play, where they are often required to take more responsibility for themselves and their friends to stay safe and negotiate play experiences with their peers (Kelly & White, 2013). Access to the outdoor environment is often identified by children as important to their enjoyment in the early childhood years (Clark, 2007). Elliott (2015, p. 43) extends on Clark's notion of enjoyment by discussing how these outdoor learning experiences 'promote feelings of agency or empower-ment, and support a child's sense of place in the world'.

In an educational sense, agency refers to the capacity of a person to act and create in a given context (Miller & Kirkland, 2010). UNCRC Article 13 states that it is the right of the child to express their ideas freely, and to be given information and the opportunity to express their ideas and opinions. From an early childhood education perspective, agency can be viewed as 'young children [being] able to contribute ideas, energy and creativity towards the management and solving of local issues' (Davis, 2010, p. 25). However, Davis's definition of agency is not always well understood or recognised by adults and teachers, because teachers sometimes feel that what they say and suggest is, in some way, superior to what the child is suggesting (Hudson, 2012). In the busy daily program of the early childhood setting, there can be a tendency to give children less space and time than is necessary for them to express their voice in issues that impact on their lives.

The early years are significant times in a child's life, where exploration is a major focus: the exploration of the environment as well as of language, feelings, relationships and ideas. Adults who closely observe and scaffold various explorations with the child are supportive of children who express good ideas and seek out solutions for the problems that impact on their lives. Sobel (2006), a place-based educator, writes that as children participate in solving problems in the outdoors they become creators rather than just consumers of knowledge. Meaningful participation occurs when children are part of the construction of knowledge, decision-making and possible solu-tions. The outdoor environment is an ideal context in which to encourage these outcomes, especially when early childhood philosophy, curriculum and teaching practice are based on a commitment to democratic processes and collegial relationships between children, and staff and families.

The child already has agency

Children have a desire to exercise their agency, so will look for ways to make a difference, showing that they are competent in influencing others through their actions and creative decision-making (Ritchie et al., 2010; Vaealiki & Mackey, 2008). Teachers who support children's agency are likely to be open to working with children in a collaborative, democratic way to support and celebrate the child's desire to make a difference. Moss (2007) presents a clear case for children's participation in a democratic environment within the early childhood setting—an environment where other perspectives are openly and safely expressed; where all children are able to express their ideas and opinions, interests and fears; where tensions arise when decisions do not always please everyone, but the greater good of the group is seen as desirable. Lee (2005) relates this dilemma to the notion of 'separability', where the tension between individuality and independence is balanced with the need to be attached and dependent. The ability to act independently as well as 'recognising dependency in relation to other human beings' is seen as important learning for a sustainable future (Hägglung & Pramling Samuelsson, 2009, p. 59). Johansson (2009) discusses a similar moral issue in relation to sustainable development, where there is tension between individuality and community—the freedom of the individual versus the responsibility we have for others with whom we are connected, as shown in Figure 8.1. In the scenario depicted in the figure, once the water system is set up the children know how to avoid waste and over-use of water. Taps placed at different levels indicate when the level is dropping. Children know it is important to leave enough for other children so they remind their friends and also pass on the important information to visitors and new children.

Figure 8.1 Thinking of others; sharing out the water resources

Source: Kidsfirst Kindergartens.

The notion of separability has particular significance for indigenous peoples. In the Māori world of Aotearoa New Zealand, individuality links to interdependence, as each child lives within the *whānau*/family, and is therefore able to contribute to the wellbeing of the whole. The young child is likened to the young leaves in the *harakeke* (flax bush) that grows nurtured and surrounded by a mass of individual yet strongly connected leaves symbolic of the wider *whānau*/family of the child (Ministry of Education, 2009). The notions of identity and responsibilities to others give children confidence to practise what it is to be interdependent yet still be a citizen and an agent for change. Our work with children should extend beyond children's 'agentic participation rights' to honouring the rights of other generations, the cultures of the community and the rights of the ecosystem (Davis, 2014, p. 23) so that they guide us in how we should interact and respond to the elements that nurture and sustain life in the present and for the future.

Agency and respecting the authority of the outdoors

Our agency in the natural world is also guided by the authority of the physical and natural elements. Authority is seen by Arendt (2008, cited in Michaud, 2012) as a certain form of obedience that occurs outside of violence or coercion. Respecting the authority of the natural world allows children to understand their interaction and interconnectedness with the natural world and to respect the limits that nature places on their play and actions. Therefore, children and teachers in the outdoors need to be aware of the authority of the environment and consider the messages the environment communicates to us, such as noticing sap dripping from a tree if the bark is ripped off or the bird that cannot relocate its nest with its young if a tree is cut down or a branch is broken. There are stories here for children and teachers to share about caring and the consequences of our actions.

Jean-Jacques Rousseau (1712–78) focused much of his writing on the child in nature because of the opportunity to discover learning without the authority of another so as to avoid the learning being influenced and controlled by others. However, for a well-functioning society, there is a necessary tension between the autonomy of the child and the authority of the human and non-human worlds (Michaud, 2012). For sound reasons, the child lives in a world where the adults make many decisions about the structure of the environment and the structure of the day. Adults have sculptured parks and playgrounds for children, and created urban areas where there are safety concerns for children, but these place restrictions on their freedom to explore and play. Traditional playground structures still have a place in outdoor activity, but do not allow for children to make changes, therefore lessening their opportunities for agency. These structures have an authority of their own—for example, a swing will always be the swing with a limited number of ways in which it can be used. Many adult-designed structures may have children's best interests at heart, but we should also provide opportunities for children to plan changes, move materials and adapt their environment on a regular basis to fit the context of their play at a particular time. Such experiences strengthen agency.

Agency in the outdoors: The learning contexts

The next section focuses on the learning that strengthens agency. This learning is often not immediately observable, unlike the observation of a child discovering a new path through the trees or the colour of the leaves changing with the seasons. What is observable is children's growing confidence and sense of who they are and what they are capable of achieving. Children who regularly experience the outdoor playspace are learning much about their world that may not be put into words or expressed in a painting, construction or play. Through the everyday affirmations from trusted, caring adults, agency is nurtured. The outdoor environment provides many opportunities for children to exercise their agency by being active participants, planning and engaging with others in outdoor experiences. Observant teachers will notice the action, recognise what it means for the child/children and respond in a manner that nurtures and strengthens the child's confidence and agency.

The discussion that follows focuses on young children in outdoor environments—young children who are confident and competent in their belief that they are creative and imaginative in their play while caring for themselves, their friends and the natural world. Four interconnecting themes organise the discussion, to look more closely at what agency means in a particular context. These four themes are based on the author's interest and research in the hope that they will stimulate further discussion and debate around the opportunities other learning environments might produce.

Agency in the physical and natural world

In the context of this discussion, the physical world will include geological features, such as rocks and streams, as well as plant and animal life. When exploring the notion of agency, the focus is usually on the individual, such as the individual child who ventures into the natural environment. The child has the right to play, explore, imagine and create, but what of the rights of the natural world? In her discussion on an extended rights framework, Davis (2014, p. 29) refers to the rights of the natural world and the importance of 'recognizing biocentric/ecocentric rights', where all biodiversity—including humans—must be protected. Davis's reconsideration of a rights framework therefore suggests that we should extend our thinking and demonstrate to children how to care for the wider biosphere of life and all that supports life on Earth. If we take the position that the natural environment has rights, we must collectively take responsibility to care and protect, even in our play and outdoor experiences. With a biocentric/ecocentric approach guiding our activity and experiences in nature, teachers and children can work together to identify good practice and play that respects the authority of the natural world.

Sobel (1990) advocates for children to be given opportunities to manipulate the natural environment and, where necessary, make changes to fit their play. Participating in these experiences strengthens their agency and belief that we can improve our situation by making changes. Playing in the outdoor environment where there are moveable and malleable materials allows for creativity, collaborative planning and imagination giving the child authority over what these objects could become. Rasmussen (2004) refers to these areas as 'children's places' because they are created by the children, not created by adults for children's use. Children can make their own decisions and take action to achieve their play and exploration purposes. Exercising agency is illustrated in Figure 8.2, while Figure 8.3 shows children practising team work by planning and creating together.

In Figure 8.2, children at the kindergarten participated in a day out, where they walked to a block of manuka trees (tea tree). The manuka tree grows tall and straight with thin trunks. The children and teachers talked about the best ones to cut down and decided that the dead ones would be best and to leave the ones with green shoots. Children were involved in the cutting, using a saw, and in helping to put the branches on a truck to take back to their kindergarten.

Figure 8.2 A child purposefully selecting natural materials for construction and play
Source: Kidsfirst Kindergartens.

In Figure 8.3, the children were part of the discussion about what to build. They decided that a tepee was what was needed. This led to further discussion and interest in other types of houses. Children also became interested in the different ways by which people entered their house and what was the appropriate behaviour.

Figure 8.3 The tepee is ready for friends to come in.

Source: Kidsfirst Kindergartens.

Case study 1: Agency in the physical and natural world

Children at a Fiordland Kindergarten on the edge of the Fiordland National Park, South Island, New Zealand have access to a rich natural playground. As children set off to explore, there is a feeling of anticipation due to the unpredictable nature of the park's playspace. Nature is the 'authority' in these spaces. It is often unpredictable: it can be gentle or destructive. The Fiordland children, who regularly return to explore the same area with their teachers and families, see that nature has its own timetable; therefore, decisions made with the children in these spaces need to be from a biocentric/ecocentric viewpoint. These regular visits allow children to experience the rhythms of nature, and the varying weather conditions. The authority of changing seasons and associated weather patterns demands a certain respect and obedience, such as wearing appropriate clothing and changing daily activities in response to the conditions. Children attending the Fiordland Kindergarten demonstrate their strong sense of agency in the forest environment of their local national park by making decisions in response to variable conditions:

'Children decide collaboratively where the best place to go is for the day. Each visit is new even if we are going to the same place, as the conditions are different, expanding the possibilities of their imagination and the dynamics of the group' (Maley-Shaw, 2013, p. 65).

Agency in the social world

In the early childhood setting, children can often be observed playing and interacting with the same groups of children, using the wide range of resources available. Observations and reflections on this play, such as in the home or family corner, show that there are objects that reflect the life of most families. Selecting resources is often limited by what is available through catalogues and retail outlets, and reflects the colours, usefulness and practices of a dominant culture, such as specific gender (e.g. pink plastic tea set) or particular cultural artefacts (e.g. knives and forks). Children will use these objects, guided by the authority of the object for the purpose for which they were made, therefore excluding some children for whom these play materials are not meaningful. Moving this play into the outdoors using natural materials offers wider opportunities for agency and inclusion, where children can choose the materials, using them to represent objects that are familiar and meaningful in the context of their own lives. Using natural materials can include a wider group of peers as the resources are what the child imagines them to be.

Caring for others and the environment is an area of social agency that is often noticed in the outdoor environment. Caring for the outdoor environment in the early childhood setting can help children to strengthen their relationships with peers, teachers, parents and families, as they are more likely to show caring behaviours and demonstrate empathy for others (Ritchie, 2013). Noddings (1984, cited in Martin, 2007, p. 59) has described caring as an 'act to improve the lot of others'. Stan van Hooft (1995, cited in Martin, 2007, p. 57) suggests the idea of 'deep caring' that moves out from ourselves, into the wider contexts of our communities and encompasses 'the Earth and all of creation'. Many of us may have observed how children consider the natural world to have human feelings. Indigenous cultures, such as Aotearoa New Zealand Māori, do not see themselves as separate from the environment, but rather integrated and spiritually connected to it (Ritchie, 2014).

The outdoor environment—where there is respect for people, the culture and the environment—can evoke a feeling of peace and calm. An example from my research has shown how a young child, challenged in his relationships with peers, quickly drew them to him when he cradled a dying butterfly in his hands. It seems that the other children sensed that he was in a caring role that showed his empathy, and felt safe to engage with him (Mackey, 2014). The child's interaction with the butterfly, from the natural world, demonstrates for us how the human world is interconnected with the non-human world, such as the flora, fauna and geographical features of the land. It is hoped that showing empathy for creatures of the natural world will engender feelings of empathy in our human relationships. Empathy and feelings of injustice motivate us as humans to want to find a solution through action and to be agents of change. Children have a strong desire to participate in such action, and feel protective in their quest to express their agency.

Case study 2: Agency in the social world

Children in the outdoor environment of the Fiordland Kindergarten participate in circle time with storytelling, where children make their own choices about the direction of the story, momentarily putting aside the authority of a picture book. Agency with language through storytelling gives them the confidence to use language in many other contexts. One such context is teaching the new adults about what they have learned in the outdoors. When new adults or new children join the group, there is much to share and children competently support the learning of others. When new children or adults visit the outdoor space, children enjoy the responsibility of leading a familiarisation tour of the area. In such situations, children have the knowledge and experiences to share, and therefore are empowered by the authority that these experiences of the area give to them (Maley-Shaw, 2013).

Agency in the democratic world

Rousseau wrote of his concern that children's thinking was influenced by society, and his belief that they must learn in an environment where education began with the child, free from authority. However, Michaud (2012) argues that Rousseau's ideas on education and authority have shown how authority has adapted to democratic education. He saw the necessity to address this issue in his writings on the education of the young Emile. Centuries later, there is wide understanding of the importance of the early years in strengthening children's agentic participation through democratic processes within early childhood settings (Davis, 2014). In a more modern context, Sobel (1990, cited in Elliott, 2015) writes that by developing a sense of place and agency through making good decisions and taking effective action in their young lives, children will carry that confidence as adults when they need to stand strong to deal with the issues confronting them.

Within child-centred early childhood curricula, such as *Te Whāriki* (Ministry of Education, 1996) and the Early Years Learning Framework (EYLF) (DEEWR, 2009), there is support for the democratic practices of listening to the child's voice, responding to their interests, and avoiding testing and mean scores by highlighting dispositions and the child's strengths. In the outdoor environment with groups of friends, their abilities in democratic processes are tested as they stretch their own limits and fine-tune their skills. As children interact and plan play with friends and teachers, opinions are expressed, ideas and perspectives are shared, and decisions are made about what further activity they might all participate in. Through guided participation (Rogoff, 2003), children see how their contribution to the group can make a difference and influence outcomes, thus strengthening agency.

Creating a sense of community in the outdoors brings children, parents and often grandparents together in a less threatening, more relaxed environment (Maley-Shaw, 2013). Michael Sandel, a Harvard law professor, has presented extensively on justice and shows concern for the ways in which outdoor spaces, such as playgrounds, parks and public gathering places, are becoming unsafe. These are spaces where diverse groups of people—especially children—should feel free and safe to interact with each other, independent of adult supervision. Unfortunately, the culture of fear and a growing inequality permeate some of our towns and cities, creating a barrier to healthy communities and also to the development of democracy (Sandel, 2009). Families and groups of children need open public spaces where they can meet and nurture a sense of community, as illustrated in Figure 8.4.

Every sandpit needs an occasional top-up, but this is usually done by a group of parents on a weekend. In the scenario depicted in Figure 8.4, teachers and children talked about what needed to be done to the sandpit: measuring the depth of the sand, finding out where to purchase it and asking what the cost would be. The day came to spread the sand. Children, with parents and teachers, used their kindergarten time to fill small wheelbarrows and move the sand. It took several days, but the children were participating together, doing meaningful work and making decisions about where to place the sand. The same has been done with bark chips.

Figure 8.4 Children participate with the kindergarten community to fill their sandpit.

Source: Kidsfirst Kindergartens.

Agency in the democratic world seeks a level of justice and peaceful existence. Many questions arise when children see injustice and evidence of disharmony or conflict in the natural world. In the web of life, animals—including humans—kill and eat other animals and plants, and teachers are often involved in these sensitive conversations. Often teachers and parents have these and similar conversations prior to children raising the issue so that each is aware of values and practices of the community and early childhood setting. We all struggle with the tensions about doing the right thing, and there is no single answer regarding what is right and wrong. Through engaging in supportive and respectful conversation and action-taking, children can see that the world is not black and white, and that decisions should consider different perspectives, depending on culture and context.

Agency in the cultural world

How teachers and children plan for experiences in the outdoor environment should acknowledge the authority of cultural practices and restrictions of local indigenous communities. Agency does not suggest a 'free for all', as there are often cultural restrictions along with a caring and respect required by the cultural context in which the learning takes place. Davis's (2014) model of the five dimensions of rights for early childhood draws attention to collective rights, where the rights of social groups and those of the indigenous peoples must be honoured. Teachers and children must work together to show respect for the wisdom of indigenous peoples and to consider their sustainable cultural practices carried out in the place that is now the outdoor learning and play environment. A suitable example of this is the gathering of flax, or *harakeke*, for Māori weaving in Aotearoa New Zealand.

Through collaboration with community members and families, teachers become familiar with the traditions and cultures of the local people. Children are able to contribute to the knowledge and discussion, and to continue to respect the cultural traditions and the authority of the natural environment.

An extensive study of ten early childhood centres explored how young children care for themselves, others and the environment (Ritchie et al., 2010). The focus was on how the teachers and children understood sustainability using both Māori or indigenous perspectives and Western perspectives. The study foregrounds the children's care and concern for the amount of rubbish dropped on *Papatūānuku* (Earth Mother) and the dangers of smoke in the air affecting the lungs of *Ranginui* (Sky Father). The teachers noticed that the children in their play continued to talk about their responsibilities towards the mother Earth and were confident in their abilities to take action. The children's learning and influence were seen in their teaching of others about how we must all care for the Earth. The children were strong in their belief that they had agency.

Respecting indigenous cultures

There are several restrictions around when and how flax should be gathered and processed to respect the authority of the plant world. This is especially significant with a plant such as flax, which has been very important for providing raw materials for traditional food-gathering items, clothing and shelter. Māori begin the gathering of flax with a prayer, or *karakia*, to ask the permission of the spiritual world to take from the plant. The flax is carefully gathered to process and create according to traditional methods. Leftover pieces are returned to the base of the plant as part of the natural cycle, and not discarded in the waste bin. The tradition requires the creator to give away the first effort in craft, such as an article of weaving. This first weaving is a valued gift and creates a bond between the giver and receiver (Prendergast, 1987).

CONCLUSION

Through genuine agentic participation in the early childhood setting, educators work alongside children to support their quest for independence, while they also need to belong to a social group of friends, family and community. When we talk about rights, we also balance this with discussion about our responsibilities to each other and to the environment. The balance between agency and authority has similar understandings of our role as an individual citizen: needing to acknowledge our interdependence while having respect for biocentric/ecocentric rights of the Earth and its inhabitants (Davis, 2014). Many of our environmental issues today have arisen out of an anthropocentric focus, where humans have believed in their rights to exploit the Earth's resource with little or no regard for the interdependent nature of the biosphere (Ritchie, 2013). Children who are regularly exploring and experiencing the outdoors in their play will better understand their place in the natural world and their influence. It is therefore of utmost importance for children to strengthen their agency and awareness so that they can make a difference to benefit their own lives and that of others.

REFLECTION QUESTIONS

8.1   When have you been aware of your behaviours/practices changing as a result of an idea or comment from a young child in your care?

8.2   How can teachers support children to contribute good ideas and offer solutions to solve problems? Share what you know about democratic process and why it might be important in the early childhood setting.

8.3   Why might the discussion on 'separability' be significant in the context of agency in outdoor learning?

8.4   What is your understanding of 'authority'? How does it fit with this discussion on agency?

8.5   How might you include others—such as minority groups (e.g. in terms of disability, ethnicity and gender), parents, grandparents and community—in the outdoor experience?

8.6   Are you able to identify areas in your local community where the public space available for children is well managed and allows for safe gathering?

8.7   What do you see as some of the authority of the physical environment in your area? Will it have an impact on the way the children explore and interact with the physical environment?

8.8   From your experience with cultures different from your own, how do you understand their relationship with the natural world?

8.9   What is significant about non-indigenous peoples respecting indigenous rights in the natural world?

RECOMMENDED RESOURCES

- Enviroschools New Zealand: www.enviroschools.org.nz/enviroschools-programme/early-childhood
- Fiordland Kindergarten Nature Discovery: fiordlandknaturediscovery.blogspot.co.nz

- Jan White, Mud kitchens: https://janwhitenaturalplay.wordpress.com/tag/mud-kitchens
- Playcentre in Canterbury: www.canterburyplaycentre.org.nz
- Reggio Emilia Inspired Outdoor Play: www.letthechildrenplay.net/2013/03/be-reggio-inspired-outdoor-environments.html

REFERENCES

Ärlemalm-Hagsér, E. & Davis, J. (2014). Examining the rhetoric: A comparison of how sustainability and young children's participation and agency are framed in Australian and Swedish early childhood education curricula. *Contemporary Issues in Early Childhood, 15*(3), 231–44.

Clark, A. (2005). Ways of seeing: Using the mosaic approach to listen to young children's perspectives. In A. Clark, A. Kjørholt & P. Moss (eds), *Beyond listening: Children's perspectives on early childhood services* (pp. 29–49). Bristol: Policy Press.

—— (2007). Views from inside the shed: Young children's perspective of the outdoor environment. *Education 3–13: International Journal of Primary, Elementary and Early Years Education, 35*(4), 349–63.

Davis, J.M. (ed.) (2010). *Young children and the environment: Early education for sustainability* (pp. 43–75). Melbourne: Cambridge University Press.

—— (2014). Examining early childhood education through the lens of education for sustainability. In J. Davis & S. Elliott (eds), *Research in early childhood education for sustainability: International perspectives and provocations* (pp. 21–37). London: Routledge.

Davis, J., Engdahl, I., Otieno, L., Pramling Samuelsson, I., Siraj-Blatchford, J. & Vallabh, P. (2009). Early childhood education for sustainability: Recommendations for development. *International Journal of Early Childhood, 41*(2), 113–17.

Department of Education Employment and Workplace Relations (DEEWR) (2009). *Belonging, being and becoming: The Early Years Learning Framework for Australia.* Canberra: Department of Education, Employment and Workplace Relations.

Elliott, S. (2015). Children in the natural world. In J. Davis (ed.), *Young children and the environment: Early education for sustainability* (2nd edn, pp. 32–54). Melbourne: Cambridge University Press.

Hägglung, S. & Pramling Samuelsson, I. (2009). Early childhood education and learning for sustainable development and citizenship. *International Journal of Early Childhood, 41*(2), 49–63.

Hayward, B. (2012). *Children, citizenship and environment: Nurturing a democratic imagination in a changing world.* Abingdon: Routledge.

Hudson, K. (2012). Practitioners' views on involving young children in decision making. *Australasian Journal of Early Childhood, 37*(2), 4–9.

James, A. & Prout, A. (1997). *Constructing and reconstructing childhood: Contemporary issues in the sociological study of childhood* (2nd edn). London: Falmer Press.

Johansson, E. (2009). The preschool child of today—the world citizen of tomorrow? *International Journal of Early Childhood, 41*(2), 79–95.

Kelly, J. & White, E.J. (2013). *The Ngahere Project: Teaching and learning possibilities in nature settings.* Hamilton, NZ: Wilf Malcolm Institute of Educational Research: University of Waikato. Retrieved 21 March 2017 from <www.waikato.ac.nz/__data/assets/pdf_file/0007/146176/Ngahere-project_3-2013-03-14.pdf>.

Lee, N. (2005). *Childhood and human value: Development, separation and separability.* Maidenhead: Open University Press.

Mackey, G. (2012). To know, to decide, to act: The young child's right to participate in action for the environment. *Environmental Education Research, 18*(4), 473–84.

——(2014). Valuing agency in young children: Teachers rising to the challenge of sustainability in an Aotearoa New Zealand early childhood context. In J. Davis & S. Elliott (eds), *Research in early childhood education for sustainability: International perspectives and provocations* (pp. 180–93). Abingdon: Routledge.

Maley-Shaw, C. (2013). *Fiordland kindergarten: Nature discovery.* Invercargill, NZ: Kindergartens South.

Martin, P. (2007). Caring for the environment: Challenges from notions of caring. *Australian Journal of Environmental Education, 23*, 57–64.

Michaud, O. (2012). Thinking about the nature and role of authority in democratic education with Rousseau's Emile. *Educational Theory, 62*(3), 287–302.

Miller, S.J. & Kirkland, D. (2010). *Change matters: Critical essays on moving social justice research from theory to policy.* New York: Peter Lang.

Ministry of Education (1996). *Te Whāriki: He whāriki mātauranga mō ngā mokopuna o Aotearoa—Early childhood curriculum.* Wellington, NZ: Learning Media.

——(2009). *Te whatu pōkeka: Kaupapa Māori assessment for learning. Early childhood exemplars.* Wellington, NZ: Learning Media.

Moss, P. (2007). *Bringing politics into the Nursery: Early childhood as a democratic process.* Retrieved 5 November 2016 from <eprints.ioe.ac.uk/5603/1/Moss2007Bringing5.pdf>.

Office of the United Nations High Commissioner for Human Rights (1989). *Convention on the Rights of the Child.* Retrieved 21 May 2016 from <www.ohchr. org/EN/ProfessionalInterest/Pages/CRC.aspx>.

Prendergast, M. (1987). *Fun with flax: 50 projects for beginners.* Auckland, NZ: Reed.

Rasmussen, K. (2004). Places for children—children's places. *Childhood, 11*(2): 156–73.

Ritchie, J. (2013). A pedagogy of biocentric relationality. *New Zealand Journal of Educational Studies, 28*(1), 34–50.

—— (2014). Learning from the wisdom of elders. In J. Davis & S. Elliott (eds), *Research in early childhood education for sustainability: International perspectives and provocations* (pp. 49–60). Abingdon: Routledge.

Ritchie, J., Duhn, I., Rau, C. & Craw, J. (2010). *Titiro Whakamuri, Hoki Whakamua. We are the future, the present and the past: Caring for self, others and the environment in early years' teaching and learning.* Retrieved 21 March 2017 from <www.tlri. org.nz/sites/default/files/projects/9260-finalreport.pdf>.

Rogoff, B. (2003). *The cultural nature of human development.* New York: Oxford University Press.

Sandel, M. (2009). *Justice: What's the right thing to do?* New York: Farrar, Straus and Giroux.

Sobel, D. (1990). A place in the world: Adult memories of children's special places. *Children's Environments Quarterly, 7*(4), 5–13.

—— (2006). How fantasy benefits young children's understanding of pretense. *Developmental Science, 9*(1), 63–75.

Vaeliki, S. & Mackey, G. (2008). Ripples of action: Strengthening environmental competency in an early childhood centre. *Early Childhood Folio, 12,* 7–11.

Young, T.C., & Cutter-Mackenzie, A. (2014). An AuSSI early childhood adventure. Early childhood educators and researchers actioning change. In J. Davis & S. Elliott (eds), *Research in early childhood education for sustainability: International perspectives and provocations* (pp. 143–57). London: Routledge.

Chapter 9

The private play places of childhood

Deborah Moore

Integral to my philosophy of education as a kindergarten teacher was an awareness of children's need to be hidden at times within the kindergarten environment—to be away from the 'madding crowd' (Hardy, 1874), even for a short while. Later, in my role as a preschool field officer for local government, I watched many children in numerous early childhood settings constantly looking for ways to be hidden from view, to see others without being seen. I watched in despair as plants in these settings were pruned to the ground to purposefully prevent children from hiding, with adults considering these children to be recalcitrant and wilful. Later still, as an early years sustainability officer, I tried unsuccessfully to minimise the regulatory pruning of bushes in these settings. Supervisory regulations always trumped a child's need for privacy. In all these roles, I was conscious that my values and actions were counter to the regulatory requirements of full visible 'supervision of all children at all times' (Department of Education and Early Childhood Development, 2012, p. 1). This has been an ethical dilemma that I have contemplated for much of my career within early childhood education. This chapter presents background literature around this dilemma, together with empirical research I have conducted in which the phenomenon of privacy is of critical importance to children, and some ideas for educators to consider when enabling young children's private places for play.

Provocation

Researchers have become increasingly interested in children's use of place (Canning, 2010; Maynard, Waters & Clement, 2011), particularly how it relates to young children's experiences within their 'adult-designated spaces for children' (James, Jenks & Prout, 1998, p. 34). Furthermore, educators and policy-makers now widely acknowledge that children's sense of belonging to their 'own place' is important for their emotional wellbeing and overall development (see DEEWR, 2009). Despite this increasing interest, pedagogical spaces for children are still often adult-constructed, with little regard given to children's own knowledge of place. The priority for constant supervision of children holds a dominant position in early childhood education through the National Quality Standards (ACECQA, 2013). This can be seen, for example, in Standard 2.3.1 (ACECQA, 2013) whereby 'each child is to be adequately supervised at all times' (p. 44); furthermore, it is a legal 'offence to inadequately supervise children' (p. 45). This is the case even when children's safety is not in question. In two separate research projects I have conducted recently, young children's need to construct their own private play places within adult-designed and supervised educational settings was highly evident in their conversations and their actions. These young children's strong impulse towards private play places appeared to be markedly resilient, even though it was difficult due to 'panopticon style' (Foucault, 1979) surveillance requirements mandated by regulatory standards and policies. How, then, do educators in early childhood and primary school educational settings reconcile this tension between supervisory regulations and an increasing awareness of children's emotional need for privacy in their play places?

Background literature

In the following section, three key areas of background literature are discussed surrounding the notion of children's private play places. The first key area discusses the change in the image of the child over time, from innocent to vulnerable, so that children are now considered in need of constant protection. As a consequence of this perceived need, an incremental increase has occurred in the surveillance of children. Second, children's knowledge of place is raised, highlighting adult neglect in taking children's emotional attachment to place into account in the design of educational environments. In the third key area, classical and contemporary literature around privacy and secrecy is brought to the fore to illuminate the importance of privacy for children's play.

The image of the vulnerable contemporary child

Every era has its own view of childhood and what young children are considered capable of doing (Qvortrup, 2009). In earlier centuries, children were seen as 'miniature adults' who contributed to working life alongside parents and other adults (Cunningham, 2006). Eighteenth-century philosophers such as Froebel and Rousseau espoused the view that young children should be seen as 'innocents', and therefore were in need of protection from the world of adults (Wood & Attfield, 2005). With the advent of modernity, young children were perceived as vulnerable 'empty vessels' who needed to be filled with knowledge by knowledgeable adults (Dahlberg & Moss, 2005). From the twentieth century, dramatic and unsettling societal changes triggered an increasingly risk-averse society in which the constant protection of children was now seen as paramount in child-rearing (Giddens, 1991; Gill, 2007). These societal changes led to 'ever-greater surveillance and efforts at control, always in the name of the protection of a pure childhood that has never really existed except in the minds of adults' (Gillis, 2009, p. 124). In attempting to protect this hypothetical 'pure childhood', moral panic linked with adult anxiety around children's safety has incited a marked increase in the monitoring and supervision of children (Gill, 2007). Rooney (2012) confirms this current trend, arguing that 'the desire to control, shape, discipline or keep tabs on the child is . . . very much part of the increasing surveillance over children's lives' (p. 335) (see also Chapter 2 for further discussion of risk aversion).

Although contemporary children may be considered physically 'safer' today than in the past (Gill, 2007); they are conversely perceived to be more vulnerable than previous generations (Cunningham, 2006). As a consequence, children are now 'more hemmed in by surveillance and social regulation than ever before' (James, Jenks & Prout, 1998, p. 7). Research has shown that early childhood education, regulation and policy commonly reflect societal values and assumptions about childhood, and consequently can be seen as a gauge of contemporary discourses regarding the construct of childhood (Sandberg & Vuorinen, 2010). Therefore, these assumptions around the image of the vulnerable contemporary child have given rise to the prevalence of early childhood policy and regulation that demands 'every child should always be monitored actively and diligently . . . and always need to be in sight of an adult' (DEECD, 2012, p. 1). However, what these assumptions and policies do not reflect is the child's emotional need for their play places to sometimes be private and secluded from others.

Young children's emotional attachment to place

Classical place-based researchers found that 'spaces' with socially constructed meanings could be symbolically transformed into meaningful 'places' (Hart, 1979; Tuan, 1977). For example, Tuan (1977, p. 8) contended that a child's 'experience of place' was strongly connected with 'emotion'. Similarly, the 4- to 11-year-old children in Hart's (1979) study also spoke of their strong affiliation with particular places and the importance of seclusion. The children in Hart's study told of their search for affordances such as trees, sticks and leaves to assist in 'manipulating spaces to make places' to construct their hidden play places (p. 205). Similarly, Moore's (1986) study of children's play places indicated that their 'hidden life' was 'not well understood, acknowledged or taken seriously' by adults (p. xiv). Moore argued that this was because researchers were focused primarily on adult-organised environments for children. This gap in adult understanding may have been due to children's reticence to talk about their 'own made places', which Moore respected as children's 'private knowledge' (p. 46).

By the 2000s, an emphasis on researching children's relationship with their play places had become increasingly evident (see Clark, 2007; Rasmussen, 2004). This was seen in Rasmussen's (2004) and Clark's (2007) play place studies, where children were asked to talk about the places where they 'preferred' to play. For instance, an 8-year-old child in Rasmussen's study created his 'own town' with houses, roads and fields on a 'piece of land' with a 'special meaning and name' (p. 157). Similarly, in Clark's study, she identified a number of different 'spaces' where children chose to play, such as 'private spaces' to watch others from (p. 356). Rasmussen clearly differentiated between the meanings of the places that children constructed for themselves (i.e. children's places) and those places constructed by adults (i.e. places for children). Therefore, for Rasmussen, a built playhouse would be considered an adult place set up for children's play, whereas a 'den' or 'cubby' was a place that children constructed for themselves. Rasmussen argued that adults needed to acknowledge children's ability to 'create places that are physical and symbolic' for themselves and for their play (p. 171).

Following on from earlier studies of children's attachment to particular places for play, Lim and Barton (2010) also claim that children interpret place according to their own experiences that occur there. Lim and Barton's understanding of the deep relationship that children develop with places they construct themselves for play strengthens Rasmussen's (2004) contention about this experience. Other researchers have also confirmed these ideas around children's profound attachment to their play places (Elliott, 2010; Jack, 2010). Elliott (2010, p. 61) discusses the work of evolutionary biologists, who found that 'there appears to be an innate evolutionary drive for children to create hiding spaces or places—a vestigial survival strategy', while Jack's (2010, p. 756) discussion of the 'primordial urge' to seek places of belonging reinforces this fundamental childhood experience.

Children's privacy and secrecy in play places

Hart (1979) and Moore's (1986) classical work on children's need for seclusion in their play places was subsequently strengthened through the phenomenological study of children's secret places by van Manen and Levering (1996), who found that children's construction of secret places was an important childhood phenomenon that was not well understood by adults. Notably, they claimed there was a difference between privacy and secrecy in children's play practices. Privacy was seen as a deliberate withdrawal from others, while secrecy referred to the maintenance of relationships 'with those from whom the secrets are kept or with whom the secrets are shared' (p. 59). Furthermore, van Manen and Levering argued that it was necessary for children to first experience privacy—that is, to separate from others—followed by intentional secrecy in their play practices and play places. They suggested that children sought secret, secluded places not only for concealment away from adults and peers, but also to prompt feelings of safety and to enable 'step[ping] into other worlds' (p. 32). Their study suggested children were capable of constructing creative solutions even when they were not able to find privacy:

> Children who lack private space may have to go 'underground' and construct a double life, a secret inner world, that constitutes a place of refuge. The child leads an outer life and at the same time, there is the inner life that does not match the external norms and expectations (p. 158).

Van Manen and Levering's (1996) reference to a child's 'secret inner world' alludes to the notion of being 'hidden in plain sight' that children can skilfully develop. Hart's (1979), Moore's (1986) and van Manen and Levering's (1996) findings around children's need for privacy and secrecy have been re-emphasised in recent studies (cf. Corson et al., 2014; Roe, 2007). Collectively, these researchers have found that children need to feel hidden away from the adult gaze—to 'feel secrety', as Roe (2007, p. 477) quotes from the children in her study. In my own recent studies, I have also found young children's intense emotional need for privacy away from the gaze of adults, as well as their broader peer group, to be a primary motivation for their secret place-making (Moore, 2010, 2015b).

The following section provides some specific research examples from two of my studies, both illustrating children's resilient quest for the construction of their own private places within their educational settings.

Researching with children through narratives of private play places

For the first of these studies, I conducted a comparative case study investigating young children's outdoor play preferences in two different preschool environments. One preschool had a large space, full of bushy, natural places, while the other provided a small playground dominated by fixed climbing equipment and very limited vegetation (Moore, 2010). In the second study, I used a narrative inquiry methodological approach to prompt and examine the stories of three generations in four families about their experiences of childhood imaginative play places (Moore, 2015b).

Case study 1: 'Only children can make secret places'

Initially, in the first study, I asked the children about their preferences for their outdoor play experiences in both centres; however, this line of inquiry did not engender much interest from the children. Much later, however, the study evolved into an examination of the phenomenon of childhood secret play places when one child, John (5 years), nonchalantly mentioned his 'safe, secret place in the bamboo jungle'. John also insightfully suggested that 'the teacher knows where we are, but she doesn't know what it is'—which I interpreted to mean that while John was aware the teacher was watching him, he was also convinced she did not know he was constructing his own secret place (Moore, 2015a). Alice, another 5-year-old child in the same 'bushy' environment, explained that 'only children can make secret places' when I inquired who made the secret places she had told me about in her preschool.

I had assumed at first that the bushy environment had triggered this search for and construction of secret places. However, the children in the other outdoor setting were also very eager to make their own secret places, even when they had limited opportunities and provisions to do so. This was evident when Don, a child in this sparse outdoor space, confidently said, 'I haven't made my secret place yet . . . But I *will* make it'. Don suggested he might need to use the climbing frame 'with something over the top to make it a secret' if he could not find anywhere else. Unfortunately, I did not see any evidence of Don's secret place construction over the six-month course of the study. It should be noted that the educators in this smaller setting were particularly concerned about the need for constant supervision of the children's play. Consequently, a narrow space around the corner of the preschool building was often prohibited from children's use, with educators complaining that they were not able to supervise this space 'adequately', so children were not allowed access to play there. A small gate was locked to stop children entering this space, even though this was the only physical place for any hidden play within this early childhood setting.

Not all the children in this study wanted to talk openly about their secret places, and as Goodenough (2003) has wisely questioned, why should children discuss these important places with adults who have forgotten about their existence? However, the children who wanted to talk to me about their secret places would first look over their shoulder to check that no one else was listening, and then launch into a whispered story about the intricate details of their secret places. This occurred, for example, when Alice quietly told me a story about her secret place tree where, she explained, 'lots of people walk around this tree all the time, but they don't know it's my secret place'. Alice's construction of this symbolic place appeared to be intrinsically linked to her sense of identity as a creative place-maker, which was later confirmed when she spoke of the 'inventions' she created when she was 'inside' her secret place. I found that by not interrogating the children with a barrage of adult-directed questions, the children were happy to tell their stories to an interested other (Moore, 2014).

Alice also perceptively described another secret place in her bushy preschool playground as a place that was 'very peace and quiet, and no one can see me, not one little bit'. Many of Alice's stories demonstrated her astute understanding of the abstract notion of 'being hidden in plain sight' through her conscious use of the physical and/or symbolic secret places she constructed for herself. This understanding was also evident in other children's stories, where holding the knowledge of their own secret places 'separate from' adults and peers was of critical importance (van Manen & Levering, 1996). The overall findings from this study illustrated young children's persistence in wanting to construct their physical, and at times symbolic, secret places in a variety of early childhood settings. This was the case even when the constant surveillance from adults and the confrontation of physical barriers did not enable the actual construction of hidden places. The abstract notion of being 'hidden in plain sight' appears to be a skill children have developed in their search for private play places within their highly supervised, contemporary childhoods.

Case study 2: 'Sometimes we do some games that are a bit private to me and my friends'

For the second study, I once again entered into a research relationship with young children, and this time included their families. For this inter-generational narrative inquiry, I began by inviting grandparents, parents, early primary and preschool children in four families to tell stories about their childhood imaginative play places. While I was interested to know more about children's experience of secret places, I did not want to pre-empt this by inquiring about this childhood practice as I had in the previous case study. Therefore, for this study I invited each family member to tell me stories about their 'pretend play', using storytelling, drawing, map-making, photography and memory boxes of childhood artefacts to prompt their sensory memories and emotion-filled stories.

In the analysis of this study, privacy was found to be an over-arching criterion to enable the enactment of imaginative play practices and places across all three generations. All the child and adult participants told remarkably similar stories of how important it was for them to construct their own private place for their imaginative play. Frequently, the participants referred to these places as their 'own world' or 'kingdom', using terms such as 'quiet, uninterrupted and private' to describe their play places. While the concept of secret places did emerge in the stories told by the children and their parents, the grandparents only spoke of their preference for privacy in their play places. In their stories, the grandparents spoke of the 'ease' with which they could locate multiple places within their homes and neighbourhoods that provided privacy for their play, and so did not feel the need to make these places purposefully 'secret' from others. However, an increasing impulse toward secrecy for imaginative play beyond privacy has escalated from the 1970s to contemporary times. In particular, for contemporary children, the choice of where to construct private places for imaginative play has become increasingly restricted, and so requires more creative adaptions to create a level of secrecy for their imaginative play. Similar to the findings from my previous study, contemporary children have become increasingly skilled at the construction of private places that are symbolically 'hidden in plain sight' as a way of pushing back against the heightened supervision by adults in their homes and in their educational settings. The following stories told by the children in this later study tell of their search for privacy as well as secrecy in their play places.

The construction of private (and secret) places was a common feature in the young children's stories in this inquiry. While one agentive 4-year-old child declined to talk with me about his 'hidden' pretend play until the very end of the study, other children were more forthcoming in their storytelling from the beginning. Frank (4 years), for example, started his stories about his 'pretend play' by pointing to a small, prickly and thinly branched bush on the edge of his kindergarten playground, announcing, 'that's my secret place . . . and that's my secret place too . . . I maked it up . . . because I like to hide away'. I was astounded that Frank had exposed his secret place constructions in such a manner, especially as I had simply invited a story about pretend play. Another child, 7-year-old Ted, told a story about his 'secret tree' in his school playground, even though he initially had declared that he no longer played pretend games because he was in grade 2 now. However, during one of our research conversations walking around the school grounds, Ted changed his mind about revealing information about his current imaginative play when he said:

> I don't really know . . . but sometimes I do play over there . . . that's the other place I hide. That's our secret spot, secret stuff some- times happens here and there. It's not just mine . . . it's mine and my friends, and it's actually a tree . . . a secret tree.

Following on from this disclosure, Ted suggested that teachers thought he and his friends were 'just playing football' on the oval, when in reality they were running back and forth across the oval between the 'secret base trees in a secret game'. In this way, Ted and his friends successfully created a form of being 'hidden in plain sight' to enact imaginative play which was a secret with a few of his friends, while simultaneously a secret from adults and other peers.

Four-year-old Georgia's impulse to construct her own quiet, uninterrupted and private places for imaginative play was also clearly evident in her stories and her actions. Georgia's preschool experience included a day each week in a local national park environment in conjunction with their conventional preschool site. It was interesting to note that when talking about her pretend play, Georgia did not mention the large two-storey adult-built wooden cubby house that dominated her preschool playground; instead, she spoke at length about the multiple 'bush cubbies' she constructed with her friend in the park. Embedded in Georgia's stories were the strategies she used to protect her private imaginative play from the broader peer group in her early childhood settings, saying:

> We play very quietly . . . I wanted to be quiet, to make them know . . . kind of not hear us, because we were too quiet . . . because we play our secret game and it's very hard to get into it.

In playing quietly, Georgia was passively excluding others from her self-constructed cubby by not allowing other children to know the 'secret' rituals to gain entry into their imaginative play place. What is especially interesting in both of these studies is the evidence of children's exclusion of others in their play, despite the 'everyone can join in' discourse commonly employed in educational settings (Skanfors, Lofdahl & Hagglund, 2009, p. 107). Corsaro (2011, p. 157) also notes this dichotomy, suggesting how 'intensely difficult' it can be for young children to renegotiate adult expectations of sharing places, especially when children are anxious to protect the 'interactive spaces' they have organised to play privately away from others.

Six-year-old Sonya also employed protective strategies to enable the enactment of private imaginative play that was 'hidden in plain sight' from others. For Sonya, this was necessary due to the lack of opportunities for hidden places for her imaginative play in her inner-city school playground.

To counter this problem, Sonya and her friends constructed their 'own place' adjacent to an old peppercorn tree locked behind a gate in the school playground. Sonya told a story about how she and her friends would 'talk to that tree', and said she felt she had to protect this private play from other children:

When I hear some people that are going around I sometimes start to stop because I think they are going to be laughing, because sometimes we do some games that are a bit private to me and my friends, that's why I wait for them to go first.

Both these empirical studies—the comparative case study (Moore, 2010) and the intergenerational narrative inquiry (Moore, 2015b)—highlight examples of why and how contemporary children creatively construct and protect their private places for play. While these examples demonstrate the resilience of children's impulse to construct private places, they also show the contextual constraints with which contemporary children are confronted in their quest for privacy in place-making.

Implications for practitioners

Researchers, policy-makers and educators have become increasingly aware of children's use of place. Interestingly, government officers and policy-makers have claimed that this increasing awareness has informed policy and regulatory documents with the aim of promoting young children's capacity for autonomy, decision-making and independence in their use of 'space' in their educational settings (DEEWR, 2009). This can also be seen in a reference to Regulation 108 in the *Guide to the National Law and Regulations* (ACECQA, 2014, p. 76):

Approved providers might also consider that the outdoor environment should be a place not only for children to release energy and engage in physical activity, but also for exploration, problem solving and creative expression.

Throughout the preliminary section on Quality Standard 3 relating to the physical environment provided for children in the *Guide to the National Quality Standard* (ACECQA, 2013), references to children's creative and independent use of space are highlighted, encouraged and valued (pp. 78–81); later, prompts for reflection on the provision of multiple forms of spaces for children's play are evident:

> How can we organise environments and spaces in ways that allow children opportunities to play on their own as well as promote small and large group interactions and meaningful play and leisure? (Quality Area 3.2, p. 92)

Regardless of this regulatory call to allow children opportunities to 'play alone', in reality it is more common in educational settings to see the 'everyone can join in' discourse enforced (Skanfors, Lofdahl & Hagglund, 2009, p. 107). Regardless of the policies encouraging children's creative expression in outdoor places, the legal requirement to 'supervise all children at all times' counters the creation of hidden places for imaginative play. Similarly, while children's strong impulse for privacy in their play is illuminated in the previous studies, the notion of hidden play is explicitly forbidden and regulated against in early childhood and school playgrounds (cf. Chancellor, 2008). In Chancellor's (2008) study, the primary school children constantly risked being disciplined for choosing to play in private, hidden places among the 'out of bounds' bushy edges of the school fence line (p. 101). Juxtaposing these documents, regulations and reflections against the current research on young children's strong impulse toward privacy, the implications for practitioners urge the provision of opportunities for children to construct their own private play places in early childhood and primary educational settings.

Ironically, school-aged children have been acknowledged in the reflective notes for Standard 3.1 ACECQA (2013) as needing 'a balance' between supervision and the 'growing need for privacy' (p. 83). However, as Norwegian researchers Moser and Martinsen (2010) conclude from their study on the necessary provision of hidden places for toddlers, young children's need for privacy should also be acknowledged with a less intrusive form of supervision. Similar to Fotel and Thomson's (2004) stance on the surveillance of children,

I am not advocating for 'a "utopia" where children are able to move around without any supervision or restrictions at all' (p. 536). Instead, I advocate for an understanding that young children's emotional impulse towards the construction of their own private play places needs to be acknowledged and provided for within their heavily supervised lives.

Drawing on Rivkin's (2000) 'habitats' for children, the following suggestions are presented for practitioners in early childhood and primary school settings to enable children's construction of their own 'private places' for imaginative play.

Consider the provision of:

- 'wild' places with multiple natural materials as affordances so children can construct their own places among the plants and bushes, where it 'appears' adults are not constantly 'in charge'
- reconsidered 'out of bounds' fence line areas of school playgrounds for the emotional restoration of children rather than making 'easy' adult supervision the priority
- quiet, hidden places for reverie, reflection and creative thinking
- places where children can have a sense of ownership, attachment and belonging to their 'own place'
- multiple loose materials, accessible spaces and time for children to construct their 'own' places, understanding that it is children's choice of where/how they construct these places
- places to enable the 'illusion of seclusion' (for example, adult waist-height mazes of hedging plants so that adults can peek over the top if required) to enable children to feel 'secrety'
- most importantly, hidden places to respect the 'secretness' of children's places without overly intrusive interruptions by adults.

CONCLUSION

Researching with young children has shown that an adult cannot make secret places for children; only children can make these important places for themselves (Moore, 2010). Research has also shown that rich, symbolic and imaginative play occurs in these child-constructed private places for play (Moore, 2015b). If abstract thinking, creativity, autonomy and independence are dispositions and skills that we encourage in the early years of education, then young children's emotional needs around the construction of private play places should be taken into consideration. Further to this, if it is now understood that children's emotional wellbeing, identity and sense of belonging are connected with the construction of private play places, then the notion of being 'hidden' and/or 'hidden in plain sight' without the constant intrusion of an adult should also be encouraged within pedagogical places for children.

REFLECTION QUESTIONS

9.1   Think about your own experiences of childhood play, where you preferred to be and with whom. Did anyone know where you were? Did you want them to know? Did you feel 'safe' in your own place? Do you remember feeling especially creative in your 'hidden' places for play— places where you could experiment with play themes and abstract ideas in a way you could not do in front of adults or your peer group?

9.2   Respectfully invite children in early childhood/early years settings to tell you stories about their preferred places for play, and whether they want adults to know where and what they are playing.

9.3   Increase your awareness and sensitivity to children's emotional need for private place-making, especially in crowded 'places for children' where they are confined for long periods of time with many others.

REFERENCES

Australian Children's Education and Care Quality Authority (ACECQA) (2013). *Guide to the National Quality Standards.* Retrieved 20 December 2016 from <files. acecqa.gov.au/files/National-Quality-Framework-Resources-Kit/NQF01-Guide-to-the-NQF-130902.pdf>.

—— (2014). *Guide to the Education and Care Services National Law and the Education and Care Services National Regulations 2011.* Retrieved 20 December 2016 from <files.acecqa.gov.au/files/nationalregulations/NQF02%20Guide%20to%20 ECS%20Law%20and%20Regs_web.pdf>.

Canning, N. (2010). The influence of the outdoor environment: Den-making in three different contexts. *European Early Childhood Education Research Journal, 18*(4), 555–66.

Chancellor, B. (2008). Australian primary school playgrounds: Children's use of playspaces and equipment. *International Journal of the Humanities, 6*(5), 97–103.

Clark, A. (2007). Views from inside the shed: Young children's perspective of the outdoor environment. *Education 3–13: International Journal of Primary, Elementary and Early Years Education, 35*(4), 349–63.

Corsaro, W. (2011). *The sociology of childhood* (3rd edn). Thousand Oaks, CA: Sage.

Corson, K., Colwel, M.J., Bell, N.J. & Trejos-Castillo, E. (2014). Wrapped up in covers: Preschoolers' secrets and secret hiding places. *Early Child Development and Care, 184*(12), 1769–86.

Cunningham, H. (2006). *The invention of childhood*. London: BBC Books.

Dahlberg, G. & Moss, P. (2005). *Ethics and politics in early childhood education*. London: RoutledgeFalmer.

Department of Education and Early Childhood Development (DEECD) (2012). *Practice notes: 12—Supervision*. Melbourne: Victorian Children's Services Legislation.

Department of Education, Employment & Workplace Relations (DEEWR) (2009). *Belonging, being and becoming: The Early Years Learning Framework for Australia*. Canberra: Commonwealth of Australia.

Elliott, S. (2010). Children in the natural world. In J.M. Davis (ed.), *Young children and the environment: Early education for sustainability* (pp. 43–75). Melbourne: Cambridge University Press.

Fotel, T. & Thomsen, T.U. (2004). The surveillance of children's mobility. *Surveillance & Society, 1*(4), 535–54.

Foucault, M. (1979). *Discipline and punish: The birth of the prison*. New York: Vintage Books.

Giddens, A. (1991). *Modernity and self-identity: Self and society in the late modern age*. Stanford, CA: Stanford University Press.

Gill, T. (2007). *No fear: Growing up in a risk averse society*. London: Calouste Gulbenkian Foundation.

Gillis, J. (2009). Transitions to modernity. In J. Qvortrup, W. Corsaro & M.-S. Honig (eds), *The Palgrave handbook of childhood studies* (pp. 114–26). London: Palgrave Macmillan.

Goodenough, E. (2003). Peering into childhood's secret spaces. *The Chronicle of Higher Education, 49*(43), 1–4.

Hardy, T. (1874). *Far from the madding crowd*. London: Macmillan.

Hart, R. (1979). *Children's experience of place*. New York: Irvington.

Jack, G. (2010). Place matters: The significance of place attachments for children's well-being. *British Journal of Social Work, 40,* 755–71.

James, A., Jenks, C. & Prout, A. (1998). *Theorizing childhood*. Cambridge: Polity Press.

Lim, M. & Barton, A. C. (2010). Exploring insideness in urban children's sense of place. *Journal of Environmental Psychology, 30*, 328–37.

Maynard, T., Waters, J. & Clement, J. (2011). Moving outdoors: Further exploration of 'child initiated' learning in the outdoor environment. *Education 3–13: International Journal of Primary, Elementary and Early Years Education, 33*(3), 212–25.

Moore, D. (2010). 'Only children can make secret places': Children's secret business of place. MEd dissertation, Monash University, Melbourne.

—— (2014). Interrupting listening to children: Researching with children's secret places in early childhood settings. *Australasian Journal of Early Childhood, 39*(2), 4–11.

—— (2015a). 'The teacher doesn't know what it is, but she knows where we are': Young children's secret places in early childhood outdoor environments. *International Journal of Play, 4*(1), 20–31.

—— (2015b). A place within a place: Toward new understandings on the enactment of contemporary imaginative play practices and places. Unpublished PhD thesis, Australian Catholic University, Melbourne.

Moore, R.C. (1986). *Childhood's domain: Play and place in child development*. London: Croom Helm.

Moser, T. & Martinsen, M.T. (2010). The outdoor environment in Norwegian kindergartens as pedagogical space for toddlers' play, learning and development. *European Early Childhood Education Research Journal, 18*(4), 457–71.

Qvortrup, J. (2009). Childhood as a structural form. In J. Qvortrup, W. Corsaro & M.-S. Honig (eds), *The Palgrave handbook of childhood studies* (pp. 21–33). London: Palgrave Macmillan.

Rasmussen, K. (2004). Places for children—children's places. *Childhood, 11*(2), 155–73.

Rivkin, M. (2000). Outdoor experiences for young children. *ERIC Digest*. Retrieved 10 September 2009 from <www.ericdigests.org/2001-3/children.htm>.

Roe, M. (2007). Feeling 'secrety': children's views on involvement in landscape decisions. *Environmental Education Research, 13*(4), 467–85.

Rooney, T. (2012). Childhood spaces in a changing world: Exploring the intersection between children and new surveillance technologies. *Global Studies of Childhood, 2*(4), 331–42.

Sandberg, A. & Vuorinen, T. (2010). Reflecting the child: play memories and images of the child. In L. Brooker & S. Edwards (eds), *Engaging Play* (pp. 54–66). Maidenhead: Open University Press.

Skanfors, L., Lofdahl, A. & Hagglund, S. (2009). Hidden spaces and places in the preschool: Withdrawal strategies in preschool children's peer culture. *Journal of Early Childhood Research, 71*(1), 94–109.

Tuan, Y.F. (1977). *Space and place: The perspective of experience.* London: Edward Arnold.

Van Manen, M. & Levering, B. (1996). *Childhood's secrets: Intimacy, privacy, and the self reconsidered.* New York: Teachers College Press.

Wood, E. & Attfield, J. (2005). *Play, learning and the early childhood curriculum* (2nd edn). London: Paul Chapman.

Chapter 10

Creating a school playground in Papua New Guinea
A participatory approach with young children

Sue Elliott, Kym Simoncini, Victoria Carr,
Lalen Simeon and Elisapesi Manson

This chapter draws on a research project entitled 'Community Engagement in the Redevelopment of a Papua New Guinean School Playground: Participatory Research in Design, Construction, Play and Learning' (Simoncini et al., 2016). The aim of the project was to investigate how a playground redevelopment might impact on children's play, classroom engagement and behaviour, school attendance and the wider school community. The project team included both local and visiting academic researchers, an Australian-based playground builder as well as pre-service teachers enrolled at the Pacific Adventist University, Papua New Guinea, tradespeople, local teachers and communities. The project was to redevelop the school playground at Koiari Park Adventist Primary School located on the Pacific Adventist University campus in collaboration with children, parents and teachers. While children from Years 1 to 8 were active participants and contributors before, during and after the redevelopment, in this chapter we specifically outline how younger children from Years 1 to 2 (aged 6 to 9 years) shared their ideas about play, and later their reactions to the new playground through drawing and verbal descriptions. We begin by offering a provocation and contextualising the project, then briefly outline the research approach and share findings, insights and implications from our experiences.

Provocation

In any community, it is critically important to work in culturally responsive and child-responsive ways to help ensure positive outcomes for children's play and learning. The redevelopment of a playground offered a unique opportunity to enact these responsive ways and in doing so aligned with the United Nations Convention on the Rights of the Child (UNCRC) (Office of the United Nations High Commissioner for Human Rights, 1989), the highest levels of Hart's (1997) ladder of child participation in playspace design and agentic images of children (James & Prout, 1990).

Context

As a research project implemented in a developing country situated in the equatorial Pacific region, there are several contextual points to make. These include an overview of Papua New Guinean (PNG) education and play settings, the benefits of play in school and the promotion of young children's active participatory roles in research. The elaboration of these points supports a deeper understanding of this research project and findings.

Education and play settings in Papua New Guinea

In Papua New Guinea, the school-aged population (under 15 years) comprises some 40 per cent of the total population (Department of National Planning and Monitoring [DNPM], 2010) with a net enrolment rate in primary schools of 63 per cent, the lowest in the Asia-Pacific region (UNICEF, 2016). Schools operate from Year 1 (age 7) to Year 12 (age 19), with enrolment rates for primary (Years 3–8) at 65 per cent (UNICEF, 2015) and secondary (Years 9–12) at 12 per cent (Rena, 2011). By international standards, these enrolment rates are concerning and the PNG government is now prioritising meeting national targets in health and education infrastructure. Low enrolment rates can be attributed in part to the challenging geographical context and regionally dispersed population (87 per cent of people are located in rural villages), where young children's daily access to school facilities is a problem. Other barriers to school attendance include political instability, inability to pay school fees, gender discrimination, community unrest or discord, clan or family values, lack of schools and/or qualified teachers, and localised natural disasters (Carr, Simoncini & Manson, in press; DFAT, 2010; Department of Education, 2015). In addition, while there is much cultural richness and language diversity, with three official languages spoken (English, Tok Pisin and Hiri Motu), this likely compounds issues of effective and sustained schooling.

The second author of this chapter was the principal researcher and instigator of the playground redevelopment project. Dr Kym Simoncini had identified on previous visits to Papua New Guinea that playgrounds with equipment such as swings and slides were limited to the capital city, Port Moresby. She also observed that while school playgrounds were often generous open spaces with a few trees, the playgrounds were used mostly for sports or after-school games. When play occurred, it was typically competitive ball games enjoyed by boys. Girls were rarely seen participating and during school lunchtimes all children were prohibited from playing. The possibility of a project to facilitate children's play in more inclusive and diverse ways with the introduction of some equipment was thus envisioned, and Koiari Park Adventist Primary School, with links to the Pacific Adventist University, was identified as an ideal pilot site for a playground redevelopment.

The benefits of play in school

There is now a significant international body of research literature advocating the benefits of play in school settings. However, we must recognise that most, if not all, of this literature is by researchers in developed countries where daily access to school is less challenging and typically compulsory. This is not the case in Papua New Guinea. Further, research has often occurred in Western cultural contexts where children's lives are highly structured, top-down curriculum pressure prevails, and time for child-directed play is under threat (Ramstetter et al., 2010). In the cultural contexts of Papua New Guinea, the priorities for change are children accessing and attending school, play being valued as integral to daily learning by teachers and a diversity of outdoor play possibilities being available in the school playground. However, the role of play in schools is much less important compared with overcoming the challenges of low attendance and retention rates, poor infrastructure, limited teaching resources and teacher absenteeism, as described by the local Papua New Guinea chapter authors here.

Having clarified these differing cultural underpinnings, most literature strongly advocates play breaks, such as recess and lunchtime, during the school day. These child-directed play periods promote physical and social play, offer opportunities for peer scaffolding and sibling play, and have been shown to positively link to higher attention levels and focus in class (Dyment et al., 2009; Jarret, 2015; Verstraete et al., 2006). Further, if these outdoor play opportunities are in 'green' spaces where natural elements promote investigation, manipulation and challenge, there are also potential health and wellbeing benefits (Bagot, Allen & Toukhsati, 2015; Townsend & Weerasuriya, 2010; see also Chapter 3). Rural lifestyles—which predominate in Papua New Guinea, where 87 per cent of the population lives in rural areas—certainly enhance this possibility (DNPM, 2010). Beyond these specifics, and irrespective of cultural contexts, play is fundamental in promoting children's learning and development as enshrined in the UNCRC (OHCHR, 1989) and strongly supported by paediatricians (Ginsburg, 2007; Milteer et al., 2012).

Both the scholarly and the practitioner literature about playgrounds offer insights into the types of playground elements that best offer play affordances for children (see Chapter 6). The equipment and the playground space within which it is embedded must offer diversity of play potential and flexibility to engage the range of children's play interests and skills, particularly the wide age group in school settings (Brown, 2003; Gamson Danks, 2010; Nelson, 2012; Rivkin & Schein, 2014). In addition, the international nature play movement emphasises the potential of natural elements and spaces for play (Carr & Luken, 2014). The ideal playground offers 'natural, complex, challenging and exciting play environments' (Dyment et al., 2009, p. 272), including diverse sensory elements; manipulable loose parts both natural and repurposed; spatial and topological diversity; risk and challenge; novelty and inherent change; and cultural and geographical relevance and meaning (Elliott, 2008; Frost, 2010).

Young children's active participatory roles in research

We have acknowledged above the alignment of this project to the UNCRC (OHCHR, 1989), to which Papua New Guinea is a signatory. Of particular relevance here are Articles 12 and 13, which essentially state that children have a right to a voice, to be heard and to influence decision-making around matters that impact on their lives. Beyond this legally binding convention, young children's active participatory roles in research are increasingly promoted (Groundwater-Smith, Dockett & Bottrell, 2015). This engagement of children as capable and knowledgeable research participants is also framed by reconceptualised images of children as agentic social participants (James & Prout, 1990; Moore, 2014) and new sociology theory (Corsaro, 2015; see also Chapter 8). Further, Hart (1997) strongly argues for participatory approaches to playspace design. In his ladder of children's participation, the lowest rung is manipulation by adults, with the highest and most desirable rung being child-initiated shared decisions. Essentially, we recognise children as experts about their play, as knowledgeable daily users of their playground and shared decision-makers.

There is no one recipe for a playground or a redevelopment, and hence a localised and culturally aware consultative and collaborative research approach was taken here, one that responded to the unique PNG context as outlined above.

Research approach

The overall project employed a mixed-methods theoretical framework combining both qualitative and quantitative research methods (Creswell & Plano-Clark, 2011); however, in this chapter we particularly discuss the participatory action research approach undertaken (Kemmis & McTaggart, 2005). This approach was chosen to facilitate the playground redevelopment and create qualitative data about this change with the school community, given the contextual information offered above. Also, this approach was considered to offer possibilities for authentically and purposefully interacting with the school children throughout the playground redevelopment process. We created data with the children before, during and after the playground redevelopment as part of an evolving action research cycle process (Kemmis & McTaggart, 2005). The following paragraphs outline the Koiari Park Adventist Primary School context, methods of data creation and action research cycle phases of the study.

The Koiari Park Adventist Primary School, located on the Pacific Adventist University campus, comprises Year 1 to Year 8 classes totalling 384 students (6 to 15 years), nine classroom teachers and a principal. Children of both Pacific Adventist University staff and students residing on the university campus, and the surrounding local communities beyond the university compound, attend the school. The playground area identified for redevelopment by the school community was a large, open, grassed and sloping site bordered by well-established mature shade trees, such as mango and rain trees (see Figure 10.1). The school also has additional designated ball game areas, including an open basketball court and under-cover concreted areas suitable for various play activities.

Figure 10.1 Playground area identified for redevelopment at Koiari Park Adventist Primary School, Papua New Guinea

Source: Author's collection, Koiari Park Adventist Primary School, Papua New Guinea.

Children typically begin school at age 7 in Papua New Guinea, and the children who participated in this study were in Years 1 and 2, so most were aged between 6 and 9 years. In total, 86 children participated across these year levels. Permission was sought from parents/guardians for the children to participate in the research project and assent was also sought in the classroom context when children were invited to contribute their initial ideas and later responses to the playground design. While targeted questions inviting written responses were used with older children, in Years 1 and 2, children were invited to draw their responses. This occurred in their usual classroom settings and was implemented by three or four multilingual Pacific Adventist University pre-service teachers who explained the drawing activity to the children in the local Tok Pisin language. The pre-service teachers were supported and accompanied by one English-speaking Australian researcher, at different times either the first or second chapter author. As children drew their ideas the pre-service teachers and the researcher informally approached the children inviting their explanations of the drawings in Tok Pisin or English as preferred by each child.

This consultative activity with children occurred on three occasions as integral to three participatory action research cycles of plan, act, monitor and evaluate:

- an initial consultation with children, seeking their ideas to inform the playground redevelopment design and inviting drawings of both themselves playing and their favourite place to play (project week 1: July 2015)
- immediately post-construction of the redeveloped playground, a consultation with the children seeking their initial responses to the playground through drawings of their favourite places to play (project week 3: July 2015)
- later, a consultation with the children to seek their longer-term responses about where they liked to play most in the redeveloped playground (later on-site visit, November 2015).

Findings: Children's ideas and responses

The findings from each of the three consultations with children are described here, with a focus on the illustrative drawings and commentary offered by the children (see Figures 10.2, 10.3, 10.4, 10.5 and 10.6).

During the initial consultation activity to inform the playground design, children most frequently drew themselves playing ball games, such as soccer, rugby, volleyball and tennis, while some depicted other play activities, such as climbing trees, sliding and flying kites.

Figure 10.2 Vicklyn likes to play basketball, volleyball and soccer both at home and at school.

Source: Koiari Park Adventist Primary School, Papua New Guinea.

When subsequently inviting the children to draw their favourite place to play, the manipulable sensory elements of water and sand featured most strongly. Also, trees and places for ball games and other types of running games were noted as valuable playspaces.

These insights from the children informed the playground design in the followings ways: open spaces for running and ball games were maintained; a large slide and a sandpit were proposed; and, while a water feature was not feasible, a dry creek bed with bridge and an improvised log boat were planned. It was anticipated that tropical wet season rains would add to the possibilities here on the sloping site. All existing trees were maintained on the site. Note that members of the wider school community, including teachers and parents, were also consulted in focus groups about their ideas for the playground and their post-design responses to the initial plans.

Figure 10.3 Naomi likes the beach.

Source: Koiari Park Adventist Primary School, Papua New Guinea.

In the first post-playground redevelopment consultation, children drew their favourite places to play in the new space. Their drawings most often depicted the sandpit, the slide, the hills planted with lemongrass for going up and down, and the various repurposed tyre swings hanging under the trees.

The final consultation occurred after the children had experienced about four months playing in the redeveloped playground during school breaks, before and after school each day and on weekends. Most children described playing mainly during or after school each day. They were invited to draw where they played most, and again the sandpit, slide and lemongrass hills were most popularly depicted. A rope climbing structure installed post-redevelopment by the school community was frequently noted in the drawings too.

Figure 10.4 Kaykay says the playground 'makes her happy' and she makes sand castles in the sandpit.

Source: Koiari Park Adventist Primary School, Papua New Guinea.

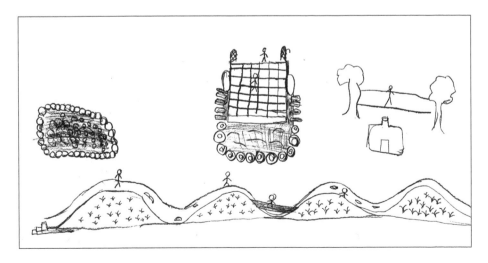

Figure 10.5 Wynstan likes the hills, sandpit, slide, ropes and cubby.

Source: Koiari Park Adventist Primary School, Papua New Guinea.

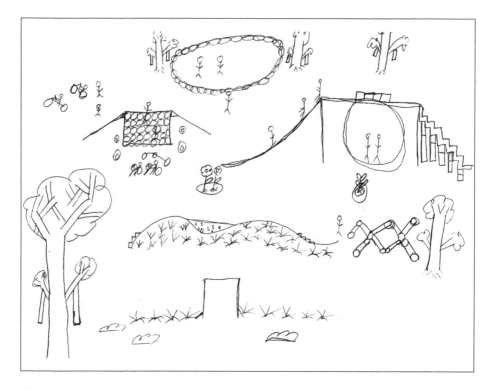

Figure 10.6 Pascal says he likes everything!

Source: Koiari Park Adventist Primary School, Papua New Guinea.

During discussions, the children also offered some insights about what else they might like in the playground. More flowers, a treehouse, toys for the sandpit, a hammock swing, a water slide and monkey bars were identified. So it is anticipated that this playground will evolve well beyond the initial research project, with ongoing support from the school community.

Insights from and implications of our experiences

Here we address insights from our experiences that may inform others wishing to consult with children as active participants in playground redevelopment, whether in a school or early childhood education setting, in Australia or elsewhere.

Building relationships is integral to participatory research approaches where relationships between participants and researchers are key to inviting engagement with the selected research methods (Groundwater-Smith, Dockett & Bottrell, 2015). We deliberately conducted the consultation activities in the children's usual classroom settings with their teacher present to offer as much physical context familiarity as possible, despite several relatively new people entering their classroom space. The Pacific Adventist University pre-service teachers promoted relationships with the children, and also clarity of communication about the drawings, by speaking predominantly in the local Tok Pisin language.

The arts, including drawing, are commonly applied as research methods for eliciting children's ideas and responses (Groundwater-Smith, Dockett & Bottrell, 2015). In this PNG school setting, the children always drew with black pencil as a medium and this was well suited to the illustrative focus in this study. The figures provided here attest to the children's skills and competencies in both observation and detailed line drawing to accurately represent their ideas. The children undertook the drawing activity with both clear intent and serious focus, and with erasers readily accessible as they corrected any aspects of their drawings as they wished. During the drawing process, conversations with the children were varied, with some children seeming keen to converse, and others more reticent; however, children's right to assent and their desired levels of engagement were respected. Overall, we believe clear understandings of the drawn depictions were achieved, with ongoing review between the pre-service teachers and the non-PNG researchers for clarification of local playground terms and their meanings. For example, the children employed the term 'seesaw' to mean a swing, while 'haus-haus', referred to domestic-type play in a pretend house or cubby setting.

Thus, a combination of the factors promoting child–researcher relationships and the drawing method employed, as noted above, facilitated not only children's willingness to participate, but the authenticity of the data created and its effective interpretation. Further, these data informed the playground design, and we believe children's participation in the playground project reflected the higher rung of adult-initiated and shared decisions with children in Hart's (1997) ladder of participation.

From the perspective of the pre-service teachers as researchers, the quality of teacher education can be promoted when student teachers are allowed to inform teaching best practice with their own research, and collaborate with one another and the community (Avalos, 2000). The pre-service teachers sought collaborations with their colleagues and the community during focus groups. Also, the pre-service teachers noticeably grew in their research roles, leading the data collection throughout the consultation period and supported preliminary analysis of the data during post-consultation debriefings. They demonstrated skills both in and outside the classroom in communication, collaboration, organisation, community participation and data analysis. Furthermore, we anticipated that there was potential for these undergraduate research experiences and skills to be carried into their future careers, and the project evaluations submitted following their participation were highly affirming.

More broadly, the research project also involved building relationships over time between researchers, teachers and parents in multiple contexts. For instance, teachers, parents and researchers participated in the physical task of playground building together, while the focus groups and teacher meetings offered forums for listening, exchanging ideas and sharing values. Such responsive relationships were instrumental to negotiating the research project within school timetables, individual classroom priorities and cultural protocols. While a playground redevelopment would seemingly be about a physical context, this is somewhat short-sighted, and socio-cultural contexts for playground change are equally, if not more, relevant in all communities.

The critical importance of parental engagement in children's learning and partnership building between teachers and parents within early childhood and school communities is well recognised in many countries (Arthur et al., 2015), yet in Papua New Guinea to date there has been limited anecdotal evidence of this occurring. Ultimately, in this PNG school, parent/community engagement in the learning of children was demonstrated through enhanced collaborations, networking and physically working together during focus groups, meetings, working-bees and so on. Similarly, parent/community involvement in the design of the playground through consultations and reflections increased the cultural awareness and cultural relevance of the playground design, so was better aligned to children's learning and play needs. In a small way, we believe this project instigated change in this respect, and therefore aligns with promoting national targets for education infrastructure improvements in Papua New Guinea.

A further quantitative aspect of this project, yet to be formally reported, is the potential impact of opportunities to play in the redeveloped playground on children's learning within their school classrooms. We looked previously at the direct benefits of outdoor play in school settings, but an indirect benefit of interest in this project was the impact for children and teachers on what happens in classrooms. Are the children attending classes more regularly, and are they more attentive in class and better able to focus on the task at hand? Anecdotally, there was emerging evidence from attendance records, interviews with teachers and classroom observations that positive changes were occurring. In the unique context of this project, we can also question the importance of the culturally designed and relevant playground in relation to positive learning outcomes for children, and we envisage further scope for research in this area.

There are a range of implications evident here, from critically examining how you might engage with young children in decision-making about playgrounds and their redevelopment to recognising the cultural uniqueness of each context and ensuring that both physical and socio-cultural dimensions are considered in any playground development process. While this study was implemented in Papua New Guinea, we believe our learning is transferable to other settings.

CONCLUSION

The intent of this project was to honour the participation of young children in this shared playground redevelopment project and, as co-researchers with children, reflect on the multiple insights gleaned from the project. Essentially, this is a story of children's participation in playground redevelopment, but it is also more broadly about building community partnerships, facilitating change and acknowledging socio-cultural and physical dimensions. We particularly anticipate that the involvement of parents, teachers and pre-service teachers in this collaborative and participatory project may inspire further creation of school playgrounds with positive long-term impacts for young children's play and learning across Papua New Guinea.

ACKNOWLEDGEMENTS

- Koiari Park Adventist Primary School children, parents and teachers
- Faculty of Education, Pacific Adventist University student teachers, administrative and maintenance staff
- University of Canberra Early Career Academic Researcher Development Program
- Port Moresby local businesses and tradespeople
- Marcus Veerman, lead designer/builder (PlaygroundIDEAS)

REFLECTION QUESTIONS

10.1 Imagine being invited to redevelop a playground in an early childhood centre or school. Where would you begin and how would you authentically engage all stakeholders, including children?

10.2 What opportunities are there in culturally diverse or unique settings for everyone to participate in the playground redevelopment, and what methods might be most appropriate?

10.3 What priorities would you identify in a playground redevelopment process: community participation, incorporation of natural features, structural elements, cultural relevance, inherent biodiversity, responsiveness to topography, local materials and tradespeople, ongoing maintenance, children's safety and other factors?

10.4 Consider the resources that might be utilised in a playground redevelopment, such as skilled or unskilled volunteers, repurposed items such as tyres and planks, and natural materials—for example, tree logs, rocks and soil.

REFERENCES

Arthur, L., Beecher, B., Death, E., Dockett, S. & Farmer, S. (2015). *Programming and planning in early childhood settings* (6th edn). Melbourne: Cengage.

Avalos, B. (2000). Policies for teacher education in developing countries. *International Journal of Educational Research, 33*(5), 457–74.

Bagot, K.L., Allen, F.C.L. & Toukhsati, S. (2015). Perceived restorativeness of children's school playground environments: Nature, playground features and play period experiences. *Journal of Environmental Psychology, 41*, 1–9.

Brown, F. (2003). Complex flexibility: The role of playwork in child development. In

F. Brown (ed.), *Playwork: Theory and practice* (pp. 51–65). Buckingham: Open University Press.

Carr, V. & Luken, E. (2014). Playscapes: A pedagogical paradigm for play and learning. *The International Journal of Play, 3*(1), 69–83.

Carr, V., Simoncini, K. & Manson, E. (in press). Early childhood education in Papua New Guinea. In J. Roopnarine, J.E. Johnson, S. Quinn & M. Patte (eds), *Handbook of International Perspectives on Early Childhood Education.* New York: Taylor & Francis/Routledge.

Corsaro, W.A. (2015). *The sociology of childhood* (4th edn) Thousand Oaks, CA: Sage.

Cresswell, J.W. & Plano-Clark, V.L. (2011). *Designing and Conducting Mixed-Methods Research* (2nd edn). Thousand Oaks, CA: Sage.

department of Education (PNG) (2015). *Education for all 2015 national review report: Papua New Guinea.* Paris: UNESCO.

Department of Foreign Affairs (DFAT) (2010). *Australian support for basic and secondary education in Papua New Guinea 2010–2015: Delivery strategy.* Retrieved 17 May 2017 from <dfat.gov.au/about-us/publications/Documents/png-education-strategy.pdf>.

Department of National Planning and Monitoring (DNPM) (2010). *Papua New Guinea—millennium development goals second national progress comprehensive report for Papua New Guinea.* Retrieved 17 May 2017 from <www.pg.undp.org/content/dam/papua_new_guinea/docs/MDG/UNDP_PG_MDG%20Comprehensive%20Report%202010.pdf>.

Dyment, J. E., Bell, A.C. & Lucas, A.J. (2009). The relationship between school ground design and intensity of physical activity. *Children's Geographies, 7*(3), 261–76.

Elliott, S. (ed.) (2008). *The outdoor playspace: Naturally.* Sydney: Pademelon Press.

Frost, J.L. (2010). *A history of children's play and play environments: Toward a contemporary child-saving movement.* New York: Routledge.

Gamson Danks, S. (2010). *Asphalt to Ecosystems: Design ideas for schoolyard transformation.* Oakland, CA: New Village Press.

Ginsburg, K.R. (2007). The importance of play in promoting healthy child development and maintaining strong parent-child bonds. *Pediatrics, 119*(1), 182–91.

Groundwater-Smith, S., Dockett, S. & Bottrell, D. (2015). *Participatory research with children and young people.* London: Sage.

Hart, R.A. (1997). *Children's participation: The theory and practice of involving young citizens in community development and environmental care.* London: Earthscan & UNICEF.

James, A. & Prout, A. (eds) (1990). *Constructing and reconstructing childhood.* London: Falmer Press.

Jarrett, O.S. (2015). Recess and learning. In J.E. Johnson, S.G. Eberle, T.S. Henricks & D. Kuschner (eds), *The handbook of the study of play* (pp. 299–318). Lanham, MD: Rowman & Littlefield.

Kemmis, S. & McTaggart, R. (2005). Participatory action research: Communicative action and the public sphere. In N.K. Denzin & Y.S. Lincoln (eds), *Handbook of qualitative research* (3rd edn) (pp. 559–603). Thousand Oaks, CA: Sage.

Milteer, R.M., Ginsburg, K.R., Mulligan, D.A., Ameenuddin, N., Brown, A., Christakis, D.A.,... Levine, A.E. (2012). The importance of play in promoting healthy child development and maintaining a strong parent–child bond: Focus on children in poverty. *Pediatrics, 129*(1), 204–13.

Moore, R. (2014). *Nature play and learning places: Creating and managing places where children engage with nature.* Raleigh, NC: Natural Learning Initiative and Reston, VA: National Wildlife Federation.

Nelson, E. (2012). *Cultivating outdoor classrooms.* St Paul, MN: Redleaf Press.

Office of the United Nations High Commissioner for Human Rights (OHCHR) (1989). *United Nations Convention on the Rights of the Child (UNCRC).* Retrieved 21 May 2016 from <www.ohchr.org/EN/ProfessionalInterest/Pages/CRC.aspx>.

Ramstetter, C.L., Murray, R. & Garner, A.S. (2010). The crucial role of recess in schools. *Journal of School Health, 80*(11), 517–26.

Rena, R. (2011). Challenges for quality primary education in Papua New Guinea: A case study. *Education Research International, 1*(1): 14–35.

Rivkin, M. & Schein, D. (2014). *The great outdoors: Advocating for natural spaces for young children.* Washington, DC: NAEYC.

Simoncini, K., Carr, V., Elliott, S., Manson, E., Simeon, L. & Sawi, J. (2016). Playground development in Papua New Guinea: Creating new play, learning and research environments. *Children, Youth and Environments, 26*(1), 179–94.

Townsend, M. & Weerasuriya, R. (2010). *Beyond blue to green: The benefits of contact with nature for mental health and well-being.* Melbourne: Beyond Blue.

United Nations Children's Fund (UNICEF) (2015). *Papua New Guinea Education.* Retrieved 17 May 2017 from <www.unicef.org/png/activities_4369.html>.

—— (2016). *Education in Papua New Guinea: An early start for a better future.* Retrieved 17 May 2017 from <https://blogs.unicef.org/east-asia-pacific/education-papua-new-guinea-early-start-better-future>.

Verstraete, S.J.M., Cardon, G.M., De Clercq, D.L.R. & De Bourdeaudhuij, I.M.M. (2006). Increasing children's physical activity levels during recess in elementary schools: The effects of providing game equipment. *European Journal of Public Health, 16*(4), 415–19.

Part 4
Cultural perspectives

Chapter 11

Indigenous perspectives on outdoor learning environments
On Country Learning

Libby Lee-Hammond and Elizabeth Jackson-Barrett

In this chapter, we provide an Indigenous perspective on the ongoing complexity of achieving equitable outcomes for Aboriginal children in education. We will share our research and experiences of two culturally centred outdoor learning projects, which we describe as On Country Learning (OCL) (Lee-Hammond & Jackson-Barrett, 2013). This research will serve as a starting point for early years educators to incorporate Indigenous perspectives into their programs in ways that honour Aboriginal and Torres Strait Islander cultures and also meet the requirements of the Australian Curriculum (ACARA, 2015), National Quality Standard for Early Childhood Education and Care (ACECQA, 2013b) and the Australian Professional Standards for Teachers (AITSL, 2011).

Provocation

At a national level in Australia, policy documents and frameworks stipulate that those working in early childhood education must demonstrate cultural competence in respect to Aboriginal and Torres Strait Islander peoples and cultures. Those working in the birth to 8 years area are expected to have the knowledge and skills to interpret and apply the standards and outcomes of the National Quality Framework and Standard (ACECQA, 2013a, 2013b), *Belonging, Being and Becoming: The Early Years Learning Framework for Australia* (EYLF) (DEEWR, 2009) and, for those working in the school sector, the Australian Curriculum (ACARA, 2015) and the Australian Professional Standards for Teachers (AITSL, 2011). In all these documents and frameworks, there are clear requirements to demonstrate a capacity to develop partnerships with families (ACECQA, 2013a, 2013b) and have the necessary repertoire of strategies for teaching ATSI children.

For example, the Australian Professional Standards for Teachers (AITSL, 2011) stipulate what knowledge and skills teachers should have in order to effectively teach Aboriginal and Torres Strait Islander students and to teach all students about Aboriginal and Torres Strait Islander languages, history and culture. The requirements are:

- Focus Area 1.4: Strategies for teaching Aboriginal and Torres Strait Islander students
- Focus Area 2.4: Understand and respect Aboriginal and Torres Strait Islander people to promote reconciliation between Indigenous and non-Indigenous Australians (AITSL, 2011).

The above standards identify two important foci that have been absent in previous Aboriginal education initiatives, and while these two areas mark a major step in readdressing Aboriginal perspectives, histories and knowledges, there is no accountability measure against which these expectations can be measured in educators' roles with children. For instance, how does one measure respect?

With reference to Aboriginal cultures, the projects reported in this chapter will assist you to consider ways in which you might effectively meet the National Quality Standard Element 1.1: Each child's current knowledge, ideas, culture, abilities and interests are the foundation of the program (ACECQA, 2013b).

How would you rate your current level of competence with regard to ATSI culture and history? In this chapter, we will demonstrate how two outdoor learning projects have enabled early years educators to be better equipped and more confident to work with young children in line with these standards and frameworks.

Policy, theoretical and cultural contexts

The significance of Professional Standards is underscored by countless reports that review and recommend as a national priority 'Closing the Gap' (Commonwealth of Australia, 2011) in educational outcomes for Aboriginal students—for example, reports from the Department of Education Western Australia (2013), the Council of Australian Governments (COAG) (2008), the Ministerial Council for Education, Early Childhood and Youth Affairs (MCEECDYA) (2010–14) and the Western Australian Aboriginal Education and Training Council (WAAETC) (2011–15). Much effort has gone into identifying the reasons for educational outcomes for Aboriginal children in Australia that differ from those of non-Aboriginal children; however, these reasons are usually ascribed to an innate 'cultural deficit' (Cowlishaw, 2012; Parbury, 1999) and at other times to sociocultural factors (Kerwin & Van Issum, 2012). These conclusions concerning Aboriginal 'disadvantage' are framed in a Western notion of what constitutes knowledge and the proper outcomes of an education.

All our official measures of success in education are standardised (e.g. NAPLAN) and relate exclusively to prescribed learning goals built on Western knowledge systems for the production of 'active and informed citizens' (Ministerial Council on Education, 2008, p. 7). These measures fail to consider how Indigenous knowledges might be esteemed and celebrated as strengths and competencies of Aboriginal children as a result of their participation in an education (Guenther, Bat & Osborne, 2014). As a way of responding to the above concerns, the Australian government has embedded Aboriginal perspectives as a cross-curriculum priority, together with professional standards for teachers through the Australian Institute for Teaching and School Leadership (AITSL). Regardless of these two initiatives, it has not been the case that radically different approaches to Aboriginal education at the 'cultural interface' (Nakata, 2007) have been seriously trialled or even attempted at a systems level. Achieving equitable outcomes in education for Aboriginal children is unfinished business, primarily because of the mismatch between what constitutes quality early years pedagogy, the actual delivery of curriculum in Western classrooms and how achievement is measured.

In this chapter, we discuss two projects, Walliabup Connections and Djarlgarra Koolunger, both situated within the urban space of Whadjuck Country of Nyungar Boodja in the southwest corner of Western Australia. Using the Leuven Wellbeing and Involvement Scale (Laevers, 1994), along with parent and teacher interviews, these projects have provided preliminary evidence that students involved in these OCL projects have increased levels of involvement, wellbeing, social confidence and cultural identity.

We argue that one significant understanding that has been a large part of the early success of this work is the primacy the project places on knowledge that has largely been overlooked by Western education in Australia (and elsewhere where colonisation has marginalised indigenous knowledge systems). That is, that Aboriginal peoples have always had, and continue to have, a vibrant, complex and rigorous system of learning involving Country. It is this learning that teaches Aboriginal children the precious cultural understandings and relationships that form the core of their identities. OCL projects such as Walliabup and Djarlgarra explore the possibilities of redesigning pedagogy to align first with Indigenous knowledge systems and then to explore and then connect with mandated curriculum (Western knowledge). These projects are therefore occurring at what Nakata (2007) describes as the cultural interface between Western scientific knowledge and Indigenous knowledge. Nakata (2007, p. 8) explains that 'Indigenous knowledge systems and Western knowledge systems work off different theories of knowledge that frame who can be a knower, what can be known, what constitutes knowledge.'

We draw on Indigenous pedagogies, as well as the outdoor play and learning literature and our own OCL research. In the initial stages of our work, we described the project as Bush School; on reflection, though, a more authentic description of our work as grounded in Country has necessitated a change of nomenclature, and we now refer to this work as 'On Country Learning' (OCL). In this chapter, the reader will see references to both names. Our work is embedded in Country with Elders' knowledge and participation as a starting point because to understand Country for those who are not Aboriginal or Torres Strait Islander is to understand that there is

an ecological web called 'country'—living things interact. Their lives are interconnected because they are here together in this place. In the same way, their stories interconnect, past connects with present, and creation is part of the contemporary life of the place and its people...Country is a place of belonging...Country gives us our identity. Our lives are formed by knowing our Country (Bird Rose, 2002, p. 16).

Country is therefore the central tenet of our OCL projects. A child's need for belonging, now enshrined in the EYLF (DEEWR, 2009), nests comfortably within the notion of Country, and enables educators to embrace this approach supported by a policy framework. We are committed to ensuring that children's identity is strengthened in the early years. Therefore, as part of the school-based projects, we explore the children's social and emotional wellbeing and their levels of involvement in the learning that takes place. In addition, we seek to make explicit the connections of OCL to the AITSL standards (AITSL, 2011) and the Australian Curriculum (ACARA, 2015). We present a pedagogical approach that embraces the multiple ways in which early years educators may co-construct educational projects grounded in Indigenous cultures and in Country (Jackson-Barrett et al., 2015).

How does OCL work in practice?

Both OCL projects we discuss here consisted of group visits to designated places On Country on a weekly or fortnightly basis. Visits were dependent on how the community and school wanted to run their projects. It was important that we listened and responded to what the community was asking for, rather than coming in with a set program to 'deliver'. The sites we visited with children were chosen by the Elders of the community in order to teach about and nurture a new generation of children with the skills, knowledge and values from that Country. Children were active participants in the experiences, and were encouraged to explore and experiment in collaboration with their peers, teachers and Elders. Through this participation, the children adopted an active role in constructing meaning from their experiences, and thus developed a deep understanding of the learning when it was linked to the regular curriculum content back in the classroom. OCL provided opportunities to make connections with curriculum subject areas. The researchers supported the classroom teachers to make connections between the learning that occurred On Country to the school curriculum. Making this connection to lived experience enabled children to draw on their 'funds of knowledge' (Moll et al., 1992), which are so important in knowledge construction. This engaged them in a central tenet of their identity: Country.

The two projects are Walliabup Connections and Djarlgarra Koolunger. These two OCL projects, while conducted in different places, shared common features in that they were both situated near *kep* (water) and had their own Dreaming stories related to the land. Both schools connected to these projects had a high proportion of Indigenous children enrolled and the school leadership understood the importance of the children learning from Country.

Case study 1: The Walliabup Connections project

Walliabup was our inaugural Bush School project, situated at Bibra Lake in Perth, Western Australia. It was conducted with twenty Aboriginal children from Kindergarten to Year 2 attending a local primary school. The research question for this initial project was to explore how learning in an outdoor environment with a clear connection to Country impacts on Nyungar children's level of involvement and engagement in learning. We had three main aims for this project: to document the engagement and wellbeing of Nyungar children in an outdoor learning environment (Walliabup Wetlands); to draw on the unique knowledge held by local Nyungar Elders; and to develop a culturally responsive school curriculum that enriched children's understanding of curriculum areas. The project involved the children leaving the school by bus and spending half a day each week at the wetlands. Once they arrived, the children and their teachers were engaged with Nyungar Elders, who told the children stories, taught them songs and helped them to learn this particular Country. Aboriginal Elder Pop Noel Morrison spoke about this experience in an interview, saying 'passing on our stories and knowledge is keeping culture alive' and 'children need to leave the classroom and [have the] opportunity to go bush and learn about culture through the natural world'. Another Elder, known as Kongk (Uncle Len Thorne), taught the children about fishing, hunting, throwing boomerangs, dancing, identifying birds and plants and about their totems. In this process, he was engaging in the ancient practice of Elders imparting cultural ways of doing and knowing about Country with younger generations. Kongk's knowledge has been invaluable and crucial for children's learning in this project. We would state categorically that local Elders must be present in On Country experiences with children, and that they must be remunerated for their time.

An example of children's learning On Country took place in the context of learning about birds nesting. The children watched a pair of mudlarks make their nest, flying back and forth to the river in tag-team fashion—the children were fascinated with the synchrony of the birds and their persistence with the task. At one point, the children commented on the enormous size of the tree in which the birds were nesting. It was a very old, very large eucalypt. We wondered together about just how big the tree was and whether it was the biggest of all the trees in that vicinity. A problem-solving exercise ensued. How can we measure the trees without any measuring tools? The children decided to use their bodies and stretched fingertips to measure the trees' circumference. They counted how many children were needed to reach all the way around. Using this non-standard measurement, they quickly began to compare the size of trees and began estimating and testing their estimates, with some children deciding to record the data they were collecting. This vignette highlights the emergent nature of the learning experience (Jones & Nimmo, 1994). As educators, we saw the intentional teaching and learning possibilities, asked questions, posed problems and provided resources and support to follow through with the children's ideas.

Case study 2: The Djarlgarra Koolunger project

Djarlgarra Koolunger (Canning River Kids) was undertaken with another urban primary school with Aboriginal children enrolled in Year 1. This OCL project was situated within the cultural space of the Canning River, where the Kent Street weir is located. The project commenced with children of Aboriginal heritage from three Year 1 classrooms.

Our experience with Walliabup had taught us much, as we engaged in reflective practice, and we jointly planned the project with Kongk to ensure that his expertise was utilised in the best possible way. We planned a series of sessions at Djarlgarra according to key cultural concepts, such as Fire, Hunting, Shelter, Gathering, Cooking, Painting and Storytelling. We used these as organising ideas for the weekly visits, but also flexibly responded to children's wondering questions and investigations. Further to this, we researched the games adults had used in the past to teach children the skills of hunting, and we introduced these to the children with great success. One of these games was based on a spear-throwing game played prior to colonisation. In an earlier time, adults would prepare a possum skin ball to roll along the ground where boys (who would one day become the hunters for their families and communities) would throw sticks fashioned as 'play' spears. The aim of the game was to hit the moving ball. When we played a modified version of this game, we used hula hoops, balls of various sizes and pieces of dowel for throwing. The children were full of excitement when one of them hit the target. Their teamwork, physical skill development and deeper understanding of ancient hunting practices made this game a very successful experience in terms of children's level of involvement and the indicators of wellbeing that we were looking at in our research.

What are some of the project outcomes for Aboriginal children?

In this section, we draw on insights and responses from children, teachers, parents and an Aboriginal Education Officer (AEO) to identify the benefits of OCL for Aboriginal and Torres Strait Islander children and their classroom educators.

Our observations of children attending the project using the Leuven Involvement Scales (Laevers, 1994) On Country indicated heightened levels of wellbeing in the outdoor environment compared with the classroom at school. Not only were the levels of children's wellbeing and involvement higher when they attended the OCL project, but they increased in this setting over time.

This finding echoes the work of Waller (2007) in the United Kingdom, which showed similar results using the Leuven Scales for children attending an outdoor play and learning project. In addition to these important outcomes, the OCL project also strengthened children's cultural identity (Lee-Hammond & Jackson-Barrett, 2013). Having a strong cultural identity is an essential component of resilience, and is known to support children's social and emotional development and learning (DEEWR, 2010; Kickett-Tucker, 2008). A strong sense of cultural identity is also a robust protective factor in the promotion of social and emotional wellbeing and the prevention of substance abuse and youth suicide (Zubrick et al., 2004).

In addition, a long list of competencies and proficiencies that the children demonstrated in these outdoor environments ranged from literacy, numeracy, spatial awareness, application of logic and divergent thinking to environmental understandings. Children experienced what could be described as heightened connectedness to their identities, to their Country and to each other. In addition, we were able to document that the project had a positive impact on Indigenous children's school attendance, with punctuality also increasing significantly. One principal stated that the project 'categorically increased our Indigenous attendance' (correspondence from principal, 2012). Teachers reported that children were demonstrating higher levels of concentration, collaboration and cooperation in this environment compared with their classroom setting, and there was a flow-on effect in improved classroom engagement.

Children attending the project needed time and space to adjust to the alternative outdoor 'classroom', and initial excitement at the change gave way to a more settled and comfortable disposition. We identified that children were engaging in what Csikszentmihalyi (1996) describes as 'flow': a state of total immersion in an experience in which energy is fully aligned with the task at hand. Flow is characterised by observing children who are focused deeply on the experience in which they are involved; they are not easily distracted and become less aware of time. Flow is also indicated when children seem unconcerned with making mistakes and are willing to meet challenges.

These elements of flow appeared to characterise the OCL experience for the children we observed. In an outdoor environment where there are no apparent assessment tasks and where children's Aboriginal identity was foregrounded and celebrated, it is conceivable that their energy was directed to being immersed in the moment rather than masking anxiety or simply trying to cope.

It was clear from interviews conducted with educators immediately following each project that children were happy and engaged with the learning when participating in OCL. Educators commented:

> When we first arrived, I was overwhelmed, I think the word would be, at just being out in that environment and automatically seeing the changes in the students from the get go. It was very natural for them to just be there. It was just a really positive experience for them.

> The children absolutely loved it; they looked forward to it each week. It was really something good that we could refer back to with our writing and they had confidence in their memories of it to be able to write about it. They really liked the activities they did, so they felt that they enjoyed writing about it. They were so passionate about going.

Parent participants also acknowledged a change in children's engagement and levels of enthusiasm about attending school:

> On those days . . . we wake up at quarter to seven. He was ready by ten to seven. I wasn't even out of bed and he was telling me 'Mum! Mum, where's my socks?' Like [he was] ready!

The same parent also noted a level of recall and detail in her son's recounts of OCL that was unusual compared with previous responses to the question, 'How was your day?' This appears consistent with the idea that the child was deeply involved and experiencing 'flow' (Csikszentmihalyi, 1996):

> I asked him about it. He could sit down, have—and I'm not lying—a good five-minute conversation and tell me

about everything that happened from the beginning to the end . . . every single thing, every little detail, every little activity that [you] did. I ask him about school and . . . there's no detail, but when I asked him about Bush School he could recall everything—it's like it all sunk in.

An AEO revealed she had observed that the children she knew well were absorbed in ways of learning that she had not seen before. She was able to articulate the connections to curriculum and identify a child-centred approach in learning On Country:

Well they're doing science aren't they? They're doing maths, they're doing things that we wouldn't be able to teach our kids [at school]. What bush food to look for . . . and [they] probably did a bit of life-cycle with some of the insects or whatever they saw. It's a whole new learning and it's different learning when you're out there than sitting in a classroom and doing it on paper . . . I hate it when you go out on excursions and the kids gotta have a piece of paper and they gotta write everything down . . . You know it wasn't the adults coming up with the ideas, it was the children that had to solve problems. There was a lot of problem-solving, which was good because it gets the kids to think.

What each of these participants either witnessed or experienced was the optimal experience of 'flow', where the participants 'feel a sense of exhilaration, and deep enjoyment' (Czikszentmihaylyi, 1996, p. 2). These examples of OCL serve to highlight the ways in which early years educators can honour local cultural protocols and create opportunities for children and educators to embrace Aboriginal ways of knowing, being and doing (Martin, 2009) through a shared approach of teaching and engaging authentically with Aboriginal perspectives in the 'right way' beyond a tokenistic add-on (for example, one-off activities like painting a flag on NAIDOC day or decorating a wooden boomerang with dot painting).

What are some of the benefits for educators?

We understand that educators cannot facilitate learning about Aboriginal perspectives with children without first having an opportunity to learn about Aboriginal culture themselves. Our OCL work offers opportunities to work alongside educators who have little or no existing knowledge of Aboriginal perspectives. As a result of their participation, educators gained a deeper understanding of Country. One educator noted how the experience deepened her understandings of the Nyungar culture:

> I thought I was okay with some Nyungar culture. I've worked with a lot of Nyungar kids, but it doesn't mean you understand the depths. There's a lot of depth with the culture and I guess we just skimmed the top so it was depth that I've seen I guess.

For us as educators and researchers, this was a profound research outcome. It highlights the transformative power of being On Country as both a professional and personal experience. Here we have identified a distinction between educators and children's perspectives for learning *about* Country and learning *on* and *with* Country. This, of course, enables educators to meet the standards of the profession discussed earlier in this chapter.

Implications for practitioners

The EYLF (DEEWR, 2009) and the *Educators' guide to the EYLF* (DEEWR, 2010) mandate that early years educators develop cultural competence as part of their ongoing professional learning and practice with children from birth. Competence is distinct from cultural awareness, and implies a deeper level of understanding, engagement and practice with regard to inclusion and diversity. To explain, the EYLF (DEEWR, 2009, p. 16) states that cultural competence is the ability to understand, communicate with and effectively interact with people across cultures. It is therefore helpful for practitioners to consider the key elements of cultural competence:

- being aware of one's own world view

- developing positive attitudes towards cultural differences
- gaining knowledge of different cultural practices and world views
- developing skills for communication and interaction across cultures (DEEWR, 2009, p. 16).

The *Educators' Guide to the EYLF* (DEEWR, 2010, p. 21) further explains why respect, understanding and including a child's culture are critical to their developing identities. The guide states:

> Culture is the fundamental building block of identity and the development of a strong cultural identity is essential to children's healthy sense of who they are and where they belong (DEEWR, 2010, p. 21).

In addition, the Australian Curriculum requires educators to ensure that Aboriginal and Torres Strait Islander cultures and histories are explicitly included as a cross-curricular priority that

> provides opportunities for all students to deepen their knowledge of Australia by engaging with the world's oldest continuous living cultures. Through the Australian Curriculum, students will understand that contemporary Aboriginal and Torres Strait Islander communities are strong, resilient, rich and diverse (ACARA, 2015, p. 53).

CONCLUSION

In this chapter, we have highlighted the central place of Aboriginal culture in two Australian outdoor learning projects. We have emphasised the relationships between learning environments and the community, between people and Country, and between learning and wellbeing. The principal role of the educator is to become a learner in this context, and to reflect deeply on their own cultural lenses, their cultural competencies and their responsiveness. When educators make a commitment to becoming more deeply engaged in the meaning of Country for themselves and the children, they co-construct curriculum in ways that are relevant and meaningful to children. We argue that educators must be prepared to take this journey.

REFLECTION QUESTIONS

11.1   Think about your personal connection to Country. Where were you born? What are some of the strong associations you have with your birthplace? How do you feel when you come home from a time away?

11.2   How comfortable are you about asking an Aboriginal Elder for support and advice in your project? How would you approach the conversation and find the appropriate person(s) to help you?

11.3   What languages, traditional place names and Dreaming stories are associated with the place where you live or work?

RECOMMENDED RESOURCES

- Cultural competence: For a deeper understanding of what cultural competence looks like in the early years, see *Understanding Cultural Competence: EYLF professional learning project*: www.earlychildhoodaustralia.org.au/nqsplp/wp-content/uploads/2012/05/EYLFPLP_E-Newsletter_No7.pdf.
- The following link to the New South Wales Department of Education's resources for Aboriginal education has some useful points on developing cultural understanding: www.dec.nsw.gov.au/what-we-offer/regulation-and-accreditation/early-childhood-education-care/aboriginal-access/aboriginal-resources.
- The Government of South Australia has produced an excellent resource titled *Early Years Learning Framework Perspectives on Aboriginal and Torres Strait Islander Cultural Competence*: www.earlychildhoodaustralia.org.au/wp-content/uploads/2014/01/Persepctives_on_Aboriginal.pdf.
- What works: This resource is extremely worthwhile as a reference point for educators committed to Closing the Gap. It is based on a three-step process of building awareness, forming partnerships and working systematically: www.whatworks.edu.au/dbAction.do?cmd=homePage.
- Secretariat of National Aboriginal and Islander Child Care (SNAICC): Best practice in early years Aboriginal education is documented thoroughly on the SNAICC website, which includes resources, reports and advocacy tools. You can subscribe to the SNAICC newsletter: www.snaicc.org.au/good-practices-in-early-childhood-education-and-care-services.
- On Country Learning: For a more detailed explanation of the types of

learning experiences utilised in the On Country Learning Project refer to our earlier work: Lee-Hammond, L., and Jackson-Barrett, E. (2013). Aboriginal children's participation and engagement in Bush School. In S. Knight (ed.), *International perspectives on forest school: Natural spaces to play and learn* (pp. 131–45). London: Sage.

- Eight ways of Aboriginal learning: This is a resource to support educators to connect with Aboriginal perspectives: https://8ways.wikispaces.com.

REFERENCES

Australian Children's Education and Care Quality Authority (ACECQA) (2013a) *Guide to the National Quality Framework*. Canberra: ACECQA.

—— (2013b) *Guide to the National Quality Standard*. Canberra: ACECQA.

Australian Curriculum, Assessment and Reporting Authority (ACARA) (2015). *The Australian Curriculum*. Retrieved 31 October 2016 from <www.acara.edu.au/default.asp>.

Australian Institute for Teaching and School Leadership (AITSL) (2011). *Australian Professional Standards for Teachers*. Retrieved 28 August 2016 from <www.aitsl.edu.au/docs/default-source/apst-resources/australian_professional_standard_for_teachers_final.pdf>.

Bird Rose, D. (2002). *Country of the heart: An Indigenous Australian homeland*. Canberra: Aboriginal Studies Press.

Commonwealth of Australia (2011). *Closing the gap: Prime Minister's Report 2011*, Retrieved 30 March 2016 from <www.fahcsia.gov.au/sites/default/files/documents/05_2012/2011_ctg_pm_report.pdf>.

Council of Australian Governments (COAG) (2008). *Indigenous reform: Closing the gap*. Retrieved 18 July 2016 from <www.coag.gov.au/node/291#Indigenous%20Reform>.

Cowlishaw, G. (2012). Culture and the absurd: The means and meanings of Aboriginal identity in the time of cultural revivalism. *Journal of the Royal Anthropological Institute, 18*(2), 397–417.

Csikszentmihalyi, M. (1996). *Flow and the psychology of discovery and invention*. New York: HarperCollins.

Department of Education, Employment and Workplace Relations (DEEWR) (2009). *Belonging, being and becoming: The Early Years Learning Framework for Australia*. Canberra: Commonwealth of Australia.

—— (2010). *Educators being, belonging and becoming: Educators' guide to the Early Years Learning Framework for Australia*. Retrieved 9 November 2016 from <www.deewr.gov.au/Earlychildhood/Policy_Agenda/Quality/Documents/EYLF_Ed_Guide.pdf>.

Department of Education Western Australia (2013). *Aboriginal education*. Retrieved 9 November 2016 from <www.det.wa.edu.au/aboriginaleducation/detcms/aboriginal-education/aboriginal-education/docs/aboriginal-education-plan-2011-2014.en?oid=com.arsdigita.cms.contenttypes.FileStorageItem-id-7148382>.

Guenther, J., Bat, M. & Osborne, S. (2014). Red dirt thinking on remote educational advantage. *Australian and International Journal of Rural Education, 24*(1), 51–67.

Jackson-Barrett, E., Price, A., Stomski., N. & Walker, B.F. (2015). Grounded in country: Perspectives on working within, alongside and for Aboriginal communities. *Issues in Educational Research, 25*(1), 36–49.

Jones, E. & Nimmo, J. (1994). *Emergent curriculum*. Washington, DC: National Association for the Education of Young Children.

Kerwin, D. & Van Issum, H. (2012). An Aboriginal perspective on education: Policy and practice. In R. Jorgensen, P. Sullivan & P. Grootenboer (eds), *Pedagogies to enhance learning for Indigenous students* (pp. 1–20). Singapore: Springer Science+Business Media.

Kickett-Tucker, C. (2008). *Koordoormitj culture, identity and self-esteem*. ARACY Grid Access, August. Retrieved 30 November 2012 from <www.aracy.org.au/index.cfm?pageName=publications_library&theme=A16D8A05-1EC9-79F9-594530ECF1FF2620>.

Laevers, F. (1994). *The Leuven Involvement Scale for young children*. Manual and video. Leuven, Belgium: Centre for Experiential Education.

Lee-Hammond, L. & Jackson-Barrett, E. (2013). Aboriginal children's participation and engagement in Bush School. In S. Knight (ed.), *International Perspectives on Forest School: Natural spaces to play and learn* (pp. 131–45). London: Sage.

Martin, K. (2009). Aboriginal worldview knowledge and relatedness: Re-conceptualising Aboriginal schooling as a teaching-learning and research interface. *Journal of Australian Indigenous Issues, 12*, 66.

Ministerial Council for Education, Early Childhood Development and Youth Affairs (MCEECDYA, 2010–14). *Indigenous education action plan*. Retrieved

1 January 2017 from <www.mceecdya.edu.au/mceecdya/indigenous_ed_action_plan_2010-2014_consultation,29978.html>.

Ministerial Council on Education, Employment, Training and Youth Affairs (2008). *Melbourne Declaration on Educational Goals for Young Australians*. Melbourne: Curriculum Corporation. Retrieved 1 January 2017 from <www.mceecdya.edu.au/verve/_resources/National_Declaration_on_the_Educational_Goals_for_Young_Australians.pdf>.

Moll, L.C., Amanti, C., Neff, D. & Gonzalez, N. (1992). Funds of knowledge for teaching: Using a qualitative approach to connect homes and classrooms. *Theory into Practice, 31*(2), 132–41.

Nakata, M. (2007). The cultural interface. *The Australian Journal of Indigenous Education, 36*, Supplement, 7–14.

Parbury, N. (1999). Aboriginal education: A history. In C. Rhoda (ed.), *Teaching Aboriginal Studies* (pp. 63–86). Sydney: Allen & Unwin.

Waller, T. (2007). The trampoline tree and the swamp monster with 18 heads: Outdoor play in the foundation stage and foundation phase. *Education 3–13, 35*(4), 393–407.

Western Australian Aboriginal Education and Training Council (WAAETC) (2011). *Strategic plan: Our vision* (2011–2015). Perth: Government of Western Australia.

Zubrick, S.R., Dudgeon, P., Gee, G., Glaskin, B., Kelly, K., Paradies, Y., Scrine, C. & Walker, R. (2004). Social determinants of Aboriginal and Torres Strait Islander social and emotional wellbeing. In N. Purdie, P. Dudgeon & R. Walker (eds), *Working together: Aboriginal and Torres Strait Islander mental health and wellbeing principles and practice* (pp. 75–90). Perth: Telethon Institute for Child Health Research.

Chapter 12

Outdoor play in Norwegian and Australian early years settings
Differences in theory, pedagogy and practice

Leyla Eide

Despite large amounts of research evidence attesting to the importance of outdoor play for healthy development and learning, many children in Western countries, including Australia, have had their outside play opportunities greatly reduced. Yet some countries, such as Norway, consistently break with this trend. Although both Australian and Norwegian early childhood educators recognise the benefits of outdoor play, the outdoor experiences of children attending formal early childhood education settings vary greatly between the two countries. This chapter explores the differences in outdoor play provisions for Norwegian and Australian children attending early childhood education services. The particular focus is on the potential reasons behind these differences, including cultural underpinnings, the objectives in the Norwegian and Australian early childhood curricula for care and education, and the main theories and philosophies that lay the foundation for Norwegian and Australian pedagogy. I acknowledge that there are many differences within and between the provisioning of outdoor play in both Australian and Norwegian early childhood education services, but, for the purposes of this chapter, a generalised approach has been taken. Before continuing, it is important to note that while each topic was researched extensively to present the most current findings, certain issues I considered important to include do not appear to have been investigated in the existing literature. In these instances, statements reflect what I have observed consistently in practice and through my own research in Western Norway and New South Wales, Australia, as well as what I have learnt through in-depth discussions with educators and colleagues across Norway and in New South Wales.

Provocation

The following observations are from two regular early childhood education centres, one in Bergen, Norway, the other in Sydney.

Today the children climbed trees, crawled up and then rolled/slid down steep hills and small mountains. Highest up was a boy and a girl, who climbed about 7 metres up a fir tree. When it got close to lunchtime, the children used an axe to chop wood for the fire (which they tended themselves), and then prepared and heated cordial over the flames, to drink with their packed lunch. Later, two educators engaged in play fighting and fencing matches using sticks with groups of children. A third educator had brought along a piece of rope, which he attached to a sturdy stick, and made into a provisional swing hanging from one of the largest trees. The educator hung it so that the children needed to climb part-way up the tree in order to get onto the swing (in his words, this was done to increase the challenge for them). To disembark, they were required to hoist themselves down, so that they were hanging from the swing by their arms, before dropping about 1.5 metres to the ground. Three children took off by themselves to explore the forest, returning 45 minutes later, full of excitement, as they had found a patch of lemon clover to enjoy on their way. The pre-schoolers spent four hours in the forest, with the children all engaged in child-initiated free play. *(Research notes—hiking trip with pre-schoolers. Norway, March 2016)*

After the wooden climbing frames were deemed too unstable almost three months ago, the children only had one opportunity for climbing: a small tree. The children were allowed to climb to the branch that was approximately 1 metre above the ground. This branch extended onto the roof of the wooden tunnel, and today one of the boys crawled from the branch onto the tunnel. Immediately, one of the educators called out from down on the cycling path: 'Get down! You know you're not allowed to climb onto the tunnel!' The boy called back, 'But I can do it! I won't fall down!' The educator responded, 'It doesn't matter! You know you're not supposed to climb onto the roof!' The boy made his way back to the branch, down the tree, and wandered off kicking at the dirt, muttering, 'But I was being careful.' The educator explained that the children used to be allowed to climb onto the tunnel, but that it recently had been deemed too unsafe. *(Research notes—outdoor play at centre. Australia, November 2015)*

These anecdotes demonstrate accepted practices in two countries that value children's opportunities for outdoor play, so how can the outcome be so different? This chapter aims to explore the underlying values and attitudes towards outdoor play and factors that influence the variations both within and between these two countries.

Outdoor play in Norway

As a young child growing up outside one of Norway's largest cities in the late 1980s, I spent more or less all day outdoors. Even before school age, my peers and I would roam the neighbourhood freely without adult supervision. We were in charge of looking after our younger siblings, and would go tree climbing and hiking in the nearby woods, ride our bicycles (with the youngest perched on the rear carrier racks), climb steep cliffs to collect shiny crystals and wander down to the ocean to search for crabs and shells when the tide was low. In winter, we sledded or skied down hills and mountainsides, and went ice-skating on the lakes. The time to go home was either when it was dark or when one of our parents called that dinner was ready. We had enormous amounts of freedom, and we relished the sense of responsibility and trust our parents bestowed upon us.

Norway has a strong cultural tradition when it comes to enjoying and utilising the wild and rugged outdoors (Sandseter, 2014). Being outside is considered part of the way of life, and even has its own term, first used in a poem by Norwegian playwright Henrik Ibsen (1899), to describe it: *friluftsliv* (free air life). *Allmannaretten* (right to roam) ensures through legislation the right of everyone to access any area, as long as it is open country, regardless of who owns the land (Norwegian Ministry of Climate and Environment, 1957). The old Scandinavian saying that 'there is no such thing as bad weather, only bad clothing' holds strong: come rain, hail, snow or shine, Norwegians of all ages venture outside, enjoying the transformations that happen in nature due to the changing seasons and weather (Gullestad, 1992). While no external regulations exist for early childhood education settings to follow, an online search indicates that most municipalities recommend that children aged 1 to 3 years are brought inside if temperatures are below –10°C, and the older children at –15°C. However, these are guidelines only, and Lie, Vedum and Dullerud (2011) found that none of the ten centres referred to in their study had established temperature limits for outdoor activities.

Early childhood education in Norway: Traditions and curriculum

In Norway, early childhood education settings are called *barnehager* (indef. form, plural; indef. form, singular: *barnehage*; def. form, singular: *barnehagen*), a direct translation from the German *kindergarten*. *Barnehager* are prior-to-school settings primarily intended for children aged between 1 and 6 years, and by law all children in this age bracket have the right to attend a *barnehage*. While *barnehager* are part of the educational system in Norway, they are separate from formal schooling, which commences the year a child turns 6. Norwegian parents can choose between 49 weeks of fully paid parental leave or 59 weeks at 80 per cent coverage. Consequently, there are very few children under the age of 1 year enrolled in *barnehager*. In 2014, nine out of ten children aged between 1 and 6 years attended a *barnehage*, and 93 per cent of these were enrolled full time (Statistics Norway [SSB], 2015). These numbers reflect the Norwegian view held by most policy-makers that the education and development happening in *barnehager* lays the foundation for lifelong learning (Norwegian Ministry of Education and Research [NMER], 2006) and active participation in a democratic society (NMER, 2005).

The *Kindergarten Act* (NMER, 2005) and the Norwegian Framework Plan for the Content and Tasks of Kindergartens (henceforth referred to as the Framework) (NMER, 2006) have been developed by the Norwegian government, and are the main documents for the construction of curricula in Norwegian *barnehager*. The Framework (NMER, 2006) provides a binding document for personnel in terms of planning, implementation and evaluation of a *barnehage*'s experiences. While adult-initiated learning is given weight, both the *Kindergarten Act* (NMER, 2005) and the Framework (NMER, 2006) stress the importance of free play, and that unstructured, child-initiated play should be the primary focus when outdoors.

The Framework (NMER, 2006) states that children are physically active, and express themselves largely through the use of their bodies. Through physical activity, children learn about and get to know the world and themselves, gaining experience, skills and knowledge through movement and sensory experiences (NMER, 2006). Opportunities for physically active play outside are considered important for motor skill development and body control, but even more so for the development of positive self-perceptions and beliefs through physical mastery (NMER, 2006). Additionally, much value is placed on 'experiencing nature for pleasure, as an end in itself' (Nilsen, 2008, p. 46). As part of the curriculum, educators must contribute to ensuring that all children are provided with positive and diverse experiences relating to outdoor life and activities every day, during all seasons and in all types of weather (NMER, 2006).

Norwegian *barnehager* typically have large outdoor play areas, often with many natural elements like boulders, grass, trees, bushes and hills, as well as a wide variety of fixed play equipment, such as swings, cubby houses, slides and forts. There are no specific requirements in relation to the size of an early childhood education setting's outdoor space, but the Norwegian Ministry of Education and Research advises that there should be approximately 33 square metres per child under the age of 3 years, and 24 square metres for each child over the age of 3 years (NMER, 2005). Researchers have found that, on average, Norwegian *barnehager* have between 47 (Moser & Martinsen, 2010) and 50.5 square metres (Vassenden et al., 2011) available per child. Moser and Martinsen (2010) suggest that access to such large areas affords children abundant and rich experiences in the outdoors, resulting in both an immersion in nature and the possibility to 'sneak away' to secret places where privacy and calmness can be found.

The amount of time spent outside in Norwegian *barnehager* is also significant. Moser and Martinsen (2010) found that, on average, Norwegian children spent 70 per cent of their time outside at *barnehager* during summer, and 31 per cent during winter. Intentionally using, and actively exploring, the local area is part of Norwegian *barnehager*'s curricula (NMER, 2006), and most *barnehager* have at least one day per week where they hike to local nature areas, spending a minimum of half a day playing there. The Framework (NMER, 2006) asserts that children have a right to investigate and discover the outdoor environments available in their local community, and that educators should actively use the resources there to facilitate children's development and learning. Perhaps, as argued by Borge, Nordhagen and Lie (2003, p. 606), the large amount of time spent outdoors reflects most Norwegian parents' view that 'happy children are children playing outside most of the day irrespective of season and weather'.

According to Guldberg (2009), the nation's passion and love for *friluftsliv* is what makes Norwegians particularly reluctant to restrict children's opportunities to move about freely outside. However, a comprehensive national survey by Sandseter and colleagues (2013) shows that directors in Norwegian *barnehager* are experiencing increased pressure—including from parents, playground inspectors and the media—to curtail children's free engagement with the outdoors, and to focus more on child safety to prevent injuries. There is little evidence supporting the arguments regarding injury prevention; statistically, children in Norway have never been safer. There has been a steep decline in child injury rates and deaths over the last 50 years (Ellingsen, 2008), and, looking specifically at *barnehager*, Sandseter and colleagues (2013) found that few minor injuries and extremely few moderate to severe injuries occurred. Despite the statistical evidence, pressure from outside has led some directors to limit the types of play permitted in the outdoors (Sandseter & Sando, 2016). This development gives cause for concern that Norwegian educators must now advocate to preserve children's access to extensive and diverse outdoor play.

Theories and philosophies as foundations for pedagogical practice in Norway

Educators in Norway draw upon numerous theories, but most dominant are those proposing a nonlinear, bottom-up approach to human development (Sandseter, Little & Wyver, 2012). Dynamic systems theory (Thelen & Smith, 1998) and Hendry and Kloep's (2002) lifespan model lay the foundation for most Norwegian educators' philosophies. These theories posit that learning and developmental growth are fuelled by direct encounters with, and mastery of, challenging experiences rather than through age-related maturation. For instance, I have heard numerous Norwegian educators express the importance of allowing young children to occasionally feel uncomfortable—for instance, by being wet and/or cold, or scared/anxious. A strong belief that these experiences are invaluable not only for learning self-help skills (e.g. how to dress appropriately according to the weather), but also in terms of building knowledge, independence and resilience, is in line with the nation's cultural values of nature and the outdoors (Nilsen, 2008). From a theoretical perspective, this means that Norwegian educators adhere to the competent child paradigm, which views children as having an inherent aptitude for competency and capability (Smith, 2007).

Particularly influential in relation to outdoor play is Gibsonian theory (Gibson, 1988). Gibson coined the term 'affordances' to describe the features of an environment from a functional perspective: the specific actions an individual can undertake with the objects and surroundings present. For example, trees and large boulders afford climbing and jumping down from; sticks afford sword-type play; small stones afford throwing; and steep hills afford rolling, running or bicycle riding. Gibsonian theory has been extended through the works of Heft (1988) and Kyttä (2004), who have focused specifically on affordances in relation to children's outdoor environments. According to Gibsonian theory, the types and number of affordances found in an environment are infinite, but the actualised affordances will differ from person to person, based on their contextual circumstances, such as physical stature, abilities and personal interests (Kyttä, 2004). It is only by perceiving their environment through direct interaction that an individual will discover the potential affordances it holds for them (Gibson, 1988). Consequently, for Norwegian educators, opportunities for direct engagement with nature are an essential part of their pedagogy, and any limitations imposed on such explorations must be considered carefully (Sandseter et al., 2012).

Norwegian educators view the outdoors as distinctly different from indoor environments in terms of what it offers children. As part of their pre-service training, Norwegian educators learn that the natural environment should be considered an educator in its own right. Indoor toys (e.g. puzzles, blocks and train tracks) are generally not brought into the outdoors, and educators do not plan or set up outside in preparation for the day, but rather seize the spontaneous teachable moments that arise. The choice of what to do is up to the children, who can access the equipment shed independently. Loose play materials are often limited to sandpit equipment, a selection of bicycles/scooters/tricycles, witches' hats, sled boards (during periods of snow) and/or a selection of balls. Trees for climbing and fixed play equipment, such as slides, swings, climbing frames, cubby houses, forts and flying foxes, situated within a natural playground are largely seen as more than sufficient in terms of meeting children's play needs. In these environments, there are many affordances for rich, challenging and diverse experiences.

Outdoor play in Australia

Traditionally, Australia has been considered a country of people with a great fondness of the outdoors. Activities such as bushwalking, fishing, playing in the streets, frolicking at beaches, having picnics and barbecues, and impromptu sports in the countless parks have been regular occurrences for many children and families. The image of Australians as stoic sun-kissed, khaki-clad, nature wranglers out camping to observe the natural bush and its wildlife gained traction across the globe through movies like *Crocodile Dundee* and the late Steve Irwin's TV series *The Crocodile Hunter* (Little & Wyver, 2014; Scott, 2010). The value placed on engagement with the outdoors seems to be reflected in current national research, with over 90 per cent of Australians expressing a belief that outdoor play is beneficial for children's development and learning (Planet Ark, 2011). Despite this, there is presently little congruence between the above descriptors and highly urbanised Australian life, where children are kept inside, in very close proximity to their homes or behind fences on small playgrounds (Little & Wyver, 2014).

While 73 per cent of children growing up a decade ago played outside more than they did inside, the equivalent proportion of children today is just 13 per cent, and as many as 10 per cent only engage in outdoor play once a week or less (Planet Ark, 2011). For some children, the main context for outdoor free play is at their early childhood education service. Yet, even in these settings, access to the outdoors is often limited. Many centres do not take children outside when it rains or is windy, and keep them inside during colder days in winter. Additionally, an estimated 84 per cent of early childhood education settings do not allow outdoor play during the middle of the day when UV radiation is high (Ettridge et al., 2011), despite Cancer Council Australia's attestation that all children can spend time outside during these hours as long as necessary sun-smart precautions are taken (see www.sunsmart.com.au).

Early childhood education in Australia: Traditions and curriculum

Belonging, Being and Becoming: The Early Years Learning Framework for Australia (EYLF) (DEEWR, 2009), the Education and Care Services National Law, the Education and Care Services National Regulations (both henceforth referred to as the Regulations) (ACECQA, 2014) and the National Quality Standard (NQS) (ACECQA, 2013) are the main documents impacting on the facilitation of outdoor play in Australian early childhood education settings. Of particular importance for pedagogy and curriculum development is the EYLF, which is comparable to the Norwegian Framework. The EYLF provides guidance for educators in their daily planning, documentation and evaluation of practice. While outdoor play is far from the primary focus of the document, outdoor environments are addressed specifically in some sections, with the importance of natural elements, opportunities for risk-taking and the unique affordances available outside highlighted.

The importance of outdoor environments is reinforced in the NQS (ACECQA, 2013) and the Regulations (ACECQA, 2014). The NQS (ACECQA, 2013) emphasises the inclusion of environments and equipment designed to foster easy access for all, and flexibility in terms of the utilisation of, and interaction between, indoor and outdoor environments. The Regulations (ACECQA, 2014) offer further support by requiring that outdoor play-grounds permit exploration of, and experiences with, natural environments for all children. While all three documents encourage risk-taking in play, they also have a strong focus on safety. The challenge for educators, then, is to determine how they can balance risk and safety in outdoor play provision (see Chapter 2).

Small playgrounds are one of the potential hindrances to sufficient quality outdoor play in Australian early childhood education settings. Under the Regulations (ACECQA, 2014), the minimum requirement for outdoor space per child is 7 square metres. Little (2015) conducted a survey to ascertain the actual sizes of outdoor spaces across Australian early childhood education services. Of the 245 participating centres, 39 per cent were found to meet the required minimum, 58 per cent exceeded it and 3 per cent had outdoor spaces below the required minimum. While it is promising that over half of the centres had playgrounds larger than necessary, it was not investigated how much above the minimum requirement they were, and it is likely that few matched the Norwegian average of 47–50 square metres per child. Consequently, it is difficult for Australian centres to offer children numerous, diverse and complex outdoor physical play equipment. This difficulty is also compounded by height restrictions (1.8 metres maximum fall height) on fixed play equipment and impact area requirements of 1.5 to 1.7 metres around any apparatus with a fall height of 0.6 metres or more (Standards Australia, 2014), which mean vertical solutions to small play areas are not an easy option. Mauffette, Fréchette and Robertson (1999) advise that a minimum of 13.5 square metres per child is needed in order to provide a sufficient variety of outdoor experiences while maintaining adequate safety standards.

Limited information exists on the amount of time spent outdoors in Australian early childhood education services. A national survey conducted by Little (2015) found that three-quarters of participating centres spent between 18 and 36 per cent of daily operating hours during summer outside, and that 69 per cent of all centres maintained this amount in winter. While these numbers provide some information about outdoor playtime, they do not give an indication of the average amount of time children spend outside. Considering that children at some services might spend as little as 9 per cent of their time outdoors (Little, 2015), the average percentages for Australian early childhood education settings could be quite low. However, the implementation of indoor/outdoor programs for some or all parts of the day, where children freely choose whether to play inside or outside, has recently increased in popularity in Australia. While some centres have run these programs for many years, the recent growth may be due at least partly to the introduction of the NQS (ACECQA, 2013), which states that 'Facilities are designed . . . to allow flexible use, and interaction between indoor and outdoor space' (p. 10). This type of programming gives children the opportunity to regulate how much time they spend outdoors, which may well increase the amount of outdoor play for some children. However, it could also mean that children who, for various reasons, prefer indoor play, end up spending very little or no time at all outside.

Compared to Norwegian *barnehager*, excursions to natural outdoor playscapes with the purpose of child-initiated exploration and free play appear less frequent for Australian children in early childhood education settings. In my experience, most centres do have excursion policies, but rarely make use of them; most prioritise taking children to non-play locations like museums, zoos, and art galleries when they do leave the centre. Rigorous and time-consuming risk-assessment is required under the Regulations (ACECQA, 2014) prior to visiting new and/or non-regular excursion sites, parental permission is compulsory and additional adults accompanying the group are generally a necessity. This effectively means that there is no room for spontaneous decision-making when unexpected opportunities for play and learning outside the centre present themselves. These conditions undoubtedly also make it challenging to bring children to large, possibly densely forested, unfenced terrain, and let them play freely. The potential consequence is that many Australian children attending early childhood education services may experience little variation in their outdoor playspace, are rarely seen in the community, and gain limited knowledge of and connection to, their local natural environments. Yet some centres manage to take children on play-based excursions to sites such as national parks or public playgrounds within the regulatory framework and, as will be discussed later, the increase in Bush Kinders illustrates that further changes are underway (see Chapter 13).

Theories and philosophies as foundations for pedagogical practice in Australia

Australian educators express a strong belief in the importance of outdoor play for children's learning and positive development (Little, Sandseter & Wyver, 2012), yet a misalignment has been found between pedagogical beliefs and practices (Little et al., 2012). Little and colleagues (2012) argue that at least some of this disparity may be ascribed to the theoretical approaches that lay the foundation for pedagogical practice. As previously stated, Norwegian early childhood education practice is underpinned by bottom-up theories relating to child development. Bottom-up approaches favour hands-on engagement with challenging environments, and non-linear maturation processes (Sandseter et al., 2012). Conversely, Australian perspectives are largely top-down (Sandseter et al., 2012). Such approaches are defined by a belief that higher-order thinking and linguistic structures that mature and increase in a linear, age-related manner are the driving force for all learning and development (Sandseter et al., 2012).

While a range of theories/theorists influence pedagogical approaches to early childhood education in Australia, the most dominant stem loosely from Piagetian/post-Piagetian and socio-cultural theory (Soto & Swadener, 2002). Within the field of early childhood, both professional practice and scholarly research in Australia have focused mainly on these (Sandseter et al., 2012), and while acknowledging critical theories and post-structuralist theories, the EYLF (DEEWR, 2009) accentuates socio-cultural theory and, to a lesser degree, developmental theories. Although the emphasis on socio-cultural theory has undoubtedly resulted in a series of progressive pedagogical changes, Little and colleagues (2012, p. 171) assert that it also has limitations, which could make it problematic for educators to 'establish alignment between theory and practice in outdoor spaces'. While the most popular Norwegian theories emphasise the importance of direct exploration of physical environments, rich social relationships and interactions are considered imperative to children's progress across all domains within socio-cultural theory. Both Piagetian and socio-cultural theories allow for the construction of beliefs among educators about developmental growth and learning that place limited importance on the physical environment (Sandseter et al., 2012).

An important aspect of the EYLF (DEEWR, 2009) is play-based learning coupled with children's right to agency, decision-making and active participation. However, there is also a very strong focus on intentional teaching and the provisioning of planned experiences. How educators are to achieve the appropriate balance between teacher-facilitated and child-initiated experiences is not expanded upon within the document, and recent research suggests the balance might be skewed. Sandseter and colleagues (2012) interviewed seventeen educators about what influenced the types of provisions made available to children outside. The results indicate that Australian educators have a particular focus on planning and intentional teaching. For outdoor play, this meant activities offered fostered development of specific skills, or related directly to children's interests as previously observed, rather than inviting them to freely choose how they engaged with the affordances available.

While Norwegian educators see the outdoors as markedly separate from the indoor environment, and limit adult-initiated play outside, research indicates that this may not be the case in Australia. As Little and colleagues' (2012) study suggests, educators spend time planning and detailing children's outdoor activities. This corresponds with my experience, both personally and through conversations with educators at various centres. There appears to be an increased focus on providing playground activities based on written plans derived from a combination of children's observed interests and educators' ideas. Another occurrence observed consistently by myself and colleagues in the field is that inside toys (e.g. books, painting/drawing materials, puzzles/ games, car mats and blocks) are made available in various spaces throughout the playground at many centres. As a result, much of the often already limited space is taken up, and opportunities to facilitate those types of play that are only available outdoors may be lost. Thus many of the provisions available promote seated/standing activities rather than physically active play. Indeed, current Australian research has found that, of the time spent outdoors in early childhood education services, between 46 per cent (Dyment & Coleman, 2012) and 66 per cent (Sugiyama et al., 2012) comprises sedentary behaviours. These numbers indicate that there are many more unique affordances available outside that Australian educators can capitalise on.

In Australia, a risk-averse society and fear of litigation may have contributed to the development of an environment in early childhood education with a focus on safety, and the prevention of even minor child injuries (Sandseter & Little, 2012). This emphasis on risk-minimisation was reflected in a rigid regulatory environment, which felt limiting to the facilitation of outdoor play for many educators (Sandseter et al., 2012). The new Regulations (ACECQA, 2014) have become less stringent, and acknowledge the positive contribution of risk-taking for child development. While some educators have experienced an increase in terms of the types and variety of outdoor experiences they can now offer children, the Regulations still appear restricting and daunting to others (Little, 2015). On a positive note, some educators identified a heightened sense of autonomy as a consequence of the new Regulations, and felt they were now able to argue their case, and justify the provisioning of previously prohibited outdoor experiences (Little, 2015).

While, in general, Norwegian early childhood education settings have always had natural outdoor playgrounds, there has been a tendency to replace natural with artificial materials in Australia (Elliott & Davis, 2008). However, the last decade has seen a return to providing nature-based playgrounds in all types of early childhood education services. There is also a growing trend in Australia for early childhood education settings to provide opportunities for children's immersion in natural environments. Inspired by the Scandinavian focus on nature and outdoor *barnehager*, and the United Kingdom's forest schools, Bush Kinders began appearing in Australia in 2011. These are regular early childhood education services that routinely (e.g. once a week), and regardless of the weather, take a group of children (often the oldest) to a local nature area for a full-day or half-day program. While there, children engage in free play, utilising resources and affordances available in the environment. They climb trees, dig for worms, roll in the mud, run and jump down from rocks/boulders. Westgarth Kindergarten in Melbourne was the first of its kind, and piloted a Bush Kinder program. Results were unequivocally positive for all involved—children, educators and parents (Elliott & Chancellor, 2014). What is particularly interesting, and promising, is that these Bush Kinder programs adhere to the Regulations (ACECQA, 2014), and base their practice on the EYLF (DEEWR, 2009). Clearly, it is possible to offer young Australian children varied, rich and diverse affordances during outdoor play. The challenge now is for educators to embrace different theories, change their practices and step out of centre-based comfort zones.

Implications for practitioners

Increasing the amount of time children spend outside should be easily achievable for most Australian educators. Conversely, expanding the amount of available outdoor space is likely to be impossible in most cases. However, if additional thought and planning is given to existing spaces, it is possible to capitalise on the unique potential the outdoor environment offers in terms of learning. For instance, different groups of children can have access to the outdoor playground at different times, open-door programmes that entice all children to venture outside can be provided, tables and mats set up with resources that replicate indoor experiences can be removed in favour of more open spaces, and increased room can be made for varied types of challenging play equipment.

It may seem particularly challenging to provide high-quality outdoor play experiences in an environment where so much of what can be done is regulated by external agencies. In such a context, it is important to continuously lobby relevant authorities for further recognition of early childhood educators' professional expertise and their individual decision-making capabilities related to young children's outdoor play. A shift in educators' thinking around the Regulations (ACECQA, 2014) is also needed. Rather than viewing them in terms of what cannot be done, the focus should be on what can be achieved within the existing limitations. Bush Kinders have been able to successfully offer children diverse and challenging outdoor experiences in large, natural environments outside of the centre gates—while complying with the Regulations (ACECQA, 2014). Contact could be made with one or more of these centres in order to establish professional partnerships and seek valuable mentoring regarding the practical requirements for designing and implementing such programs. Finally, educators should be aware of council-run and/or privately operated outdoor play initiatives in the local community, and plan ahead for excursions that can utilise these organised opportunities for varied outdoor play throughout the year.

CONCLUSION

Australia and Norway are two countries with a historical love of nature and the outdoors. Yet the outdoor play affordances available to children in Norwegian and Australian early childhood education settings are very different. As outlined in this chapter, there are several reasons behind these differences, but some might have a larger impact than others. It appears that the pedagogical approaches underpinning early childhood education practice in Norway permit educators to theorise in depth about the purpose and benefits of children playing outside more than their Australian counterparts (Sandseter et al., 2012). Gibsonian and dynamic systems theories place children's learning and development in a direct relationship with hands-on engagement in diverse environments. This provides Norwegian educators with a strong theoretical justification for prioritising play in the outdoors (Sandseter et al., 2012). It is evident that some misalignment exists between what Australian educators believe constitutes good practice and what they are actually offering children in terms of outdoor play. Socio-cultural theory is an important theoretical framework for Australian early child-hood education pedagogy in most areas. However, it provides no support for educators when it comes to decision-making relating to play in outdoor environments (Sandseter et al., 2012). It is perhaps more desirable to look to the EYLF's (DEEWR, 2009, p. 11) requirement that educators draw upon 'critical theories that invite early childhood educators to challenge assumptions about curriculum, and consider how their decisions may affect children differently' when facilitating and planning for outdoor play.

REFLECTION QUESTIONS

12.1   Both Norway and Australia are contexts that in theory recognise the importance of outdoor play and engagement with nature, yet there appear to be vast differences in the implementation of this belief. Why might this be the case?

12.2   After reading this chapter, what are some thoughts and reflections regarding your ideas and approaches to outdoor play?

12.3   How has your thinking about what constitutes high-quality outdoor play been challenged?

12.4   As a future early childhood educator, how would you advocate for diverse, varied and challenging outdoor play with families?

12.5   How would you inspire future colleagues to critically examine their thinking around outdoor play?

12.6   Norwegian educators believe that children must sometimes be allowed to feel uncomfortable in order to learn important skills and develop independence. What are your thoughts about this?

12.7   Ask your parental figure/s about their outdoor play as young children. How do their experiences compare with yours a generation later?

12.8   Is it challenging to find a suitable balance between adult- and child-initiated activities in the outdoor environment? What are some ideas to support a balanced approach?

REFERENCES

Australian Children's Education and Care Quality Authority (ACECQA). (2013). *Guide to the National Quality Standard*. Retrieved 20 December 2016 from <www.acecqa.gov.au>.

—— (2014). *Guide to the Education and Care Services National Law and the Education and Care Services National Regulations 2011.* Retrieved 20 December 2016 from <www.acecqa.gov.au/National-Law>.

Borge, A.I.H., Nordhagen, R. & Lie, K.K. (2003). Children in the environment: Forest day-care centers. *The History of the Family, 8*(4), 605–18.

Department of Education, Employment and Workplace Relations (DEEWR). (2009). *Belonging, being and becoming: The Early Years Learning Framework for Australia.* Canberra: Commonwealth Government.

Dyment, J.E. & Coleman, B. (2012). The intersection of physical activity opportunities and the role of early childhood educators during outdoor play: Perceptions and reality. *Australasian Journal of Early Childhood, 37*(1), 90–8.

Ellingsen, D. (2008). *Tryggere, men kanskje kjedeligere* [Safer, but perhaps more boring]. *Sikkerhet* [Safety], *5*. Retrieved 4 October 2016 from <https://brage.bibsys.no/xmlui/bitstream/handle/11250/178924/Kap4-Ellingsen.pdf?sequence=1>.

Elliott, S. & Chancellor, B. (2014). From forest preschool to Bush Kinder: An inspirational approach to preschool provision in Australia. *Australasian Journal of Early Childhood, 39*(4), 45–53.

Elliott, S. & Davis, J. (2008). Introduction: Why natural outdoor playspaces? In S. Elliott (ed.), *The outdoor playspace naturally: For children birth to five years* (pp. 1–14). Sydney Pademelon Press.

Ettridge, K.A., Bowden, J.A., Rayner, J.M. & Wilson, C.J. (2011). The relationship between sun protection policy and associated practices in a national sample of early childhood services in Australia. *Health Education Research, 26*(1), 53–62.

Gibson, E.J. (1988). Exploratory behavior in the development of perceiving, acting, and the acquiring of knowledge. *Annual Review of Psychology, 39*, 1–41.

Guldberg, H. (2009). *Reclaiming childhood: Freedom and play in an age of fear.* New York: Routledge.

Gullestad, M. (1992). *The art of social relations. Essays on culture, social action and everyday life in modern Norway.* Oslo: Scandinavian University Press.

Heft, H. (1988). Affordances of children's environments: A functional approach to environmental description. *Children's Environments Quarterly, 5*(3), 29–37.

Hendry, L.B. & Kloep, M. (2002). *Lifespan development: Resources, challenges and risks.* London: Thomson Learning.

Ibsen, H. (1899). *Samlede værker. Fjerde bind* [Complete works. Volume 4]. Copenhagen: Gyldendalske boghandels forlag.

Kyttä, M. (2004). The extent of children's independent mobility and number of actualized affordances as criteria for child-friendly environments. *Journal of Environmental Psychology, 24*(2), 129–98.

Lie, S., Vedum, T.V. & Dullerud, O. (2011). *Natur-, frilufts- og gårdsbarnehager: Hva kjennetegner disse? Hva betyr de for barnas utvikling?* [Nature-, outdoor- and farm kindergartens: What characterises these? What do they mean for children's development?] (Rapport Nr. 8 [Report No. 8]). Hedmark: Hedmark University of Applied Sciences.

Little, H. (2015). Promoting risk-taking and physically challenging play in Australian early childhood settings in a changing regulatory environment. *Journal of Early Childhood Research, 43*(4), 337–45.

Little, H., Sandseter, E.B.H. & Wyver, S. (2012). Early childhood teachers' beliefs about children's risky play in Australia and Norway. *Contemporary Issues in Early Childhood, 13*(4), 300–16.

Little, H. & Wyver, S. (2014). Outdoor play in Australia. In T. Maynard & J. Waters (eds), *Exploring outdoor play in the early years* (pp. 141–56). Maidenhead: Open University Press.

Mauffette, A.G., Fréchette, L. & Robertson, D. (1999). *Revisiting children's outdoor equipment: A focus on design, play and safety.* Hull, QC: Gauvin.

Moser, T. & Martinsen, M. (2010). The outdoor environment in Norwegian kindergartens as pedagogical space for toddlers' play, learning and development. *European Early Childhood Education Research Journal, 18*(4), 457–71.

Nilsen, R.D. (2008). Children in nature: Cultural ideas and social practices in Norway. In A. James & A.L. James (eds), *European childhoods: Culture, politics and childhoods in Europe* (pp. 39–60). Hampshire: Palgrave Macmillan.

Norwegian Ministry of Climate and Environment (1957). *Lov om friluftslivet (Friluftsloven)* [Act Relating to Outdoor Recreation (Outdoor Recreation Act)]. Retrieved 4 October 2016 from <https://lovdata.no/dokument/NL/lov/1957-06-28-16>.

Norwegian Ministry of Education and Research (NMER) (2005). *Lov 17 juni 2005 nr 64 om barnehager (barnehageloven) med forskrifter og departementets merknader til bestemmelsene* [Act no. 64 of 17 June 2005 relating to Kindergartens (the Kindergarten Act) including regulations and the ministry's comments regarding the provision]. Retrieved 17 June 2014 from <www.udir.no>.

—— (2006). *Rammeplan for innhaldet i og oppgåvene til barnehagen* [Framework plan for the content and tasks of kindergartens]. Retrieved 17 June 2014 from <www.udir.no>.

Planet Ark (2011). *Climbing trees: Getting Aussie kids back outdoors.* Sydney: Planet Ark. Retrieved 4 October 2016 from <http://treeday.planetark.org/documents/doc-534-climbing-trees-research-report-2011-07-13-final.pdf>.

Sandseter, E.B.H. (2014). Early years outdoor play in Scandinavia. In T. Maynard & J. Waters (eds), *Exploring outdoor play in the early years* (pp. 114–25). Maidenhead: Open University Press.

Sandseter E.B.H. & Little, H. (2012). *Rom for risikofylt lek i barnehagen—En komparativ studie av fysiske omgivelsers betydning for risikofylt lek i Australia og Norge* [Room for risky play in early childhood settings—A comparison of physical environments' impacts on risky play in Australia and Norway]. In F. Rønning, R. Diesen, H. Hoveid & I. Pareliussen (eds), *FoU i Praksis 2011: Rapport fra konferanse om praksisrettet FoU i lærerutdanning* [FoU in practice 2011: Report from conference regarding practicum-oriented FoU in teacher education] (pp. 409–19). Trondheim: Tapir Akademiske Forlag.

Sandseter, E.B.H., Little, H. & Wyver, S. (2012). Do theory and pedagogy have an impact on provisions for outdoor learning? A comparison of approaches in Australia and Norway. *Journal of Adventure and Outdoor Learning, 12*(3), 167–82.

Sandseter, E.B.H. & Sando, O.J. (2016). 'We don't allow children to climb trees': How a focus on safety affects Norwegian children's outdoor play in early-childhood education and care settings. *American Journal of Play, 8*(2), 178–200.

Sandseter, E.B.H., Sando, O.J., Pareliussen, I. & Egset, C.K. (2013). *Kartlegging av hendelser og ulykker som medfører skade på barn i barnehage* [Mapping of happenings and accidents that result in child injury in childcare centres]. Trondheim: Queen Maud University College of Early Childhood Education.

Scott, C. (2010). *Bogue nation: Walking with Bogans.* Retrieved 5 October 2016 from <www.brendanlee.com/site.php/Main/BogueNationWalkingWithBogans>.

Smith, A.B. (2007). Children as social actors: An introduction. *International Journal of Children's Rights, 15*(1), 1–4.

Soto, L.D. & Swadener, B.B. (2002). Toward liberatory early childhood theory, research and praxis: Decolonizing a field. *Contemporary Issues in Early Childhood, 3*(1), 38–66.

Standards Australia (2014). *Playground Equipment and Surfacing. Part 1: General safety requirements and test methods.* Sydney: Standards Australia.

Statistics Norway (SSB). (2015). Kindergartens 2014, final numbers. Retrieved 21 May 2015 from <www.ssb.no>.

Sugiyama, T., Okely, A.D., Masters, J.M. & Moore, G.T. (2012). Attributes of child care centers and outdoor play areas associated with preschoolers' physical activity and sedentary behavior. *Environment and Behavior, 44*(3), 334–9.

Thelen, E. & Smith, L.B. (1998). *A dynamic systems approach to the development of cognition and action* (3rd edn). Cambridge, MA: MIT Press.

Vassenden, A., Thygesen, J., Bayer, S.B., Alvestad, M. & Abrahamsen, G. (2011). *Barnehagens organisering og strukturelle faktorers betydning for kvalitet* [The kindergartens' organisational and structural factors' importance for quality]. Report IRIS—2011/029. Stavanger: International Research Institute of Stavanger.

Part 5
The outdoors and beyond

Chapter 13

Beyond the fence
Exploring forest preschool/school approaches in Australia

Sue Elliott and Barbara Chancellor

The origins of forest preschool/school approaches are attributed to Scandinavian countries, where children can frequently be found playing outdoors in all weathers as an integral aspect of their education programs (Knight, 2013a; Williams-Siegfredsen, 2012). Such approaches are linked intrinsically to Scandinavian culture and landscape, specifically in Denmark, where Williams-Siegfredsen (2012, p. 7) describes *friluftsliv*, or the 'free air life', as a long-standing cultural tenet. While forest preschools for young children up to the school-entry age of 6 years have been common in Scandinavia for decades, only in the 1990s was the forest preschool approach introduced into the United Kingdom. Since the 1990s, there has been an exponential growth in this approach across both preschools and schools, and internationally in many countries, including Australia, Canada, Japan, New Zealand and the United States (Knight, 2013b). In Canada and the United Kingdom, this growth has recently led to over-arching professional associations, the Canadian Forest School Association and the United Kingdom Forest School Association, which offer guiding principles, practical information, publications, research and collaborative potential.

A challenge for each country has been for educators to both translate and adapt the principles and pedagogies of a forest preschool/school approach to the culture, landscape and education policies within each country and, more specifically, each local community context. For example, in New Zealand, building on the strengths of the bicultural early childhood curriculum Te Whāriki (NZ Ministry of Education, 1996), forest preschool programs are interwoven with local Māori culture and stories (Kelly & White, 2013; Maley-Shaw, 2013). In Canada, an innovative early childhood–primary team-teaching approach at a school site has forged new collaborative partnerships, not to mention the challenges of cougars and bears in the uniquely Canadian landscape (Hoyland & Elliot, 2014). In Japan, educators have instigated localised forest preschool programs, yet these are not currently recognised by government as part of the range of registered preschool programs available. As Bentsen and colleagues (2010, p. 236) state, 'it is important to be aware of local, regional and national contexts, and of how curriculum and outdoor educational practices are framed and shaped by cultural, social, political and geographical factors'. Similar to the uptake of Reggio Emilia principles internationally since the 1990s (Edwards, Gandini & Forman, 1998), one cannot simply replicate an approach in each country; a period of translation and interpretation, as framed and shaped by local factors, is essential.

Provocation

Forest preschool and school approaches have emerged in Australia over recent years as part of a worldwide movement that now recognises play in nature as highly beneficial for young children. Many educators are moving beyond the fence in early childhood services, and at times in schools, to explore local urban and rural natural environments, such as parks, bushland, farmland, beaches and waterways. How can educators wishing to explore opportunities for nature-based pedagogies in their local communities meld current guiding policies with this educator-led grassroots movement?

In Australia, the framing and shaping of a forest preschool approach began around 2010, led by a handful of educators in the state of Victoria inspired by the Scandinavian models. A pioneer in this field was the community of children, educators and parents at Westgarth Kindergarten in inner urban Melbourne, which established a pilot Bush Kinder in the kindergarten's local Darebin Parklands. An evaluative study of this pilot program (Elliott & Chancellor, 2012), and subsequent on-site professional learning opportunities and networking among interested educators, ultimately led to the establishment of a Victorian-based professional group, Early Childhood Outdoor Learning (ECOLearn). While Victoria was the starting point and continues to have the most programs, it has been estimated that there are now some hundreds of Bush Kinder and/or Bush School programs across Australia.

In part, this momentum has been fuelled by state government-funded nature play initiatives and instrumental organisations, including Centennial Parklands in Sydney, New South Wales and the Royal Botanic Gardens in Melbourne and Cranbourne, Victoria. Further, a Sydney TAFE initiative to offer an Early Years Bush Connections Training program has supported educators from varied backgrounds to build skills for facilitating outdoor learning since 2013, while some educators have travelled overseas to Denmark and the United Kingdom to undertake training.

There is now a significant international research and publication base to support the rapid emergence of forest preschool/school programs. Cited benefits noted include:

- children's increased confidence, motivation and concentration; increased social, physical and language skills; deeper conceptual understandings; and respect for the natural environment (O'Brien, 2009; O'Brien & Murray, 2006)
- children's increased social and imaginative play (Fjortoft, 2004)
- children's more varied risk-taking behaviours and positive dispositions towards risk and challenge (Waters & Begley, 2007)
- forest preschool participants practising a community of care, where everyone takes responsibility for the safety and wellbeing of the group (Coe, 2016)
- the enhancement of attitudes within families and the wider community towards natural places for play (Knight, 2013a; O'Brien, 2009)
- positive wellbeing benefits for diverse groups, including disadvantaged or challenging youth, children with autism and drug-addicted adults (Knight, 2011)

- a deepening of teachers' understandings of and relationships with the children through sustained shared thinking and more frequent child-initiated interactions with teachers, prompted by the natural environment and found loose parts (Elliott & Chancellor, 2014; Waters, 2012).

In summary, forest preschools/schools as a context for learning offer unplanned, unknown, unpredictable encounters; these are significant provocations for learning (adapted from Waters, 2012). Research to inform and deepen understandings of this approach in an Australasian context is just emerging. In particular, Lee-Hammond and Jackson-Barrett (2013) have examined Aboriginal children's participation and engagement in a bush school program (see Chapter 11); Kelly and White (2013) have engaged in action research in the bicultural bush preschool settings of New Zealand; and Grogan (2014) has investigated Bush Kinder pedagogies with a focus on education for sustainability. There are many more possibilities yet to explore.

Context

While the term 'Bush Kinder' has been informally adopted in the Australian early childhood field, the physical contexts for such programs can be quite diverse. In long-settled landscapes, such as England, a forest preschool or school space might be remnant woodland on a country estate or a small overgrown urban plot. In defining forest preschool/school, Knight (2013a) suggests that any space is possible; thus a forest preschool/school is defined by the ethos or approach and is quite simply not the usual space designated for children's outdoor play. In Australia, the space choices are diverse, and current practice indicates that urban bush parks and waterways, private farmland, public or botanic gardens, national parks, beaches and foreshores, and extensive forest-like school grounds offer suitable sites.

A number of factors are taken into consideration when selecting a local site for a program. Some guidance can be sought from Doyle and Milchem (2012), Robertson and colleagues (2009) and, locally, Elliott and Chancellor (2012):

- The site needs to be readily accessible by walking, public transport, bus hire or parents delivering children on site. Often travelling to the site is part of the learning experience, with potential to build stamina and self-management skills along the way.

- The play affordances must be considered—for example, diverse vegetation to facilitate hiding, balancing, swinging or climbing—to support construction or imaginative play with natural materials and to engage all the senses.
- The terrain may offer possibilities for clambering over rocks, moving up or down hill and perhaps sliding or ephemeral water ditches for mud play.
- The open spaces may provide a focal point to congregate for larger group play experiences, snacks or discussions, or to leave bags. The scale of the site must offer sufficient variety, but be manageable for supervising adults.
- The supervisory sightlines both within and beyond the space, proximity to hazards, such as water bodies or animal habitats, and landmarks to define the boundaries of the playable space need to be considered. An approach at Westgarth Bush Kinder (Elliott & Chancellor, 2012) has been to define the play boundaries by walking them with children while employing physical landmarks to tell a story, thus reinforcing the play boundaries in meaningful ways with children.
- The logistical considerations will include consultation and legal approvals to utilise a site, proximity to toilets or other services, and potential for extreme weather impacts, including bushfires.

Working systematically and collaboratively through these considerations may be time consuming, but ultimately it will offer the most suitable site or sites. Some programs, both in Australia and overseas, utilise multiple sites for each program, varying the location according to the preferences and interests of participating children and adults, prevailing weather or other risk-management priorities. In the dry climate and poor soils of Australia, it has been observed anecdotally that some programs are negatively impacting on vegetation, the amenability of the space and local animal habitats, so multiple and rotating site use is to be advocated.

Ecoliteracy

Ecoliteracy can be defined as understandings of the interdependent inter-relationships between the Earth's physical parameters and its inhabitants—the plants and animals, including humans. There is acknowledgement that every human action has an impact on the complex ecosystems that we inhabit and that sustain us (Stone & Barlow, 2005). Ecoliteracy informs worldviews aligned with ecocentrism, as opposed to anthropocentrism, and the ethics of sustainable ways of living and being with the Earth. Currently, humans—particularly in Western countries—are living well beyond the carrying capacity of the Earth, without recognition of the Earth's ecosystems as integral to the future of human life—and, in fact, all life (Steffen & Hughes, 2013). Despite some vocal sceptics, there is overwhelming scientific evidence that humans are the cause of climate change and irrevocable change is now underway (Steffen & Hughes, 2013). Building the critical skills and understandings of ecoliteracy in the early years is foundational, and this has long been espoused in the guise of environmental education (Gough, 1997). Further, there is support for environmental stewardship evident in the current EYLF (DEEWR, 2009) and the Australian Curriculum (ACARA, 2015). Bush Kinder contexts offer unique opportunities for exploring ecoliteracy, constructing different worldviews and examining Indigenous worldviews that have embraced sustainable ways of being over centuries in Australia.

However, field experience and recent literature (Elliott & Young, 2016; Taylor, 2013) suggest that educators may be taking a 'nature by default' approach in such settings rather than grappling with 'big-picture thinking' aligned with ecocentrism. A Bush Kinder/School program is deeper than sensory exploration of plants and animals; it also examines their interrelationships and problematises the nature/human dichotomies that have fuelled climate change. Such programs acknowledge visionaries such as Carson (1998 [1956]) who recognised the role of adults,

> If a child is to keep alive his [sic] inborn sense of wonder . . . he needs the companionship of at least one adult who can share it, rediscovering with him the joy, excitement and mystery of the world we live in (Carson, 1998, p. 55).

At Bush Kinder/School, adults can take on the challenge of finding ways to rethink worldviews through pedagogical relationships with children. Educators need to recognise the full potential of programs and contexts by drawing on a pedagogical repertoire that is informed by critical theory and transformative approaches. The aim is to shift thinking beyond stewardship *of* nature to ways of living *in* nature. Bush Kinder/School is a context for curriculum and pedagogical reimaginings in many ways (see Chapter 4).

Curriculum and pedagogy

Educators in Bush Kinders/Schools and similar settings often need to reimagine their approaches to curriculum and pedagogy to achieve the vision underpinning this philosophical approach to early years provision. Notions of pre-planning activities or games and challenges for children are unsuitable because the teaching is spontaneous and emergent. During our research into the first Bush Kinder at Westgarth Kindergarten, Victoria, educators explained this way of teaching by saying, 'It's all in the moment', 'It's about letting go' and accepting that the bush setting will provide the play and learning opportunities for children (Elliott & Chancellor, 2012, p. 14). From first-hand experience and a willingness to allow the children and the natural environment to take the lead, the educators at Westgarth Kindergarten found that open-ended, child-directed curriculum approaches were essential.

Because there are typically no materials brought into a Bush Kinder space, the available natural materials become central to children's interests and learning. This requires teachers to have a preparedness to allow the materials chosen by children for play and the children's interest in and responses to those materials to become central to any pedagogical approaches. Turning the story over to children and opening up spaces for their voices and actions to be heard and seen—that is, centralising their perspectives—is all too frequently not achieved (Chancellor & Sellers, 2017) and without this, the philosophy underpinning Bush Kinder approaches will not be realised.

At Bush Kinder, the voices of the educators should be quietened and not be the dominant sound, as so often is the case in early childhood education settings. In a bush setting, power relations are turned upside down and inside out as children drive the play and the learning, creating new geographies of/with/in the Bush Kinder space (Chancellor & Sellers, 2017). Without the buildings, fences and curriculum structures, children determine where and how they play, moving through the landscape on their own terms in ways that enhance their social learning and wellbeing. The many meanings and kinds of 'children's places' should make us aware of children as social and cultural actors who create places that are physical and symbolic, and call attention to 'the interfaces' between adults' understanding of what one can and should do in a place for children and children's understandings of this matter (Rasmussen, 2004, p. 171).

Children operating in these kinds of spaces are leading the way for optimising their socialising and learning experiences—primarily among themselves, but also in more equitable relations with the adults in the setting and in corporeal relations with the natural resources surrounding them (Chancellor & Sellers, 2017). This is different from the power relations, spatial and moral dimensions of practices and responses of children and educators more commonly played out in early childhood settings. In a similar way to Pike and Kelly's (2014, p. 9) description of children in schools, children are cajoled, directed, encouraged and rewarded to behave in certain ways that sustain unequal power relations. When children are viewed as powerful players—figuratively and physically—and the voices of teachers are quiet(ened), then spaces for equitable and complementary interrelationships are opened up (Chancellor & Sellers, 2017).

Bush Kinder settings challenge notions of curriculum design because emergence of the pedagogies requires new ways of viewing the overall curriculum. Educators are unable to predict and measure outcomes, as they may choose to do in their home kindergarten program. Relationships come to the fore and educators work hard to strengthen the sense of belonging for the children and families involved, and also to draw the wider community into the Bush Kinder experience. As the Westgarth Kindergarten teachers noted:

> It's all about relationships, belonging and community . . . the difference is there is no stuff, so the relationships are intensified, your role as a teacher is freed and you become stronger without clutter, it is really quite empowering (Elliott & Chancellor, 2012, p. 14).

Educators find that with increased awareness of the importance of relationships, they can spend more time talking with children, rather than engaging in educator-led and directed conversations. This is a very big shift for many educators new to the Bush Kinder philosophy and pedagogy.

While significant shifts in curriculum and pedagogical approaches can be challenging, Bush Kinder educators have found that this can be a time of professional reinvigoration. They have described it as an opportunity for professional growth, 'an opportunity to push myself' and gain 'new life in my teaching' (Elliott & Chancellor, 2012, p. 14).

Practicalities

There are a number of practicalities to be considered by those establishing a Bush Kinder/School. While some factors are applicable to all, others will be specific to local communities.

The over-arching structure behind all curriculum and pedagogical approaches in early years settings in Australia consists of the National Framework documents: the National Quality Standard (NQS) (ACECQA, 2013), *Belonging, Being and Becoming: The Early Years Learning Framework for Australia* (EYLF) (DEEWR, 2009) and the Australian Curriculum (ACARA, 2015). When planning a Bush Kinder/School, strong links must be evident with all aspects of these documents. At a local level, policies that relate to the operation of the program should be developed and, most importantly, reviewed by successive management committees. In early childhood settings, this may involve alterations to licensing agreements to facilitate groups of children attending the Bush Kinder/School site while the centre-based program is also operating.

Every Bush Kinder/School must have a risk-management policy that is comprehensive and aligns with relevant regulatory considerations (ACECQA, 2013). In consultation with successive groups of parents, concerns about safety must be reflected in updated risk-management policies, including those related to first-aid; adverse weather events, including bushfire; other users of the public open space, including dogs; and, importantly, policy that covers site management in relation to inspection before children arrive (see Chapter 2). Practically focused policies covering a wide range of possibilities also need to be developed and revised regularly. These might include policies about the use of manufactured toys or tools on site, drop-off and pick-up arrangements for children, toileting procedures and bushwalks when children leave the designated space.

Clear communication with all stakeholders is essential, and educators need to find suitable ways of reaching parents and the wider community for not only practical reasons, but also for promotion of the Bush Kinder/School philosophy. Furthermore, given that Bush Kinders/Schools attract interest from a range of bodies and individuals—such as local community groups, early years professionals and families of children attending—a policy for visitors is useful. Without intending to impact on children's play opportunities, visitors could unknowingly intrude and disrupt the program. For this reason, many programs now provide a visitors' brochure that outlines visiting rights and responsibilities.

Other considerations for Bush Kinders/Schools include guidelines for children's clothing during colder months, which may include gumboots and wet weather gear. Individual programs develop their own arrangements, with some recycling of wet weather gear from group to group. Some services engage children in washing the wet weather gear back at the home centre or school as both practical and integral to taking responsibility. Clothing rules need to be understood clearly by parents, and a procedure put in place for children who arrive inappropriately dressed. Sponsorship from outdoor clothing companies may be feasible if the cost of wet weather gear is prohibitive.

As with all education programs, scheduling needs to occur in consultation with management, staff and parents. Engagement of parents is critical to success, as they will be essential partners through membership of the local community, assisting with aspects of the program, working with regulators and land owners and informing others about the program. On-site orientation days are a particularly useful way to demonstrate unique aspects of the program and an opportunity to address parent concerns. Partnerships with parents are foundational in the early years, and can be strengthened through Bush Kinder/School programs where parents are critical and necessary to success.

Two vignettes from practice

The following examples offered by two early childhood centre directors from Victoria illustrate how programs are developing in the field in Australia, and reinforce the discussion and literature cited in this chapter.

Case study 1: Coburg Children's Centre

Coburg Children's Centre is a 62-place, not-for-profit long day care centre located in the inner northern suburbs of metropolitan Melbourne, operating from 7 a.m. to 6 p.m. on weekdays for children aged from 6 months to school age. The centre also offers an integrated 3-year-old and a funded, integrated 4-year-old preschool program. The centre comprises many nationalities and is well known for its commitment to sustainable practices, strong links with the local community and inclusive practices.

The Coburg Bush Kinder program is viewed as an extension of the nature-based outdoor programs offered for over twenty years at the centre, and was inspired by the Scandinavian forest preschool movement and the local Westgarth Kindergarten Bush Kinder previously noted. The program began in 2012 with weekly three- to four-hour visits by the 4-year-old group to a local creek and parkland area within walking distance (approx. 1.4 kilometres/25 minutes' walk). The walk to and from the site is an integral part of the whole Bush Kinder experience. Prior to each session, a management staff member drives to the site and sets up equipment, including the portable toilet, lunch and drinks, and tarps for shelter, and conducts a safety check of the area. The site is set back from the creek and characterised by an open grassy area, a large deciduous tree suitable for climbing and bushy secret areas inviting play (see Figure 13.1). Adjacent to the site is the end of a no through road for any vehicle access required, and a large market garden borders one side. The number of children participating varies from 18 to 24, and four educators are involved as a minimum, while additional adults might include parents, students on placement or visiting educators.

Figure 13.1 Bushy, secret areas inviting children's play

Source: Coburg Children's Centre.

An initial program challenge was finding a suitable site within walking distance from the centre and then finding a temporary alternative site due to creek bank stabilisation works. While the children enjoyed a local park alternative, it was a very different experience and highlighted the importance of having an alternate suitable site. Three benefits of the program to be highlighted include community connections and engagement, Indigenous awareness and connections to nature. Examples of community connections and engagement include staff from the market garden sharing produce with the children; council revegetation works rescheduled to include the children in the planting; and an award-winning project where children raised concerns about rubbish in the creek with a local politician, resulting in a community clean-up day organised by children letter-dropping in their neighbourhood. Indigenous awareness includes daily acknowledgement of the traditional owners, the Wurunjeri-willam clan, who once camped along the creek. An Indigenous early childhood consultant has also provided an authentic interpretation of the plants, animals and history with the children. Connection to nature has been facilitated through creative play with natural materials, climbing trees and building cubbies. In planning ahead, the 3-year-old children attend the local community garden fortnightly in small groups, laying the groundwork for their transition to Bush Kinder as 4-year-olds.

Contributed by Michelle Hocking, Assistant Director and Educational Leader, Coburg Children's Centre, Victoria

Case study 2: Yarralea Children's Centre

Yarralea Children's Centre is located in a small leafy community of Alphington in Melbourne's inner northeast. It is a not-for-profit, community children's centre that operates five days per week from 8 a.m. to 6 p.m., 48 weeks per year, and it is licensed for 44 children. Yarralea provides sessional and long-day preschool for 3- and 4-year-olds, as well as a multi-age preschool program (for children from 1–6 years). The Bush Kinder program was piloted in 2013–14 and fully established in 2015. It was provoked by current literature around children's decreasing opportunity for unstructured play in natural settings and the documented effects on health and wellbeing. It is viewed as an extension of Yarralea's preschool program and philosophy, which values outdoor play in rich, engaging natural environments and the importance of embedding sustainability as a way of life.

Children in the 4-year-old program attend Bush Kinder one morning per week as part of their funded 15 hours of preschool, and are dropped off at the local Darebin Parklands site at 8.30 a.m. by their parents and later walk 1 kilometre back to the centre at 11.30 a.m. as a group. Staff wheel a wagon from the centre containing wet weather gear and a tarp, and carry a backpack with children's medical requirements, the sign-in book, camera, sunhats and the Bush Kinder phone. The other equipment (including a camping toilet, toilet tent, first aid kit, witches' hats and water containers) is kept on-site in a rented storage container. The children are encouraged to wear appropriate clothing, including gumboots or snow boots, and to bring a snack, lunch and a drink bottle. Up to 27 children attend each session and a 1:7 adult-to-child ratio is maintained. This is achieved by having three staff: one teacher, two co-educators and a rostered parent helper. If the forecast predicts winds over 40 kilometres per hour, thunderstorms, hail or temperatures over 30°C at midday (as we walk back in the middle of the day), Bush Kinder is cancelled by group text message and the session resumes at the centre.

The Yarralea community has worked through challenges along the way. At the inception of the pilot, the full spectrum of parent response was evident, ranging from complete opposition to enthusiastic impatience to get the program off the ground; however, most families were somewhere in between. They were interested to learn more about the program, and consequently the more they understood and experienced the more they appreciated and supported the program. To educate families, they were provided with information and consulted in a patient manner, thus facilitating understandings at their own pace. Developing a risk-assessment policy was challenging: initially it was overly long and stated only risks. A more balanced risk–benefit assessment policy now clearly articulates both benefits and risks (see Figure 13.2).

Figure 13.2 Risky play is integral to Bush Kinder programs.
Source: Yarralea Children's Centre.

The key benefits identified include children's rights, environmental and social sustainability, and mental health and wellbeing. Children's rights to unstructured outdoor play in nature, and access to fresh air, sunlight, wind, rain, mud, trees and personal space are foundational. Environmental and social sustainability is manifest in authentic connections to the local Indigenous environment, fostering of education for sustainability principles and finding creatures that are researched and respectfully acknowledged as co-inhabitants of the ecosystem.

The benefits for the mental health and wellbeing of all participants is evident: there is time to just be, to contemplate, to sit together or alone, and to talk or be silent. In light of these varied benefits, the 4-year-old program will soon be extended to a full day for the latter part of the preschool year and a pilot program for 3-year-olds will commence.

Contributed by Stephanie Willey, Director,
Yarralea Children's Centre, Victoria

CONCLUSION

With an increasing number of Australian early childhood services and schools embracing this worldwide movement, based upon the benefits of children's play in nature, many educators are moving beyond the fence to utilise natural spaces within their wider communities as part of their program design. Engaging with relevant nature-based pedagogies provokes a reimagining in the field, where current national policy documents tend to focus on curriculum and pedagogies within traditional boundaries of indoor/outdoor programming and reinforce worldviews aligned to nature stewardship only.

The four key areas addressed in this chapter are illustrated in the vignettes from Coburg Children's Centre and Yarralea Children's Centre. Understandings of ecoliteracy are explored and linked with climate change, fuelled by nature/human dichotomies and Indigenous worldviews where humans in their environments coexist harmoniously. Curriculum and pedagogical approaches are emergent rather than pre-planned, and require an opening up by teachers to the importance of relationships, with discussions often led by the children. Practicalities are supported by national curriculum guidelines and policies, and policies specific to each setting are revisited to remain relevant.

This grassroots-led movement represents an ambitious and challenging approach to education that acknowledges the environmental challenges we face today and seeks to explore connecting children with nature in inspiring and innovative ways within their local communities.

REFLECTION QUESTIONS

13.1   Is Bush Kinder/School more than simply taking young children outside to play in nature?

13.2   Is Bush Kinder/School about children surviving outdoors? What limits and practices need to be in place for the best interests of children's wellbeing?

13.3   Are tools and explicit teaching of skills, such as rope work, fire lighting or whittling, as evident in the United Kingdom essential to Bush Kinder/School in Australia? What other skills might be more relevant here?

13.4   How could you implement Bush Kinder/School in ways that reflect current early years' philosophies, pedagogies and the EYLF (DEEWR, 2009) or Australian Curriculum (ACARA, 2015)? What links can you identify?

13.5   How can we manage risk with children in uniquely Australian contexts? What risks need to be considered and what are possible risk-management options?

13.6   Is specific training to work in Bush Kinder/School essential or optional? What type of training might be most relevant in Australia?

13.7   How can we acknowledge and incorporate Indigenous perspectives in Bush Kinder/School settings?

13.8   How can we care for and maintain the natural spaces that we use for play in the longer term? How might an ethic of stewardship be conveyed through the program with children, families and the wider community?

13.9   To extend further, how might we explore beyond 'sentiments of nature stewardship' with children to ethical worldviews reflecting all dimensions for a sustainable future?

RECOMMENDED RESOURCES

- Early Childhood Outdoor Learning Network (ECOLearn): earlychildhoodoutdoorlearning.weebly.com

- Early Years Bush Connections Training, TAFE NSW, available via Fran Hughes at Randwick Campus. Contact Fran Hughes (TAFE NSW): Tel: +61 9469 8625; email: fran.hughes@det.nsw.edu.au
- Forest school Canada: www.forestschoolcanada.ca/home/about-us
- Insideoutnature study tours in Denmark with Jane William-Siegfredsen: www.insideoutnature.com
- New Zealand outdoor learning: www.playandlearn.net.nz
- *Danish Forest Kindergartens* by Amos Roberts, SBS TV, broadcast 23 February 2016: www.sbs.com.au/news/dateline/story/kids-gone-wild
- United Kingdom Forest School Association: www.forestschoolassociation. org

REFERENCES

Australian Children's Education & Care Quality Authority (ACECQA) (2013). *Guide to the National Standard.* Retrieved 20 December 2016 from <files.acecqa.gov.au/files/National-Quality-Framework-Resources-Kit/NQF03-Guide-to-NQS-130902.pdf>.

Australian Curriculum, Assessment and Reporting Authority (ACARA) (2015). *The Australian Curriculum V8.2.* Retrieved 31 October 2016 from <www.australiancurriculum.edu.au>.

Bentsen, P., Jensen, F.S., Mygind. E. & Randrup, T.B. (2010). The extent and dissemination of *udeskole* in Danish schools. *Urban Forestry & Urban Greening, 9*(3), 235–243.

Carson, R. (1998 [1956]). *The sense of wonder.* New York: Harper & Row.

Chancellor, B. & Sellers, M. (2017). Bush Kinder: Thinking differently about privileged spaces through/with/in children's geographies. In P. Kelly & J. Pike (eds), *Neo-liberalism and austerity: The moral economics of young people's health and wellbeing* (pp. 277–94). London: Palgrave Macmillan.

Coe, H.A. (2016). Embracing risk in the Canadian woodlands: Four children's risky play and risk-taking experiences in a Canadian Forest Kindergarten. *Journal of Early Childhood Research.* Retrieved 17 May 2017 from <http://journals.sagepub.com/doi/pdf/10.1177/1476718X15614042>.

Department of Education, Employment & Workplace Relations (DEEWR) (2009) *Belonging, being and becoming: The Early Years Learning Framework for Australia.* Canberra: Commonwealth Government.

Doyle, J. & Milchem, K. (2012). *Developing a forest school in early years provision.* London: MA Education.

Edwards, C., Gandini , L. & Forman, G. (eds) (1998). *The hundred languages of children*. Reggio Emilia, Italy: Reggio Emilia.

Elliott, S. & Chancellor, B. (2012). *Westgarth Kindergarten Bush Kinder evaluation report*. Melbourne: Westgarth Kindergarten & RMIT University. Retrieved 17 May 2017 from <bushkinder.blogspot.com.au/2012/10/bush-kinder-evaluation-report.html>.

——(2014). From forest preschool to Bush Kinder: An inspirational approach to preschool provision in Australia. *Australasian Journal of Early Childhood, 39*(4), 45–53.

Elliott, S. & Young, T. (2016). Nature by default in early childhood education for sustainability. *Australian Journal of Environmental Education, 32*, 57–64.

Fjortoft, I. (2004). Landscape as playscape: The effects of natural environments on children's play and motor development. *Children, Youth and Environments, 14*(2), 21–44.

Grogan, L. (2014). Investigating pedagogical practices in a Bush Kinder setting in relation to early childhood education for sustainability to inform pre-service courses in early childhood education. MEd dissertation, Charles Sturt University, Bathurst.

Gough, A. (1997). *Education and the environment*. Melbourne: Australian Council for Educational Research.

Hoyland, T. & Elliot, E. (2014). Nature kindergarten in Sooke: A unique collaboration. *Canadian Children, 39*(2), 46–50.

Kelly, J. & White, J. (2013). *The Ngahere Project: Teaching and learning possibilities in nature settings*. University of Waikato, New Zealand. Retrieved 17 May 2017 from <www.waikato.ac.nz/__data/assets/pdf_file/0007/146176/Ngahere-project_3-2013-03-14.pdf>.

Knight, S. (2011). *Forest schools for all*. London: Sage.

——(2013a). *Forest schools and outdoor learning in the early years* (2nd edn). London: Sage.

——(ed.) (2013b). *International perspectives on forest school: Natural spaces to play and learn*. London: Sage.

Lee-Hammond, L. & Jackson-Barrett, E. (2013). Aboriginal children's participation and engagement in bush school. In S. Knight (ed.), *International perspectives on forest school: Natural spaces to play and learn* (pp. 131–45). London: Sage.

Maley-Shaw, C. (2013). *Fiordland kindergarten: Nature discovery*. Te Anau, NZ: Kindergartens South.

New Zealand Ministry of Education (1996). *Te Whāriki: Early childhood curriculum.* Wellington, NZ: NZME.

O'Brien, L. (2009). Learning outdoors: The forest school approach. *Education 3–13, 37*(1), 45–60.

O'Brien, L. & Murray, R. (2006). *A marvellous opportunity for children to learn: A participatory evaluation of forest school in England and Wales.* Farnham: Forest Research. Retrieved 17 May 2017 from <www.forestry.gov.uk/pdf/fr0112forestschoolsreport.pdf/$FILE/fr0112forestschoolsreport.pdf>.

Pike, J. & Kelly, P. (2014). *The moral geographies of children, young people and food: Beyond Jamie's school dinners.* London: Palgrave Macmillan.

Rasmussen, K. (2004). Places for children—children's places. *Childhood, 11*(2), 155–73.

Robertson, J., Martin, P., Borradaile, L. and Alker, S. (2009). *Forest Kindergarten feasibility study.* Glasgow: Forestry Commission Scotland.

Steffen, W. & Hughes, L. (2013). *Australian Climate Commission Report: The critical decade 2013. Climate change science, risks and responses.* Canberra: Commonwealth Government.

Stone M.K. & Barlow, Z. (eds) (2005). *Ecological literacy: Educating our children for a sustainable world.* San Francisco: Sierra Club Books.

Taylor, A. (2013). *Reconfiguring the natures of childhood.* London: Routledge.

Waters, J. (2012). Talking in wild outdoor spaces. In S. Knight (ed.), *International perspectives on forest school* (pp. 12–26). London: Sage.

Waters, J. & Begley, S. (2007). Supporting the development of risk taking behaviours in the early years: An exploratory study. *Education 3–13, 35*(4), 365–77.

Williams-Siegfredsen, J. (2012). *Understanding the Danish forest school approach.* Oxford: Routledge.

Chapter 14

Urban environments and outdoor learning

*Shirley Wyver, Jennifer Kent, Paul Tranter, Geraldine Naughton,
Lina Engelen, Anita Bundy and Kam Tara*

The previous chapters of this book have examined outdoor spaces in specific contexts, with most of these contexts being educational. Such contexts are often considered places for children and spaces that will meet children's needs. The aim of this chapter is to look beyond those contexts and consider broader environments in which spaces for play are less likely to be prioritised. This chapter will consider the relationship between built environments and opportunities for children to be physically active and engage in outdoor play. The term 'built environment' is used regularly in disciplines such as human geography and urban planning. The built environment encompasses human-modified places, including homes, schools, workplaces, parks and playgrounds, farms, roads and railways. It is now widely recognised that modern built environments can have significant adverse impacts on human health (Jackson, Dannenberg & Frumkin, 2013), and these impacts may become increasingly important as more and more people live in cities (Srinivasan, O'Fallon & Dearry, 2003).

> **Provocation**
>
> Assume that, as part of a celebration of Australia's new status as a republic, the government has decided to revitalise a country town that was thriving until the 1980s, but is now almost abandoned. The

town will be symbolic of Australia's new approach, and the success of the town will be used to expose problems in existing towns and cities that often lead to less than optimal outcomes for individuals, families and communities. Some of the iconic structures of the country town will be retained, but most other structures, such as the school built in the 1950s, the roads and some of the housing, will be removed. The new town is seen as an opportunity to start planning based on current knowledge. The key indicators for success relate to the resilience and wellbeing of young people. One of the methods to achieve this is to ensure that early childhood centres and school buildings act as meeting places, but the entire town is considered to be a place for children's and young people's learning. Learning can occur anywhere in the town. Teachers will facilitate learning and as a group will have a strong knowledge base of all aspects of the town. Children and teachers will be involved in all town planning decisions. Based on your knowledge from other chapters in this book and your own experiences, do you believe the town will achieve its goals?

What do you consider to be the main benefits and the main difficulties in implementing a vision of this kind? What methods would you use to promote this new way of learning? How would you evaluate whether the town has been successful in achieving its aims?

Urban environments and children's health

Children today walk less than ever in the history of humanity (Roberts & Edwards, 2010, p. 39).

The links between the built environment and health, including children's health, are now well researched. The ways in which our urban environments are structured and managed contribute to an array of contemporary health issues, including the burgeoning impacts of lifestyle diseases such as diabetes, heart disease and some cancers (Frank et al., 2006; Giles-Corti et al., 2016). Obesity and overweight are particularly concerning risk factors in many developed and developing countries, and children are by no means exempt from this concern. In Australia, for example, almost two out of every three adults are overweight or obese, and overweight or obesity is the second highest contributor to the national burden of disease. Over 25 per cent of Australian children are overweight or obese (AIHW, 2016).

Built environments are implicated in rising rates of obesity in a number of ways. The places where we live, work and play are characterised by rushing and busyness, with car dependence, poor access to public recreational spaces, increased exposure to high-energy convenience food options and decreased opportunities for day-to-day neighbourhood interactions, reducing opportunities for physical activity, community connection and healthy eating patterns (Kent & Thompson, 2014). A principle of public health is to build healthy choices into our lifestyles, so that we practise healthy behaviours by default (Downs, Lowenstein & Wisdom, 2009; Halpern, Ubel & Asch, 2007). Good examples are making walking or cycling easier and more appealing than the private car, or ensuring that stairways in buildings are an attractive, fun and obvious choice in preference to a lift or escalator. Instead, built environments are designed for inactivity, inferring that the optimum modern life is one that is sedentary, convenient, disconnected and efficient. The child is removed from this presumption, and as such our cities are increasingly less healthy and less child friendly.

Child-friendly cities embody the principles of the UN Convention on the Rights of the Child (UNCRC) (OHCHR, 1989). The rights of the child include the child's 'right to play' (Article 31), which is often seen as optional, or as less important than protecting children and promoting safety, or providing education or stimulating adult-organised activity. Yet this article is based on the recognition that play is fundamental to every child's development: physical, social, intellectual and emotional. Children in a child-friendly city are not only protected from all forms of abuse, violence and exploitation; they are also involved in the city and invited to participate in community life. They are provided with a range of well-maintained, open public spaces, and the means to travel safely between them. Child-friendly transport modes are active modes, such as walking, cycling, scooting and public transport use. The ability for a child to travel independently unlocks opportunities for new and diverse physical and social experiences, and is particularly important. Indeed, nations that have high levels of active transport use also score highly on indicators of child wellbeing. The Netherlands, for example, where cycling is a common choice for all trips and all ages, is a clear leader in indices of child wellbeing (Adamson, 2013). As we discuss, by merging principles of child-friendly cities with healthy built environment aspirations, we can encourage children to spend time outdoors, and remove the built and cultural barriers that currently keep them inside (Carver, Timperio & Crawford, 2008).

A recent systematic review has underscored the long-suspected importance of experiences of physical activity in the early years on healthy behaviour in adult life. In particular, the review highlights the impact of socio-economic status and its relationship to parental role modelling, facilities and other factors that relate directly to physical activity (Elhakeem et al., 2015). Providing equitable access for all children and families to undertake day-to-day physical activity should therefore be a key consideration, rather than exclusion through privatisation or practices such as 'alley gating' that restrict movement and are sometimes argued to be in place to stop less affluent individuals entering gentrified communities (Atkinson & Blandy, 2013).

Myths about regulations, laws and children's time outdoors

> Autonomous young people appear to be automatically perceived
> to disrupt the moral order of the street (Valentine, 1996, p. 596).

Children's outdoor activity can be curtailed by mistaken beliefs about access. Recent research has shown misunderstandings about the current regulatory requirements and different understandings, and this translates into a very conservative approach to play, such as restrictions on climbing trees even when the height that can be climbed is within regulations (Little, 2017). Eide (see Chapter 12) has similarly noted that the majority of early childhood centres in her study kept children indoors on sunny days despite the Cancer Council of Australia advising that outdoor time is acceptable if appropriate sun protection is used. Clearly, it seems that a bias exists towards restricting children's outdoor activity even when regulatory and other authorities have not indicated that the restriction is either necessary or desirable.

There is also a myth that there are strict laws about Australian children's independent mobility, such as walking to a school or a park. It is often stated that it is illegal for a child under 12 years to cross a road, go to a corner store or engage in other simple neighbourhood journeys in the absence of an adult (e.g. 'Do your kids walk?', 2016). Laws relate to contexts rather than age; thus, if a child's independent mobility was indicative of neglect, relevant state authorities would take action (NSW Government, 2016). Legislation has been written to protect children, but not to restrict their mobility. It is important to challenge this myth, as its perpetuation potentially restricts the independent mobility of children with parents and carers fearing a breach of the law should they allow their child to walk to a friend's house or run a neighbourhood errand.

Active not passive transport

> Australian children are amongst the most chauffeured young people in the developed world (Garrard, 2011b).

The Longitudinal Study of Australian Children is one of many studies to demonstrate that walking or cycling to school is limited. The study found that less than 20 per cent of 10–11-year-olds accessed school on foot or by bike independently (Mullan & Edwards, 2013). Children from lower socio-economic groups were more likely to walk or cycle to school independently, and this was thought to be attributable to schools for those children generally being closer to home. A study of the trends of children's mode of transport to school from 1971 to 2003 demonstrated a decline in walking to school from 58 to 26 per cent, and an increase in being driven to school by car from 23 to 67 per cent over the course of 30 years (van der Ploeg et al., 2008). This trend is not likely to have reversed in the last decade. Indeed, it has been noted that Australian children are highly likely to be driven to school, and the decision to drive children to school is made if distance to school is 500 metres or greater, which is well below the levels in countries such as Denmark (Garrard,

2011a). That converts to a minimum of a seven- to eight-minute walk for 5-year-olds, based on the finding that the average child of this age takes 13.5 seconds to walk 15 metres (David & Sullivan, 2005). A Belgian study found that the acceptable distance for children to walk to school was dependent on the child's age, and varied from 1.4 kilometres for 10-year-olds up to 3 kilometres for 14-year-olds (Chillón et al., 2015). Distance from home to school is an important factor in determining whether children walk to school, and it has been argued that this should be a consideration in the structure and design of new urban environments, as well as regulations for school catchment areas, because of the importance of accumulating physical activity for children (Hinckson et al., 2014).

According to the Australian National Centre for Social and Economic Modelling (NATSEM) (Pillips, 2013), transport is the highest cost associated with raising children from birth through to the end of schooling for low- and middle-income earners, accounting for around 20 per cent of costs. In the NATSEM calculations, transport cost includes increasing the size of the car, child seats, public transport tickets and driving children to sports. Transport exceeds the cost of food and the combined costs of childcare and education. Perhaps because transport is viewed as a transition between contexts, there is a lowered level of scrutiny applied to the role played by transport in children's lives. Nonetheless, children can spend many hours per week being mobile, and in cities shaped and accustomed to private car use, these hours are more than likely spent in a private car. The negatives associated with this are multiple and complex. Increased car time results in increased exposure to traffic accidents, and contributes to both the accumulation of and exposure to poor air quality (Douglas et al., 2011). Furthermore, car time enforces large periods of sedentariness, robbing the child of time for activity, learning and social interactions.

As shown in Figure 14.1, enabling, measuring and understanding children's independent mobility is complex. Barriers can be built, cultural or perceived. For example, a child may live within metres of the school entrance, friends' houses, green spaces or recreational opportunities, yet cannot access these facilities due to the lack of a pedestrian crossing. Concerns about traffic are frequently listed by parents as a reason to restrict children's mobility (Garrard, 2011a).

Figure 14.1 Australian suburb with no pedestrian crossings to support children in independently accessing the green space

Source: Jandrie Lombard, Shutterstock.

Issues arising in one geographical context will not necessarily be an issue in another. A recent study of 8- to 10-year-olds in South Australia, for example, used a range of innovative methods to elicit children's experiences in their local environments. Rural children had access to a larger geographical area and dangers to be avoided tended to be animals and natural hazards. Urban children had quite restricted spaces, and often played in their own backyards or close to home. They perceived local parks as 'big', even though they were much smaller than those explored by their rural counterparts. Major concerns for the safety of urban children related to traffic and strangers. Interestingly, the urban children were more likely to have restrictions imposed by adults, and often needed adult assistance to get to locations such as parks. Rather than merely accepting adult-imposed rules, rural children were more likely to negotiate with adults regarding ways of managing risks in their independent explorations (MacDougall, Schiller & Darbyshire, 2009). This study uncovered many of the complexities in children's independent mobility. For example, one urban parent wanted to allow her child more freedom but feared criticism from other parents. Place-based approaches to research can offer relevant and solution-focused outcomes.

School grounds access

> An emerging body of evidence is illustrating those children and adolescents with access to existing school recreational facilities outside of regular school hours are more likely to be active (Healthy Active by Design, 2017).

Previous chapters have discussed play in early childhood centres and schools during usual opening hours. In particular, schools are ideal sites for outdoor play and physical activity (Bundy et al., 2011) and schools have a positive impact on children being sufficiently physically active. A series of studies from the United States found that children partake in less physical activity during the summer vacation and sometimes gains made in physical activity behaviours during term are lost during this period (Baranowski et al., 2014; Franckle, Adler & Davison, 2014). Schools are familiar, and there is an expectation that the grounds are sites for outdoor play, yet these play contexts are regularly locked up for significant periods of the year. School administrators are often reluctant to allow out-of-school-hours access due to fears of property damage and accusations of negligence should an injury occur (Rooney, 2014). In recognition of the latter, two states in the United States—Virginia and Texas—have reformed laws to ensure that a greater burden is required to prove wilful negligence if legal action by a park or other public space user is to succeed (Kozlowski, 2010).

Creating playspaces in urban environments

> One should be able to play everywhere, easily, loosely, and not forced into a 'playground' or 'park'. The failure of an urban environment can be measured in direct proportion to the number of 'playgrounds' (Ward, 1990, p. 73).

Although the ideal is usually to develop more green spaces and make connections to those spaces easy for children, this is an expensive option with protracted negotiations with many stakeholders. Our opening quote suggests that if planners rely on parks and playgrounds as the only way to create a child-friendly city, this is an admission that the rest of the city is not suitable for children. MacDougall and colleagues (2009) also warn against adults reminiscing about open spaces of their own childhood, noting that child participants in their study enjoyed the spaces available to them and recreating environments of the past may not be realistic.

Researchers from many disciplines are interested in collective decisions to promote the creation of green spaces. One of the difficulties, as noted by Tranter (2016), is that neoliberal societies emphasise individual rather than collective responsibilities. At an individual level, driving a child to an early childhood centre or school may be an appealing option, but on a larger scale it leads to greater hazards for children and threats to their mobility. Australia's performance on indicators of children's physical activity has been poor (Schranz et al., 2014; Schranz et al., 2016) and reductions in independent mobility are a contributor (Schoeppe et al., 2016). Nonetheless, there are examples of communities, local governments and other organisations attempting to improve mobility, not just with a health focus, but also to improve social connectivity, aesthetics and a range of other benefits. One example is the GreenWay currently under development in Sydney, which connects the Parramatta and Cooks Rivers. GreenWay integrates light rail, cycling and walking with connections to recreational facilities that include spaces for outdoor play (Thompson & McCue, 2017). Such initiatives can serve as important models for future urban planning, and potentially can open up greater possibilities for outdoor community classrooms, as discussed in our provocation. At a broader level, though, it has been noted that, at an urban planning level, green infrastructure is not well understood. Black, Tara and Pakzad (2016) argue that there is a gap between theory and practice in Australia, with theory largely emanating from the United States while implementation and action plans emanate from the United Kingdom. Their work indicates the importance of multidisciplinary approaches and strong connections between theory and practice. Because of the health and social benefits, it is also important to ensure all members of the community can take advantage of green infrastructure rather than the disproportionate distribution of such spaces noted to occur in affluent communities in the United States and China (Wolch, Byrne & Newell, 2014).

CONCLUSION

> Australia must overcome the tyranny of the motor car, or face the destruction of its major cities as decent centres of our culture, our community, our civilisation (Whitlam, 1972).

Gough Whitlam's comments were made almost half a century ago, yet they continue to resonate today. Urban environments have a significant impact on all quality of life indicators. However, as discussed in this chapter, much of the built environment has emanated from decisions related to restricted interests and use. Nonetheless, there are opportunities to retrofit and redesign urban spaces to make these more accessible, interesting and challenging learning environments for children.

REFERENCES

Adamson, P. (2013). *Child well-being in rich countries: A comparative overview.* New York: *UNICEF.* Retrieved 2 March 2017 from <www.unicef-irc.org/publications/683>

Atkinson, R. & Blandy, S. (2013). *Gated communities: International perspectives.* Abingdon: Taylor and Francis.

Australian Institute of Health and Welfare (AIHW) (2016). *Australia's Health 2016.* Canberra: AIHW.

Baranowski, T., O'Connor, T., Johnston, C., Hughes, S., Moreno, J., Chen, T.-A., . . . Baranowski, J. (2014). School year versus summer differences in child weight gain: a narrative review. *Childhood Obesity, 10*(1), 18–24.

Black, J., Tara, K. & Pakzad, P. (2016). Mainstreaming green infrastructure elements into the design of public road reserves: Challenges for road authorities. *International Journal of Environmental Protection.* doi: 10.5963/IJEP0601001.

Bundy, A.C., Naughton, G., Tranter, P., Wyver, S., Baur, L., Schiller, W., . . . Charmaz, K. (2011). The Sydney Playground Project: Popping the bubblewrap. Unleashing the power of play: A cluster randomized controlled trial of a primary school playground-based intervention aiming to increase children's physical activity and social skills. *BMC Public Health, 15.* doi.org/10.1186/s12889-015-2452-4

Carver, A., Timperio, A. & Crawford, D. (2008). Playing it safe: The influence of neighbourhood safety on children's physical activity—a review. *Health & Place, 14*(2), 217–27.

Chillón, P., Panter, J., Corder, K., Jones, A.P. & Van Sluijs, E.M.F. (2015). A longitudinal study of the distance that young people walk to school. *Health & Place, 31,* 133–7.

David, K.S. & Sullivan, M. (2005). Expectations for walking speeds: Standards for students in elementary schools. *Pediatric Physical Therapy : The official publication of the section on pediatrics of the American Physical Therapy Association, 17*(2), 120–7.

Do your kids walk or ride to school by themselves? You could be breaking the law. (2016, 5 August). *Courier Mail* (Brisbane). Retrieved 5 March 2017 from http://www.couriermail.com.au/news/queensland/do-your-kids-walk-or-ride-to-school-by-themselves-you-could-be-breaking-the-law/news-story/d45f1daefac034cb0a7aef961285c88b.

Douglas, M.J., Watkins, S.J., Gorman, D.R. & Higgins, M. (2011). Are cars the new tobacco? *Journal of Public Health, 33*(2), 160–9.

Downs, J. S., Lowenstein, G. & Wisdom, J. (2009). Strategies for promoting healthier food choices. *American Economic Review, 99*(2), 159–64.

Elhakeem, A., Cooper, R., Bann, D. & Hardy, R. (2015). Childhood socioeconomic position and adult leisure-time physical activity: A systematic review. *International Journal of Behavioral Nutrition and Physical Activity, 12*(1), 92.

Franckle, R., Adler, R. & Davison, K. (2014). Accelerated weight gain among children during summer versus school year and related racial/ethnic disparities: A systematic review. *Preventing Chronic Disease, 11*(12), E101.

Frank, L., Sallis, J., Conway, T., Chapman, J., Saelens, B. & Bachman, W. (2006). Many pathways from land use to health and air quality. *Journal of the American Planning Association, 72*(1), 75–87.

Garrard, J. (2011a). *Active travel to school: Literature review.* Retrieved 5 March 2017 from <www.timetotalk.act.gov.au/storage/Active travel to school Literature Review.pdf>.

—— (2011b). Why aren't more kids cycling to school? *The Conversation,* 17 October. Retrieved 2 March 2017 from <https://theconversation.com/why-arent-more-kids-cycling-to-school-3531>.

Giles-Corti, B., Vernez-Moudon, A., Reis, R., Turrell, G., Dannenberg, A.L., Badland, H., . . . Owen, N. (2016). City planning and population health: A global challenge. *The Lancet, 10062*, 2912–24.

Halpern, S.D., Ubel, P.A. & Asch, D.A. (2007). Harnessing the power of default options to improve health care. *New England Journal of Medicine, 13*(27), 1340–4.

Healthy Active by Design (2017). *Shared facilities: Healthy active by design.* Retrieved 2 March 2017 from <www.healthyactivebydesign.com.au/design-features/shared-facilities>.

Hinckson, E.A., McGrath, L., Hopkins, W., Oliver, M., Badland, H., Mavoa, S., . . . Kearns, R.A. (2014). Distance to school is associated with sedentary time in children: Findings from the URBAN Study. *Frontiers in Public Health, 2*, 151.

Jackson, R.J., Dannenberg, A.L. & Frumkin, H. (2013). Health and the built environment: 10 years after. *American Journal of Public Health, 103*(9), 1542–4.

Kent, J.L. & Thompson, S. (2014). The three domains of urban planning for health and well-being. *Journal of Planning Literature, 29*(3), 239–56.

Kozlowski, J.C. (2010). State immunity laws limit public play liability. *Law Review, September.* Retrieved 2 March 2017 from <http://cehdclass.gmu.edu/jkozlows/lawarts/09SEP10.pdf>.

Little, H. (2017). Promoting risk-taking and physically challenging play in Australian early childhood settings in a changing regulatory environment. *Journal of Early Childhood Research, 15*(1), 83–98.

MacDougall, C., Schiller, W. & Darbyshire, P. (2009). What are our boundaries and where can we play? Perspectives from eight- to ten-year-old Australian metropolitan and rural children. *Early Child Development and Care, 179*(2), 189–204.

Mullan, K. & Edwards, B. (2013). *8 Safe environments, parental concerns and children's unsupervised time, time outdoors, and physical activity: The Longitudinal Study of Australian Children annual statistical report 2013.* Canberra: Australian Institute of Family Studies. Retrieved 2 March 2017 from <www.growingupinaustralia.gov.au/pubs/asr/2013/asr2013h.html>.

New South Wales Government (2016). *Children and Young Persons (Care and Protection) Act 1998.* Retrieved 2 March 2017 from <www.legislation.nsw.gov.au/#/view/act/1998/157>.

Office of the High Commissioner for Human Rights (OHCHR) (1989). *Convention on the Rights of the Child.* Retrieved 21 May 2016 from <www.ohchr.org/en/professionalinterest/pages/crc.aspx>.

Pillips, B. (2013). *The cost of raising children in Australia.* Canberra: NATSEM, University of Canberra.

Roberts, I. & Edwards, P. (2010). *The energy glut: The politics of fatness in an overheating world*. London: Zed Books.

Rooney, T. (2014). Higher stakes: The hidden risks of school security fences for children's learning environments. *Environmental Education Research, 4622*(June), 1–14.

Schoeppe, S., Tranter, P., Duncan, M.J., Curtis, C., Carver, A. & Malone, K. (2016). Australian children's independent mobility levels: Secondary analyses of cross-sectional data between 1991 and 2012. *Children's Geographies, 14*(4), 408–21.

Schranz, N.K., Olds, T., Boyd, R., Evans, J., Gomersall, S.R., Hardy, L., . . . Tomkinson, G.R. (2016). Results from Australia's 2016 report card on physical activity for children and youth. *Journal of Physical Activity and Health, 13*(11), Suppl. 2, S87–94.

Schranz, N., Olds, T., Cliff, D., Davern, M., Engelen, L., Giles-Corti, B., . . . Tomkinson, G. (2014). Results from Australia's 2014 report card on physical activity for children and youth. *Journal of Physical Activity and Health, 11*, S21–5.

Srinivasan, S., O'Fallon, L.R. & Dearry, A. (2003). Reviewing the evidence. Creating healthy communities, healthy homes, healthy people: Initiating a research agenda on the built environment and public health. *American Journal of Public Health, 93*(9), 1446–50.

Thompson, S. & McCue, P. (2017). Health infrastructure is what planners do. *Newplanner, 16*, 16.

Tranter, P. (2016). Children's play in their local neighborhoods: Rediscovering the value of residential streets. In P. Tranter, *Play, recreation, health and wellbeing* (pp. 1–26). Singapore: Springer.

Valentine, G. (1996). Angels and devils: Moral landscapes of childhood. *Environment and Planning D: Society and Space, 14*(5), 581–99.

van der Ploeg, H.P., Merom, D., Corpuz, G. & Bauman, A.E. (2008). Trends in Australian children travelling to school 1971–2003: Burning petrol or carbohydrates? *Preventive Medicine, 46*(1), 60–2.

Ward, C. (1990). *The child in the city*. London: Bedford Square Press.

Whitlam, E.G. (1972). *It's time: Gough Whitlam's 1972 election policy speech*. Retrieved 2 March 2017 from <http://whitlamdismissal.com/1972/11/13/whitlam-1972-election-policy-speech.html>.

Wolch, J.R., Byrne, J. & Newell, J.P. (2014). Urban green space, public health, and environmental justice: The challenge of making cities 'just green enough'. *Landscape and Urban Planning, 125*, 234–44.

Acknowledgements

Although there are threats to outdoor play in modern communities, every day we learn of innovation and change promoted by the broad spectrum of educators, designers, policy-makers, public servants, community members and researchers who have a role in outdoor play. The editors of this book particularly wish to acknowledge the children, families and educators from early years settings whose experiences and commitment to providing outdoor learning environments have informed this publication. The examples in this text illustrate their responses over the last decade to the challenges of and possibilities for the re-envisioning of outdoor learning environments.

We trust that by reading this book, everyone will recognise that they have a contribution to make to the quality of outdoor play for young children—whether it be as an individual or as an organisation.

We are donating all proceeds from the sale of this book to Mia Mia Child and Family Study Centre, Macquarie University, Sydney, to support the centre's ongoing innovation and leadership in outdoor play pedagogy.

Index